SON
of
SAINTS

To: Sister Octavia in
the struggle.
D. Carl Smith

SON
of
SAINTS

My Challenge and Growth
Towards Truth, Knowledge, and Consciousness

D. CARL SMITH

MILL CITY PRESS

Xulon Press
2301 Lucien Way #415
Maitland, FL 32751
407.339.4217
www.xulonpress.com

Paperback ISBN-13: 978-1-66284-981-7
Hard Cover ISBN-13: 978-1-66284-982-4
Ebook ISBN-13: 978-1-66284-983-1

CONTENTS

PICTURES AND ILLUSTRATIONS

SYNOPSIS OF BOOK

B orn during the early 1950s and having recently retired, I share my developmental, professional, and life experiences through the prism of my African heritage and the residual of my American chattel past. All areas are inclusive with an emphasis on my career in education. It presents those people and influences most consequential regarding my personal challenges and growth as the primary subjects of the book.

Reared and educated during the racially charged transitional period of the 1960s, I chronicle my early life and scholastic years in a small segregated southern town in eastern North Carolina. My collegiate experiences were had at a Historical Black College (HBCU) where I matriculated in the field of education as a history major. My academic concentration coupled with the prevailing Black ethos of the day, became a motivating catalyst for beginning the process of rethinking and critically evaluating much previously internalized heretofore concerning myself and especially that of African people.

An impetuous departure from my education career for military service provided a real-world awakening and push factor for my return back to education. The overwhelming response to my tour of military service and travel became an intense craving for truth, meaningful knowledge, and growth in consciousness concerning the Black human.

My honorable discharge resulted in a return to public school education. Additionally, and importantly, I, by organizing and collaborating with like-minded individuals resulted in our founding African-Centered study groups, which elevated my participation and promotion of events such as Kwanzaa, Juneteenth, and other culturally based activities fostering self-knowledge.

Unquestionably, my greatest learning curve and appreciation was derived from the Afrocentric Scholars from various fields of study including history, psychology, psychiatry, sociology, mathematics, etc. found in Chapter 9. These African-Centered thinkers and scholars have and continue to lay the plight, recovery, and foundational discovery for consciousness essentials for the 21st Century Black Human and others.

AUTHOR'S NOTES

My interest in the discovery of Ancient Africa and Kemetic study began initially while reading and listening to speeches by Malik El-Hajj Shabazz (Malcolm X). Among the countless points he made crystal clear were the facts of identification and connection with Mother Africa were purposely lost and denied in substantiation and support for the institution of chattel slavery in America. Further, these historical occurrences along with the colonization of Africa were only the most recent events from a culmination dating back into ancient times. There were Africans then and now uninformed and misinformed to think erroneously they lost nothing.

Concerning both groups, Malcolm asserted "you lost your name, you lost your mind, and you lost your culture". All of which were devastating for sustaining "knowledge of self" which is the doorway to "wholeness, elevated consciousness and spirituality".

Our challenge continues as (will and intent) to study and internalize the work of our scholars even to the extent of becoming one. They have very courageously accepted the challenge to rediscover that classical knowledge base across the full scope of the sciences, arts, and humanities. Why? This has been warranted in order to know what we once knew but not for the purpose of retreating backward. Rather, our classical past once recovered and properly contextualized shall become our springboard of departure from the residual of slavery both physical and mental as a lingering state of "conceptualized bewilderment" of sorts, back to one of world leadership.

Acknowledgments

My acknowledgments for this work are of critical importance since the individuals recognized are truly the subjects and sources for much of its content. We do not learn and become acculturated, neither do we experience consciousness growth or any phase as an initiate in a vacuum. I am eternally grateful to my late parents Mr. Emanuel and Mrs. Janice King Smith for their selfless cooperation, guidance, and provisions. In addition to me, they provided and directed my siblings: Evelyn, Emma, Johnny, and Grossie with the initial sustenance, orientation, and values for the goals of independent thought and self-reliance.

I am likewise indebted to my many elementary and secondary school educators who masterfully compensated for an underfunded and underequipped segregated learning facility. Educational excellence and behavioral discipline thereby became their watchwords and methods. Without compromise, they very professionally and tactfully utilized limited available resources tirelessly, for the strategic purpose of deferred gratitude and for "keeping our eyes on the prize, oh lord"!

I am thankful that one of the three foundational pillars of the Black community was the Black Church establishing an ethical and moral foundation for our people during very difficult and challenging times. Much of our local beliefs, aspirations, and mental toughness were manifested in church-related fellowship. I am equally thankful that our own Little Creek FWB Church and others were such major supporters of schools and the local community.

I must express appreciation for North Carolina Central University and all Historically Black Colleges and Universities for providing undergraduate and higher education studies for African American students when most predominant colleges and universities would not. Professor Corbett Jones and Dr. David Bishop were cornerstones of the history department from which I learned much of my own history, which includes the value of historiography, and experienced the initialization of much of the foundation for "knowledge of self" and "consciousness growth".

My appreciation is extended to Mr. Willie Nicholson, Mr. William Price, and the other men employed at the Pitt County Schools Maintenance Department. From these men, I learned much during a government-sponsored summer employment program for college students.

Acknowledgment, gratitude, and immeasurable indebtedness by many are owed to the historians, scholars, educators, scientists, clinicians, and writers presented in chapter nine of this book. Their courage and personal sacrifice in their pursuit of historical objectivity, proper interpretation of the data, and their willingness to search beyond established paradigms and belief systems contribute immeasurably to our truth, understanding, consciousness growth, and an Africentric Reality.

Finally, in addition to previously mentioned individuals and groups, a tremendous debt of appreciation is given to contributors otherwise not mentioned such as auxiliary content providers, editors, administrative support, and clerical assistance. These incredibly special individuals include Shirley Carmon, Ken, and Evelyn Hammond, Rander and Virginia Harris, Calvin Henderson, Donna Dixon, Coach Danny Hill, Gloria, and Jarvis Pridgen, Theresa Simmons, Donald Smith, Aunt Virgie Mae Smith, Herman Waters, and last but not least, my children (Vonnetta Smith Gaddy, Byron Dion Smith, and Danyel Imani Smith). Thanks to you a million and one times over.

INTRODUCTION

It has been the fundamental nature of humans to grow and develop both physically and mentally during the process of evolving and surviving as a species. We are keenly aware that from the dawn of the human experience there existed basic needs such as food, water, shelter, and a desire for safety within the competitive environments in which they existed.

Basic physical needs have been and remain essential, quasi-generic, and universal within the human family and only divergent to the extent dictated by geographical/climatic, cultural, and/or political mandate upon human groups.

What then are the most impactful factors on the mental condition and/or psychological essence of anthropological groups? Unlike core physical needs, it is my belief that the collective mental states of demographical groups bare their greatest contrasts and distinctions from their respective historical, cultural, and political evolution.

Public education became my lifelong profession and passion; except for a brief six-year tour of military duty in the U.S. Navy. During the early years of a thirty-two-year career in public education, I thought education was the greatest factor in any individual's cognition. It became apparent along the way that as impactful as formal education has become on contemporary society, general culture has a much greater influence than all the grade schools, colleges, universities, and "bastions of organized institutions of education" combined. After all, the institution of education within a culture is necessarily but a product of said culture or society. It is a certainty that the educational system within a culture is a subset of that culture, and supports the mores, norms, and ethos of that culture. However, the educational system would collapse profoundly if not continuously supported by the culture which produced it.

Africa and its peoples have suffered a catastrophic disconnect from much of its classical cultural foundations. This fact is due to successive Euro/Asian waves of invasions and destruction at the hands of foreigners currently dating back into ancient times. Likewise, African cultural recovery and development were again traumatically disrupted more recently by the Atlantic slave trade and European colonization of the continent. It was during the 17th-19th centuries Africa once again found herself being robbed of valuable human resources for the purpose of The Atlantic slave trade, then of its land, natural resources, and self-governance for the purpose of European colonialism. All mentioned here resulted in separation and denial of African people of their Indigenous culture, knowledge of self, and most significantly the resulting reduction in authentic African consciousness.

Clearly, through such a long-standing historical devastation Africans on the continent and those in the Diaspora have struggled mightily. The challenges have been physical, mental, and profoundly persistent. The millenniums of disastrous contact and waves of destruction hurled at African humans and their culture have been a threat to their survival and very existence by those determined to advance and progress at their expense.

A significant tactical objective is the arousal and solidification of our consciousness through availed Afro-centric scholarship and revival of authentic spirituality. African minds and hearts both at home and in the Diaspora with a higher level of urgency have collectively begun to use their eyes to see, ears to hear, mouths to speak, and hands to build through a newly awakened 21st-century knowledge of self and consciousness. Victory shall be our reward for the rescue, restoration, revitalization, and rebirth of land and a people so deserving of "Mother Africa".

There have been many along the road of my life experiences that became my sources for: education, motivation, morale-boosting, truth-finding, African-Centered-Thought, consciousness-seeking, and spirituality-pursuance. This book is an effort to acknowledge my respect and appreciation, for those individuals all of whom I consider (Saints). It is a dedicated effort that I now reach out to share my lessons learned and consciousness growth with others. Hence, this author is humble and grateful in my outreach and sharing with you as the **SON OF SAINTS** My Challenge and Growth towards Truth, Knowledge and Consciousness.

CHAPTER 1

EARLY YEARS

A Tenant Farmers' Perils

I t was the spring of 1953 and our family had recently moved into Green County near the township of Maury, North Carolina. I was not yet two years of age and had no memory of what had precipitated the sudden and abrupt move from the old Spear farm near Ayden, North Carolina. I learned much later that my mother had a confrontation with the daughter-in-law of the farm owner Mrs. Clara Spear.

It seems that Susan (daughter-in-law of Mrs. Clara) had threatened to whip my sisters (Juanita and Jean). My mother upon receiving this information located a tobacco stick and had to be restrained by my father after chasing Susan with the intent of causing bodily harm.

My father, Emanuel Smith, and my mother, Janice King Smith, a couple with a young growing family had married on November 20, 1945. They took first residence on the Spear Farm where my father and his family had lived and worked as tenant sharecroppers until the time of his becoming a young adult. Over the years, he and his family had developed a considerable appreciation for the Spear

1

family. It was well established that they had grown to respect if not admire much about Mrs. Clara and her family.

The departure from the Spears was not without reservations on his behalf nor his mothers' (Charlotte) affectionately known as (Mam-muh). Other tenant families lived on the Spear farm (neo-plantation) who thought highly of Ms. Clara and were somewhat baffled by our sudden departure. June Moye, a lifelong friend of my father, was particularly puzzled and sadden by the outcome.

My maternal grandmother Ida Pugh King (Punch) who resided in Baltimore, MD., was not among those heartbroken by the decision. She had left rural eastern N.C. for the prospects of a better life in the urban northeast several years earlier. She felt that my mother and father would do well to make a similar decision as had her three other children (Lester, Osborne, and Juanita). Although the move away from the Spears was not away from eastern N.C., I always believed she viewed it as a progressive decision by leaving the Spears. I never had the feeling that Punch had quite the same regard nor perspective of the Spears as did my fathers' family and several other tenants.

Punch always reminded us that although she was not there with us she was always thinking of us. Juanita, Jean, and I could depend upon her occasional packages through the mail. They would some-times include clothing, such as shoes, pants, and dresses, and food items such as potato chips, candy, cookies, and other eatables.

William McKinley Smith (Uncle Chig second of my Dad's four brothers) became my first memory and my earliest interaction with any family member outside the immediate family. The love from his consideration, attention, and affection shown by him became the foundation for my perspective on extended family. I remember vividly how my Uncle Chig would stop at the old mailbox and yell, "Come on Duck". I would quickly run and board my uncles' car for Ms. Winnie Stocks' store nearby where he would purchase candy or cookies for me. Something I will never forget. Years later, I realized there were several children my uncle could have been treating at the store. However, this was how our family developed the bonds over the years, which materialized into something more than cher-ished memories.

Understandably, my recall of this incredibly early period in my life is quite limited. However, there were certain events that became memorable even for a very young mind.

My sister Jean was less than five years old when a very fright-ening incident occurred. Her sleepwear caught fire from a wood heater. She immediately began to run. Our father was able to catch her and extinguish the fire before the incident became tragic. This is significant because there were to be two other similar cases involving similar aged female cousins (Gertrude Smith and Susan Bissell) who were not as fortunate as my sister Jean and lost their young lives in this very manner.

The tenants on the Lawrence Moye farm like elsewhere were expected to help with the process of cultivating and harvesting the primary cash crop (tobacco). The harvesting of tobacco typi-cally began in early summer and culminated in early fall roughly (July-September). Locally the harvesting of tobacco was referred to as "putting in tobacco". The process required the leaves to be cropped from the stalks, packed onto trucks by "primers" and carted to the barns where the leaves would be attached to tobacco sticks with twine for curing. During the course of the workday, the workers would have breaks during which they would order snacks from a nearby store. It was during these times that my sisters and I would visit my mother at the barn to share her snack. It was during one such visit that I learned a valuable lesson in obedience and self-discipline. As I recall there were apples on the ground that had fallen from a nearby tree. My mother had explicitly expressed to us not to eat the fruit because it was infested with yellow jackets (stinging insects).

Of course, once she was no longer focused on me, I began eating one of the fruit. I was immediately stung all around inside my mouth as she had warned. My mother first picked me up and began a spanking I would not soon forget. Then afterward only did she deal with my stings due to my disobedience colloquially known as (hard-headedness). She made it clear by spanking me before attending to the stings that obedience was of high priority. I thereby learned early in life that there were unpleasant consequences for disregarding appropriate warnings.

Grading and preparing the tobacco for the annual market was done at a "packhouse" the last step before its movement and auctioning for buyers at the warehouse. During this juncture neighbors, visitors and family would sometimes visit, and offer assistance. My Aunt Martha Smith Hooker would often spend the night after lending her help in this way. This was an enjoyable time for me and my sisters because she would play little entertaining games and call us her favorite nickname "Little Sneak Up".

An old sharecropper's farmhouse was not much to place confidence in during the destructive forces of hurricane Hazel in the fall of 1954. My mother sat me and my sisters in the hallway with strict verbal instructions to remain both still and quiet during the storm. These instructions were typical for any storm with the underlying understanding that we were always expected to do so when, as stated to us "God was doing his work". It was during the time of year when crops had been harvested and my father would take seasonal employment at a tobacco warehouse in a nearby town. He was thereby caught in Kinston, N.C. during the storm. This was to occur again over the years with another hurricane event at our next place of residence in Winterville, N.C. In both cases, he made it safely home through the storms despite our anxiety and much to our relief. I will never forget the site of the very large tree, which we observed, had fallen on the back porch the next day. I would learn that the fear of destructive wind and flooding of hurricanes would be recurring events growing up in eastern North Carolina.

Thankfully, the stay at the Moye's farm was a short one, when in the fall of 1955 my parents decided they had enough of the farm life. Uncle John Waters and his wife Janie Smith Waters (Dad's sister) convinced them to move from Green County to join them in the small town of Winterville, N.C. in Pitt County.

Although the move was only a short distance of 10 miles, it seemed at the time a vast and expansive change from the nearly exclusively rural and farming lifestyle of Green County. Just the proximity of houses nearby, the site of neighbors, and the regularity of passing cars was a welcome site for a young set of eyes and mind to ponder.

Within a larger perspective, the frequency of Black-family relocations from rural farm life to nearby towns during this period might be considered a smaller subset of the "great migration." The urban centers of the northeast, Midwest, west, and elsewhere were the recipients of thousands upon thousands from the south between the years of 1915-1970 (Jr. Bennett 1966, 288-289; Karenga 1993, 147-149). All were attempting to escape southern racism, bigotry, and hatred in search of better employment, economic, social, and/ or political freedom.

Previously mentioned was the fact that my mother's immediate family had relocated to Baltimore, M.D. earlier. By 1959, many of my Dad's family had likewise left the south. Several of my Dad's sibling's children including the following Sam Smith's; Thelma, Annabelle, Marie and Kurt, Chig Smith's; Florence, Julia, Earl, Bobby, Sandy, Stout, Faye and Bettie; and sister Marybelle Smith Forbes' son Gene

Forbes. It was during this time of life-changing decisions that these family members had gone north seeking a better life and good fortune for themselves.

Many family decisions to move from their sharecropping status to small towns were similar in purpose as the participants in the "Great Migration North" if only on a smaller scale. Movement off sharecropping farms to small vicinity towns seemed to offer similar if less dramatic outcomes.

Other significant municipalities in Pitt County include Greenville (county seat), Farmville, Ayden, Bethel, and Grimesland. The oddity of the small town upon small town within a relatively short distance remains a commonality to most of eastern North Carolina. Other significant regional towns in proximity were Washington, Kinston, Newbern, Goldsboro, and Rocky Mount. The state is divided into three major regions. They are located east to west accordingly firstly the coastal plains which is mostly rural and flat with numerous small towns and mostly agrarian; secondly the piedmont mostly urban, industrial, and hilly; and the third geographical region (mountains) which is back to mostly rural and agricultural with Asheville being the major urban center of the region.

Most North Carolinians reside in the urban piedmont. Those who affiliate themselves with the piedmont then and now make little distinction between the small eastern N.C. towns and the outright rural areas within eastern North Carolina. They usually consider the entire coastal plains region as rural or "the country".

Returning visitors from the northern urban cities usually referred to the entire state as "country". Both assessments were inaccurate. For the residents of eastern North Carolina, there was and remains a different perspective of their self-image, likewise is true for the piedmont despite the attitudes of those from the larger cities of the northeast and elsewhere.

<u>Winterville, N.C. Community during the '50s</u>

In 1955, Winterville, N.C. was a very small and segregated town of about 1600 residents. Communities, schools, hotels, restaurants, and basic places of public accommodations such as barbershops, movies, libraries, etc. were subject to lawful mandatory separation of the races (segregation). Black and White neighborhoods were usually divided by boundaries such as railroad tracks, dead-end streets, and mutually accepted unmarked boundaries. Winterville High School located in south Winterville was understood to be for Whites Only as Robinson Union School located in north Winterville was understood to serve Blacks only. The Dixie Queen Soda Shop and Grill located in south Winterville was another example of the times. Blacks could enter the store and make purchases but could not sit at the bar to "take a load off" nor consume purchased food items at the counter in the store.

My family's new found community was located in the Newtown section of North Winterville. The Newtown Community had no welcome wagon awaiting our arrival but did convey a sincere, friendly, and hospitable attitude toward us as a new family entering the neighborhood.

One of my first memories at our new home was the scolding from my Mom for urinating in the front yard. "Don't ever do that again she yelled from the front door, you're not in the country any-more", she explained. She chose not to become the laughingstock of the neighborhood and I needed to make friends with the kids of Newtown. My behavior with that stunt would not be helpful.

Our next-door neighbors on either side seemingly became open and friendly immediately. Ms. Holloway and her nephew Mack Arthur lived on the left and Mr. Pedro Boyd, Mrs. Burt (wife), and their children Fred and Belle lived to our right. Everyone in both houses was older than me. Mack Arthur and Fred both became popular basketball players on the Robinson School team. The early admiration for their status and athletic skills were to have a significant impression on me.

Mrs. Leyla Carmon, a neighbor located a couple of houses down from Ms. Holloway operated a small store from inside her home. Sometimes adults but mostly children would make visits to purchase bottled sodas and other small items Ms. Leyla had for sale. It was not uncommon to use a "short cut" through a neighbor's yard to reach a nearby destination. Mr. Clem and Mrs. George Ann Lawson were not the only unfortunate homeowners of such a property. Others found their property being used similarly for throughways to school, church, or other areas of town. There were no sidewalks, few paved streets, and only about ten or less lights to be found on the streets of all North Winterville in 1955.

It is presently difficult to imagine that was the reality early in my lifetime. The following commodities: television (black and white), wired phones, electric ovens, oil and gas heating and a family car were all considered to be quasi luxuries. Laptops, cell phones, satellite TV, GPS or microwaves did not exist. Neither did McDonald's, Kentucky Fried, IHOP or any other national fast-food franchises exist at the time. Likewise, there were neither local shopping malls nor giant discount stores such as Roses or Wal-Mart. If there were examples of these types of stores or retailers, they were found in the large urban areas but certainly not in eastern North Carolina.

Winterville was in many ways a satellite to Greenville, N.C. as were the other smaller towns in Pitt County. They depended upon the larger Greenville merchants for many retail items, entertainment, and public services not available in their smaller respective towns.

The General Store owned by Fannie Mae Ainge, Worthington's Grocery Store owned by Will Worthington, and Boyd's Dime Store were the principle retailers of Winterville located "uptown". The Do-Drop-In store and grill provided hot sandwiches and small purchase items on the very north side of town. According to Jack Forlines, Wilbur Hardee, the founder of the Hardees Franchise was the owner of the Do Drop Inn and owner of the first Hardees located on 10th Street in Greenville, N.C. in 1960 (Forlines 2007). Nicks Cabinet Shop, Eastern Lumber Company, and Winterville Machine Works were businesses which provided employment for some Winterville residents. Hines Auto Service, Nobles Esso (Exon), and Tapp Worthington Service Station were the gas and service stations in town. Businesses located in North Winterville (Black Businesses) during the 1950s and '60s include Miller's Grocery later (Little Joe Daniels Grocery), Hammond Grocery, Jessie Hooks Store, Jimbo Patrick Variety Store, and Joe "Hauling Nelson" Dirt and Gravel Delivery. Mr. Nelson was also a part-time photographer. He took many pictures for customers especially on Easter Sunday in their beautiful Easter outfits. Ms. Helen Cannon operated a very highly patronized cosmetology business. Worthington Family Dry Cleaners was located "uptown" Winterville initially. You could depend on Mr. Amos Worthington, Mr. Frank Worthington, and other family members to render outstanding care in dry cleaning and pressing clothing to perfection. They were later forced to move from downtown to North Winterville ostensibly to comply with the segregation norms of the day according to family members.

My tenure as the baby in the family was about to expire with the arrival of our brother Johnnie Ray as I then became the "knee baby" but it was a great feeling having the new baby brother addition to the family. Also, I recall the birth of another youngster in the community during this time to parents Mr. and Mrs. Willizard Elbert. Little did I know the important and pivotal role that he and the other men of the Pitt County Schools Maintenance Department would have on my maturation, working ethics/skills, and philosophical development as a young man later through my affiliation and employment with the P.C.S.M.D.

The birth of a new family member was a happy occasion for the extended family as well. Visiting family after church on Sundays was a very common event during the 1950s. Parents would be seated in the front seat of the car with children in the back. This would evoke immediate excitement as we would look forward to play and laughter usually outside as the adults would sit inside involved in conversation usually after dinner. Our relatives albeit at different times would visit in this manner. Our most frequent visitors include Uncle Dewey and family; Aunt Vinella and Ed Lewis; Uncle Kater Forbes and his family; Aunt Marybelle, Louise and Curtis, and Uncle Mark and his family; Aunt Virgie Mae, and children at the time, Kelly, Donald, Leon, and Celestine. Such Sunday visits would be the bulk of our entertainment for the week. The other source of entertainment was the once weekly visit to Uncle John and Aunt Janie's house to watch television. Since we did not own one at the time our entire family would visit to watch my Dad's favorite show (Sea Hunt) starring Lloyd Bridges.

The first similar aged friendship I developed was with Lester Patrick later to be nicknamed "Breeze" by schoolmates. Lester was the nephew of Mrs. Nellie and Windsor Barrett. They lived across the street from us. He first drew my attention because he was riding a bike, something I could not do. Lester became instrumental in my learning to ride a bike. He told me "after you fall from the bike and hurt yourself you would be able to ride it". That is exactly the way it happened. Since I could not ride, I had to push it along. So finally, when I did mount and attempted to balance and ride, I fell with the handlebars, ending straight into the stomach. When I tried again the next day, I could ride the bike. I broke not into a happy dance but a happy bike ride. Little did either one of us know that later in life I would return a wonderful favor to him. I introduced him to his future wife Linda Jones my classmate and dear friend.

My friendships in the community continued to grow as I met the nephews of Ms. Holloway. Their names were Willie and Ronald Ennis. They were the sons of Mr. Bozie and Mrs. Christine (Tot) Ennis. Willie was a year older than Ronald and me, but we all started school the same year because Willie initially had rheumatic heart problems. Later, I met and befriended Arthur King, Jr. I was informed by my mother much to my delight that he was not only a good neighborhood friend but my cousin as well. He was the son of my mother's first cousin Arthur King, Sr. and his wife Mrs. May Lee King. We all later became classmates except Lester who was one class ahead of Willie, Ronald, Arthur, and me. We were all to become schoolmates at Robinson Union.

As a little guy in the community, I began to admire the older ones who were nice dressers, good dancers, outstanding athletes, and good students. Some of this group included: Herman Waters my cousin the son of my Uncle John and Aunt Janie Waters; Skip and Dick Barrett were the sons of Mr. Simon and Mrs. Maylee Barrett. Others included Paul and Henry Suggs were the sons of widowed Mrs. Mattie Suggs, and Marvin and Milton Carr the grandsons of Ms. Leyla Carmon. I recall watching the Barrett brothers making baseballs by using a core to enwrap with twine. They would then use small trees to strip and sand into bats for hitting. Their motivation and desire thereby made it possible to play baseball in the streets of Newtown. I was likewise impressed by Milton Carr who owned an English Racer Bike. He would pass our house with a speedy peddle then begin peddling backward creating that trademark English Racer sound which was "double cool" to me at the time. Many were boy scouts. My cousin Herman was a leading and accomplished scout. Mr. Buck Bryant was the beloved scoutmaster and was well known for riding his bicycle through the streets of Winterville speaking and waving hello to all he would see along the way.

Even though my focus and admiration at the time were primarily directed toward the older boys or as we referred to them as the "big boys", I would be remiss if I didn't mention some of the many admired female youth as well. Some such role models included: Rosa and Helen Barrett daughters of Mr. Simon and Maylee Barrett; Elinor Waters daughter of Uncle John Waters and Aunt Janie Waters; Betty Pearl Patrick and sister Annie Mae Patrick daughters of Mr. John and Mrs. Sis Patrick.

The entire state of North Carolina falls within the area known informally as the Bible belt region of the country. This is an area encompassing the southern states, which practices mostly protestant but not limited to (Baptist) denominations. Parishioners in the Bible belt attend church at a higher rate and have more churches per capita than any other region of the country.

North Winterville was home to three churches accordingly. They were: Good Hope Freewill Baptist Church; Shiloh Missionary Baptist Church and Saint Rest Holiness Church where I could always enjoy the sound and excitement of tambourines. These churches all employed the services of a full-time pastor and held Sunday services at least monthly. Their organizational structures also included a complement of five to ten deacons, a motherboard, several ushers, a financial board, one or more choirs, and a host of committees. Sunday was a time to attend church.

Since service was only held at Little Creek FWB Church (our family church) on the second Sunday in rural Greene Country, we had a choice on all other Sundays. There was a household rule; if you did not go to church, you could not go anyplace else on Sunday. Since most churches had Sunday school weekly, there were several ways to satisfy these-criteria.

The churches played a very pivotal role in small town community life for adults as well as the youth. Good Hope at different times had an extremely popular youth choir, which was considered quite an honor to be a member. During one period of very high popularity, J. B. Hill was the director. Bible School held during early summer was well attended at Shiloh through the years. I particularly remember the refreshments on the last day. Those were the best cookies and push-ups to be sure! Church-sponsored Easter egg hunts, Christmas plays, and summer trips to beaches and parks were supervised and scheduled for our enjoyment and amusement as youthful church members and attendees.

There was a very memorable figure of a man often seen but quite surreal at the time but even more so today as I recollect. The name of that person was Reverend Highsmith who was as much an enigma to adults as to me. No one had the answers. I was just a tot at the time maybe five or six years of age. He never dressed in a typical manner. He would only be seen in Biblical dress attire. His appearance was that of a somewhat tall, white-bearded man, dressed in a long robe that could be seen wavering in the wind; holding a full-length shepherd staff in hand with sandals on his feet, I am not sure where he lived or if he had family nearby. He would be seen in front of Mr. Joe Nelson's house on Highway 11 "thumbing a ride". Often when you observed him there and glanced away, he would be gone when you looked back, or so it seemed. It was a well-advanced story that he was once placed in a local jail. He declared to the jailor that if not immediately released it would rain until he was released. It was commonly held by the locals that this actually happen and was a completely true story. Reverend Highsmith was considered by most to be a true man of God. I would describe him today as having been an authentic "mystic".

Our house was located on what is now Boyd Street, but I'm sure there were no street identification signs or house numbers at the time. The streets were assigned names and demarcation much later after our arrival in 1955. Residents thereby received their mail at the post office which was likewise their official address.

The Haunted Robinson House

We learned later that our home had belonged to one William Henry Robinson and family before our occupancy. He was known as Professor Robinson but pronounced colloquially as (Fes-ser) Robinson. Unfortunately, my research was unable to uncover very much concerning Professor Robinson's background prior to his arrival and employment at Winterville Colored School (Robinson Union School) later. However, his legacy as a dedicated, conscientious, and highly regarded educator has survived the annals of time as evidenced in North Winterville folklore and the current school which bears his name (W. H. Robinson). In addition to his principalship, he was also a licensed barber. Professor Robinson was a man of many talents. He actually cut hair on weekends as a second "gig". So, as it turned out, many of the heads that were subject to him as an educator at school were likewise subject to him for grooming as a skilled barber at his home.

Those currently who can recall his personality and demeanor consistently attest to his love and patience for children, especially the incredibly young ones. Mrs. Robinson was also very similar in this way. She was known and beloved for her wonderful smile, friendly disposition, and especially her home-baked cookies for the children.

So, at the time, we became the occupants of the Robinson House (1955) Professor Robinson had been deceased for several years. It was also a well-known scuttlebutt in the community that many claimed the house to be "haunted". My parents must have taken this to heart because early on they had placed a horseshoe above the interior of the front door. This was considered to be a symbol for "good luck" and to keep spirits, ghosts, or what some referred to colloquially as "haints" away. We must have needed a larger horseshoe!

On one occasion during a visit by our Aunt Martha who routinely slept with my sisters all reported having seen something very strange. They all reported having seen a hand go across the door and retreat without ever seeing the connected body. They all attested to having seen this occurrence. Our Aunt Martha told of the same incidence to other friends and family members for the remainder of her life. So did my sisters until this current time.

My experience was at night and likewise while in bed. So, one night as I recall I was settled into bed alone but not yet asleep. I slept in a single bed with the old-style newels between the bedposts. This allowed me to stick my feet between them as I often did. On this particular night, as my feet dangled between the newels, I felt the sensation of someone tickling my toes. At first, I thought it was one of my sisters Juanita or Jean pulling a prank on me, but I found them to be sound asleep in their bed. I immediately went to my mother and father's room and told them what had happened. They begin to explain that all was fine and insisted that I was only dreaming and to calm down and go back to bed. I couldn't calm down. My Dad ended up accompanying me to my room and getting into bed with me and did not leave until I was sound asleep. But I had remembered vividly what had happened the next morning and beyond. I shared my experience with all our neighbors and anyone who would listen. The most common response I received was typical of Ms. Holloway (next-door neighbor) and others. In her everyday vernacular, Ms. Holloway exclaimed "lardy boy it won't nobody but Fesser (Professor) Robinson, he loved little chillen (children) you know". I had no choice but to believe what they said to me, for I had no belief that they would fabricate such a story.

First non-sharecroppers home occupied by the Smith Family

In retrospect, I never became fearful in the "Robinson House" nor harbored concern for anything scary or spooky. I had never before seen or heard anything of that sort nor did I ever after that experience it. I believe sincerely rather that, the encounter was a spiritual precursor to the wonderful educational preparations and tenure that I and so many others would receive at William Henry Robinson High School in Winterville, North Carolina. Like Professor Robinson, later in life, I would become a public servant and lifelong educator (teacher and administrator) dedicated to the uplifting and the restoration of a people.

CHAPTER 2

THE MIRACLE OF DEAR OLE RHS

Robinson High School, Circa 1962

Segregated ecnellecxE

Although the Supreme Court Case Brown v. Board of Education Topeka, Kansas 1954 supposedly ended legal segregation in public schools, this had not become reality here by 1957. Hence, Robinson Union, and most other schools throughout the south had remained segregated.

By this time, "Winterville Colored School" had become Robinson Union School. This was the result of becoming the name-sake of outstanding visionary and previous principal (Professor

William Henry Robinson). The word Union in the name referenced its combined elementary and high school levels status consisting of grades 1-12. The other factor was the need to be divorced from the outdated and unwarranted racial identification (Colored School). Later circa 1965, it became officially Robinson High School. My formal education began here in the fall of 1957.

Mr. John W. Maye Sr. had become the principal extraordinaire, known for his highly effective instructional leadership and disciplinary qualities. He was without the services of an official assistant principal. Although Mr. Sam Hemby was considered the unofficial AP he also had the responsibilities of a classroom teacher. The school secretary was the very reliable and highly efficient Mrs. Pearl Frizzell, and Mr. Clinton Ray Anderson was the very thorough and dedicated head custodian.

The school's structural outlay consisted of four small separate buildings. Included were a wooden high school classroom building and library; a brick home economics unit combined with a small classroom building; a brick unified elementary building and a second wooden vocational education building. Later, a new brick library, cafeteria, gymnasium, and cinder block vocational education building were added to these existing structures.

My original perspective of Robinson School was mostly gathered from information received from my older sisters. They would usually often share at home what happened at school on a regular basis. This included their experiences and interactions with other students as well as those with their teachers. Not the least of which were perceptions of teacher attitudes and mannerisms. This was very important information for a "rising first-grader" who was fully intent upon having the least strict and most friendly teacher on the staff. By the time of the orientation, I had a definite choice in mind for my first-grade teacher.

At orientation, teachers were able to identify students from roster names and family affiliation. This made it possible for them to approach many new first graders with a level of familiarity. It also proved to be my situation with Ms. Bush. During scheduled activities, she approached my mother and me and stated, "Hi Danny wouldn't you like to be in my class next year"? To which I quickly and rudely replied, "No, Ms. Bush you're mean". My mother was shamed as Ms. Bush embarrassingly responded, "Danny, Emma, and Evelyn told you that". I must say here, Ms. Bush, by all accounts, was probably a wonderful and caring teacher however a five-year-old can be decidedly frank and honest when questioned!

Ms. Carrie Bess became my first-grade teacher the coming school year. The first few days as I recall were complete with receiving seating, class rules, materials, and procedures. I will always remember the folded name cards issued as guides for printing our names with the large eraser-less pencils and the brown lined paper to do so. Procedures for class behavior were emphasized with great clarity. All students were required not to speak out unless recognized; to be seated while in class and remain in a single line during movement outside the classroom unless otherwise instructed. Adherence to class rules was highly regarded by students. Teachers were often issued paddles along with their instructional supplies. Students were reminded that corporal punishment was a standard disciplinary measure at the teachers' discretion.

Especially important to classmates was the unofficial activity of socializing and cultivating new friendships. Mrs. Bess was determined to keep this student's desire in check and had the aforementioned measures in support of her cause. That meant we only had two daily breaks and lunchtime to promote this process, which we did very well.

Kenneth Hammond and John Maye Jr. became my first two buddy-type friends at school. We began by talking during bathroom breaks and sharing at lunchtime. Robinson did not have a cafeteria with hot lunches at the time. Students, therefore, brought their lunches or purchased sandwiches from the home economics class and enjoyed our lunches in the classroom. We also purchased cartons of milk delivered to our classroom. Lunchtime became a time for consuming our midday meal as well as learning more about our classmates. It was interesting what classmates brought for lunch. I recall one of our female classmates brought smoke sausage sandwiches and a male friend brought bologna sandwiches. Kenneth Waller was of special interest at lunchtime to me. He would never share any of his lunch, but he neither would accept any of your lunch. In sharing with my Mom what happened at school, I mentioned how KW handled his lunch; her response was "sounds like a good way to be". Mothers have a certain way of explaining things to make them immediately reasonable and acceptable.

Once in the morning and once in the afternoon the class would be instructed to line up and January-February-March to the bathroom to "take care of our personal needs". There were a set of stalls with a stool in each one. At the end of the bathroom, there was a long multi accessible urinal. We had been given instructions on which to use and for what and we were reminded many times by our teacher as well as Mr. Anderson (janitor). It was made clear that we were to use the urinal only for stand-up- needs (urinating) and the stalls for other needs. We had been warned both by Mrs. Bess and Mr. Anderson that Mr. Maye would often come into the bathrooms and check for compliance. It happened one day during morning break that one young man decided he was going to use a stool for urination. As his luck would have it, Mr. Maye stepped into the bathroom just at that moment. The young man was thereby caught by the seat of his pants from the rear and yanked from the stall as urine was being sprayed up and down and side to side as Mr. Maye pulled him from the stall. It was a terribly hilarious scene, but no one was laughing. We were all making our best hasty exit from the bathroom, with the understanding to never allow such a thing to happen to us. It was certain from that day forward Mr. John

Maye Sr. was most definitely a principal to be taken very seriously and was not to be trodden upon.

I speak for thousands of former students when I say Mrs. Carrie Bess was a wonderfully professional, patient, learned, dedicated, and nurturing teacher that we will always remember and admire.

In 2007 I had the great fortune to attend a banquet held in honor of Teachers from the Historically Black Schools of Pitt County. The well-attended activity was hosted at Cornerstone Baptist Church, located in Greenville, N.C. Alumni, and former staff well represented Robinson High. Other county schools including Suggs, Whitfield, South Ayden, Bethel Union, and Eppes were also represented well.

*Mrs. C. Bess along with others being honored at banquet
recognizing teachers at HBCS in Pitt County, NC*

Upon locating my seating, I was informed that Mrs. Bess was present at the activity. I told them I would return after I located her and made my presence known to her. When I sited her, I walked immediately to her table and stated, "Mrs. Bess It's been a lot of years and you've taught many students, so I don't expect you to remember me". She immediately replied, "Danny Carl Smith". Much to my surprise, she was able to call out my entire name without hesitation. Being a career educator myself, and not having taught even half the students she had, I knew I definitely could not have done the same. We then entered into a long and hearty hug as I choked back the tears. Little did I know that although there had been 38 years since I last saw Mrs. Bess, this would become the last time that I would see her, for she passed away before I ever saw her again.

Memories of the second, third and fourth grades were a period of continued growth physically, educationally, and socially under the direction of three very capable teachers/mentors. Mrs. Martha Jones was a strict no-nonsense type that stressed learning coupled with discipline in her methods and classroom management. She did not spare "the proverbial rod". All students were required to take an afternoon nap by placing their heads on their respective tables. I will always remember my day of pain and embarrassment when I raised my head from the table during nap time. I made the mistake of breaking the rule and received an abrupt "whack on the back" from Mrs. Jones' enforcer. Needless to say, I never did that again! I learned quickly that unpleasant consequences might suddenly result at times with very little warning.

Mrs. Mable Lang (third-grade teacher) and Mrs. Joyner (fourth-grade teacher) were similar in that they were basic in their instructional and disciplinary approaches. These were the grade levels in which the process of proper pronunciation, reading passages, spelling, and writing began in earnest. Although little thought was given to the fact at the time our books were usually those previously used by the (White Only) schools.

Meeting and learning more about other students' perceptions and attitudes was a source of fun. I particularly remember a new student named Ervin Winston. I recall a conversation one day when he was asked about where the pants he was "sporting" were purchased. His response was "I don't know I just wear them". I wasn't sure if he was giving a short answer, or whether he didn't know the meaning of the word purchase.

It was also during these grades that I had become infatuated with our basketball players. I had become a huge fan and was filled with school spirit, determined one day to become one. The players were high school students and being just a small elementary kid, I idolized them. Games were usually played during weeknights and were always well attended. Just about all the students knew and recognized the players whether at school or elsewhere. This included both boys and girls' players. The female players I adored and thought they were "absolutely beautiful" on the court. As for the boys, they were complete stars, studs, and role models for most of us little guys. A few of the school athletes that I admired and adored during my elementary years were Eva Leggett and her sisters Gloria and Pearlie, Lilly Robbins, Iselene Daniels, Lulu Smith, Shirley Waller, and others. When they suddenly ended girls' basketball I was traumatized, and I never understood why! Some of the boys I admired over the years were: Jimmy Worthington, Charles Wiggins, David Banks, James Ennis, Clifton (Bones) Daniels, Milton Carr, Scoop McLawhorn, David Whitehurst, Brandy Cox, Jimmy King, Lester Shields, Larry Daniels, and the great Raymond Bryant. We were not without outstanding cheerleaders through the years either with such talented beauties as Gloria Worthington, Evelyn Smith (sister), Judy Person, Nina Wilson, Doris McKenzie, Essie Marrow, Linda Jones, and others.

John, my friend was {school principal – Mr. John Maye, Sr. and school librarian—Mrs. Beatrice Mayes' son}. We nicknamed him (Slick) because of his close haircut. Kenneth Hammond, my next-door neighbor, whom we called Kent later (Hamp) had become my other buddy. By this time, we had established ourselves with classmates as the 50/50 Gang; with the student bus drivers we were the school ground hitchhikers. As the 50/50 Gang, we would encircle the class trash can during break and chant "fifth, fifth, fifth, fifth, fifth, fifth, fifth, fifth before sharing and consuming whatever we had for our break snack. We were known to the student drivers for hitching rides on their school buses after the regular riders debarked. We would board the buses and ride to their parking area then leave that bus only to board others until the morning bell sounded to report to class. One last item, in our minds we had high school girlfriends. They would sometimes play along in teasing us too. Eva Leggett was Kent's choice, Lilly Robins had Slick's eye and I was "head over hills" about Iselene Daniels all outstanding girl basketball players.

Teaching, learning, and content emphasis were to be effectively influenced by national and international events of the day. The Russians successfully launched their first Sputnik Satellite in 1957 and thusly began the era of "space exploration". In 1958 the Federal Government introduced the National Defense Education Act under President Dwight Eisenhower. The purpose of this earth-shaking and very momentous program was for the overall improvement of American Public Schools and to better promote post-secondary (college) education.

Programs, Politicians and Progress of early 60s

Many in government feared correctly, that we had allowed Russia to surpass us in the critical areas of science and technology. This occurrence necessarily required a remedy involving a targeted educational strategy. The National Defense Education Act of 1958 (NDEA) was designed to specifically attack educational deficits in the areas of math, science, and foreign languages. Since the nation's defense was seen at risk, more funding and resources were made available down the chain. Robinson as did most American schools became the recipients of the NDEA by way of more buildings, instructional equipment, science labs, math resources, foreign language courses, and improved libraries. These much-warranted changes and improvements began to come into focus at Robinson during my fifth and sixth-grade years. Ms. Lena Bell Spells and Mrs.

Ethel Thomas were my 5th and 6th-grade teachers respectfully. The 5th-grade math curriculum and the 6th-grade science curriculum were primary focal points for these grade levels.

Students became efficient with multiplication tables one through twelve. Ms. Spells excised great energy and effort from students in this area. All students were required to be able to stand and recite each table completely by memory until all were learned. This process was mandatory for each student and required mastery to be demonstrated in writing as well. Multiplication was among other areas of math emphasized during fifth grade.

Ms. L. B. Spells 5th grade teacher at Robinson Elementary School during its early years.

There was a highly unusual occurrence during this school year involving Miss Spells and one of her former students; then in the sixth grade. This student entered the classroom and became involved in an argumentative conflict with the teacher that quickly escalated into a physical confrontation. The student involved had a brother in the class. The incident in a matter of minutes became a mutual "hair pulling stalemate." A nearby teacher and passing high school student rushed into the room and ended the unfortunate incident. The brother and other students were compliant with Miss Spell's instructions to remain quiet and in their seats from the start. Neither before nor since this incident did I witness or become aware of such a situation between a teacher and student at Robinson. This was an extreme anomaly.

Mrs. Ethel Thomas was, as I recall, a very attractive and confident teacher. The sixth grade was a time of budding early adolescence, and she was definitely up to the challenge. She explained early in the school term that our growth and maturation process brought about hormone changes within our developing bodies. She further explained how it was necessary to practice good hygiene and the necessity for thorough baths before coming to school. She thereby warned the class that someone was not doing so. Finally, one day she decided to resolve the problem by checking under the arms of each student until she identified the problem. The remainder of the class was excused for a break. Yes, she did request water and soap and demonstrated to the student how it was to be done. We were told when to return to class. Mrs. Thomas had made her point and that problem of early adolescence never occurred again.

Three other events have remained very prominent for this time period. Governor Terry Sanford was an incredibly significant governor for most North Carolinians and especially to this community. Firstly, he was elected in 1960 along with John Kennedy both as "progressive candidates". Secondly, he had obtained office partially as "the education governor". His scheduled visit to Pitt County Schools and specifically to Robinson thereby became a momentous occasion. Our complete school body learned a song written by staff and practiced just for this occasion. Mr. Maye (principal) had the entire student body rehearsed the song entitled ("God Bless Our Governor") in the gymnasium where the program would take place. On the day of the visit, the program went over exactly as planned and practiced. The Daily Reflector Newspaper reported the Governors' related statement from his visit to Pitt County Schools the next day. The governor indicated that he enjoyed the visit to all Pitt County Schools, but he especially enjoyed his visit to Robinson Union where a special song was sung to him by the student body "God Bless Our Governor".

Science was stressed as an academic area of keen focus and the highly inspirational devotionals held before starting class each day. Devotional became "a morning ritual" during which we would have bible readings (ended in 1963), pledge to the flag, and sang such songs as "I Found a Horseshoe" and "This Old Man".

We had long lessons in science and copied many notes from the board. I particularly enjoyed the study of astronomy. The study of the sun, solar system, and distant stars always fascinated me. We would occasionally have a visit from a high school teacher for enrichment. Mr. John Ward would present short science lessons that would always be refreshing and enlightening. The class would be allowed to ask questions at the end of his lessons; this process was very helpful to a young and inquisitive sixth-grade mind.

The annual Science Fair afforded both elementary and high school students an opportunity to create and display "science projects" for competition in the gym. Projects were judged and awarded ribbons: blue, red, or white accordingly. There was tremendous pride in having a science project on display in the gym at the science fair. Douglas McKenzie and I had such a project while in the 6th grade. I will always remember the red ribbon received for a project demonstrating the ***process of rusting*** using steel wool pads in jars. Many thanks to Doug, my classmate, and fellow boyscout.

Ms. Dixon (H.S.'s French Teacher) would likewise occasionally present lessons of French to us. She would have us repeat often—used--phrases in French such as: do you speak French? (Parlez vous francais) and what time is it? (Quelle heure est-il). The class seemed eager to experience and explore French even if we were sometimes challenged by the mere usage of proper English.

The sixth grade is mostly remembered as a year of noteworthy physical and emotional growth. Early educational foundations were laid in areas of scientific investigation and thoughts of communication in a foreign language.

Mrs. T. A. Lawrence

For many Mrs. Thelma Lawrence, seventh-grade teacher was probably the most renowned, respected, and revered middle-grade teacher ever at Robinson. Her highly effective instructional methods, remarkable classroom management, and student discipline, matched with her extraordinary communication skills have become the stuff of legends among her former students.

Personal inspections were practiced in lower grades prior to Mrs. Lawrence but not to the extent and degree done in her class. After devotional, each student would turn and face their nearest classmate. At this time, each student would inspect each other for cleanliness of face and hands, especially fingernails, wrinkled clothing, hair for evidence of having been groomed, teeth for brushing, and shoes for polish and finally complete with a handkerchief or facial tissue. The inspection always ended with an oral report from each student. The report would be as an example: Johnny passed inspection today or Johnny did not pass inspection today because he is without a handkerchief and his shoes have not been polished. If one did not pass inspection this was of great concern to almost every student especially after being addressed by Mrs. Lawrence.

Also, whenever a student found themselves being chastised by Mrs. Lawrence each of our classmates was encouraged and given the opportunity to do the same. After Mrs. Lawrence finished expressing her disappointment, dissatisfaction, or disgust whichever she felt at the moment, classmates would stand and begin their similar verbal responses. This was the procedure in response to any adverse student attitudes or behaviors determined by Mrs. Lawrence requiring attention at any time during the instructional day. Students thereby had no choice but to remain "on their toes" throughout the day. Behaviors such as not doing homework, mis-behaving in class, or misconduct, in general, were the least of her problems with students. Believe me!

My personal experience with this method happened one day when my friend Ronnie Ennis and I became involved in a disagreement. We then decided to go into the coatroom to resolve our differences. We were not fighting but tussling as in quasi wrestling. Mrs. Lawrence detected the noise and quickly walked, overdrew the curtain and instructed us to come out to face the class. She then went back to her desk and began to use her folding fan as she often did before beginning a scolding session. I had learned previously that one had to think quickly and respond verbally with conviction in order to avoid Mrs. Lawrence's raft and classmates' rebuke. We were allowed to speak before the class had their turn to berate us. I stated to Mrs. Lawrence "I knew that you and the class heard the noise from the cloakroom, but I was not about to fight there. I have too much respect for you and the class to do so". She responded to me by instructing me to take a seat. She then stated to Ronnie "You were going to fight, weren't you? Weren't you? Ronnie ended by having to face the raft of the class and all their questions alone. Ronnie and I were great friends but by now, I had learned the value of swift thinking and shifting to survival mode in Mrs. Lawrence's class.

Almost everyone with a memory of that fateful day November 22, 1963, remember where they were and what they were doing when they received the horrific news. Mrs. Lawrence's class was the place for me. It was after lunch when a student came to the door and gave us the news. Once confirmed the president was dead everyone including Mrs. Lawrence placed their head on their desks and began to just sob and sob more.

Mrs. Lawrence was a very effective teacher with conviction. She taught well across the academic spectrum but especially in the subject area of English grammar. She placed special instructional value upon effective teaching: the parts of speech, diagramming of sentences, sentence structure, and speaking skills.

I feel that although she was immensely appreciated, she was likewise misunderstood by many as being too difficult and abrasive. In general, she had little tolerance for mediocrity, especially in the areas of personal confidence and verbal expression. She seemed to have determined intuitively that verbal communication skills, self-assurance, and critical thinking would be vital components to the advancement of a people. This has become her legacy to all who had the opportunity and great fortune to call her "my teacher".

The 8th grade was definitively a pivotal and transitional grade at Robinson. Ms. Carney became my next teacher as an eighth (8th) grader. She had been the girls' basketball coach before the team ceased to exist in 1963.

One of my earliest memories of Ms. Carneys' class was her indifference to a key method used by Mrs. Lawrence. She apparently detested students checking or questioning others as practiced under Mrs. Lawrence. Ms. Carney hastily remarked, "don't start that mess in here" as soon as students attempted to employ this procedure. This position was made very clear early in the school year. So, class processes and practices by Mrs. Lawrence ended immediately once in Ms. Carney's class.

I remember my 8th-grade year as an average academic year with significant emphasis on aesthetics, Boy Scouts, practice, and performance of plays.

Physical education and team sports especially basketball became huge in the 8th grade. Maybe this was an unofficial start for organized basketball. Mr. Kennedy would supervise our intraclass competition. Participants included: Jeffery Jones, David Wilkes, Kent Hammond, Dallas Staton, Ken Waller, Willie Pridgen, Harvey Strong, Ronald Ennis, Joseph Edwards John Maye Jr., and me. Physical education and extra-curricular activities became significant in building considerable individual and collective skills as well as camaraderie among us. Boy Scout Troop 88 under Mr. John Ward (Scout Master) was an extra-curricular activity, which had large and dedicated participation during middle-grade years.

Eighth-grade graduation was a much-anticipated event with student advancement from elementary standing to the ranks of high school. This status felt even more prominent in a union school setting with the presence of both levels on the same campus. One of my most memorable aspects of the graduation was all the pomp, attention to detail, and the focus of participants at this level.

Rander Harris, Lamonia Bryant, Mavis Jones, Margie Suggs, and my sister Emma were among the students in the class, which preceded us. All were good students and excellent models of student participation in graduation as 7th-grade marshals and 8th-grade honor students. As a graduating senior, Rander became valedictorian of his class in 1968. He was considered an extremely practical and very "bright guy" by classmates and friends. To some, he even became something of the neighborhood shrink (psychiatrist). It was a well-established fact that he would often listen to their problems and give meaningful advice. He was always a great listener and had a level of understanding beyond most.

The 8th grade graduation was a well-attended and highly ceremonial affair. It was an event which became an early marker of achievement for young learners. Equally important, it identified and encouraged exceptional academic skills among youthful students as rewarding and highly desirable.

Significant Non-School Related Events During Elementary Years

My family moved out of the Robinson House in Newtown in early 1961. My parents had purchased a home in (Old Town) Winterville on N. Mill Street. The house was constructed by (home builder Jim Walters Homes) a company that helped to make homeownership more affordable by constructing the exterior of homes while leaving much of the interior to be completed by the homeowner.

The move gave us new neighbors and friends. The Lacy family was located on our north side and the Hammonds were located shortly thereafter at our immediate south side. Kenneth Hammond and Brenda Lacy were classmates and so were Doris Lacy and my oldest sister Juanita. Other Lacy family members were Mr. S. J. Lacy, Mrs. Doris Lacy, and other children including Curtis, and Jerry. Other family members of the Hammond family were Reverend Hoyt Hammond, Mrs. Mary Hammond, Aunt Annie, and children still residing at home were David, Harvey, and Margaret. Our close proximity community relationship began as a very friendly and neighborly one. Our parents modeled the appropriate behavior and family members respectfully followed their example. This, fortunately, remained the case throughout our developmental and school attendance years.

These seem to have been the typical neighborly relations of the north Winterville community. Some additional nearby classmates and their families were those of Mr. Lester and Mrs. Mavis Jones, Mr. Frank and Mrs. Euridice Worthington, Mr. Lloyd and Mable Hooks, Mr. Sam Tucker, and others.

Like most others in the community, Emanuel and Janice Smith supported their household and family as blue-collar workers. My mother worked in domestic care early and as a seamstress at Grifton Clothing Manufacturing later.

My father's major employment was at Southern Bakery, Greenville, N.C. for several years and later with Cox Trailers Co., Grifton, N.C. until retirement. He also was self-employed as a licensed barber and proprietor of a barbershop in Ayden, N.C. only five miles from Winterville. He was there for more than 50 years.

Here at my Dad's barbershop, I found my first official work, by replacing cousin Anninias Smith who had finished South Ayden

H.S. and departed for North Carolina A&T in 1962. This event proved to go beyond just an opportunity to make a few dollars. The experience opened the door to new friendships, greater personal growth, and exposure to new insights and ideas that would impact my rapidly developing worldview in a profound way. It was here that I listen and learned from many valuable ideas, points of view, and life experiences of customers. In the midst of shining shoes, sweeping floors, and running errands I was compiling and expanding my information base. The barber shop chatter was ideas and perspectives often interesting and compelling emanating from Black men ostensibly speaking freely.

Many such conversations centered on varying views of readings and interpretations of the bible. There were equally discussions and debates on local happenings and current events, with a sprinkling of life stories and experiences. Sometimes when the conversations would become somewhat heated, I would often have an opinion, but I never injected that opinion because it was quite taboo for a child to do so during that era.

Mr. Funny Dunn and Mr. Peter Roundtree were two favorite customers because they were such provocative conversationalists. I recall heated conversations concerning "scripture", greatest boxers, baseball players, and even whether astronauts would ever go to the moon as stated by JFK in 1961. They expressed their doubt, disbelief, and total refusal to accept even the possibility of such a thing. This was well before "conspiracy theory" had become a readily utilized term. There was some disagreement in the shop from some as they went back and forth in the discussion. As I listened, it seemed so simple to me that science and technology could and would create such a reality. At the time it seemed clear that it must have been their "generational gap" that would not allow their acceptance of the inevitable. Presently we know the outcome of the moon landings. Yes? No? There are some currently from the world of conspiracy as well as the scientific community that would agree with Mr. Roundtree and Mr. Dunn. They have asserted scientific anomalies and completely rejected the "moon landings as a NASA Hoax.

Listening to customer debate and banter in the shop came in a close second when making friends and balling were possible. Leon Mayo became my first young friend in Ayden. He was the grandson of Mr. John Lewis Williams, the first of my Dad's co-barbers. Along with Mayo, I met and balled with several other similar-aged boys including Curtis Stewart, Jesse (Jump Shot) Woods my cousin Kelvin King and others. We all were about eleven or twelve at the time.

The Robinson Union Tigers and The South Ayden Eagles had already become serious rivals by now. This existential rivalry had already been established by such players as Henry Knox, Jimmy Worthington, David Banks, Clifton Daniels, Charles Wiggins, and others for Robinson. Likewise, the same had been achieved by such players as Cousin Cal Cannon, David Kilpatrick, Jimmy Brown, Charles Becton, Kermit Dixon, Thomas Reeves, Eddie McCarter, and others for the South Ayden teams. Little did we know that in just a few years we would become some of the future players sustaining the same rivalry!

Coach Bernard Haselrig (Iconic South Ayden Basketball Coach) was a regular customer at the barbershop. After his haircut, he would sometimes join us in a pickup game as both a player and coach. The coach in him would sometimes point out fundamentals to us as we played. He also stated to me on several occasions "Danny, you can attend South Ayden where you can play basketball and football since Robinson has no football team" he explained. I must say that I always had profound respect for Coach Haselrig, without a doubt, but I was a "Tiger" through and through. I never spoke those words to him and there would be no changing that fact!

High School began for my classmates and me in the fall of 1965. The Civil Rights Act of 1964 and the Voting Rights Act 1965 were focal

points on the national landscape as Malcolm X had been assassinated. The Watts Riot exploded, and the Viet Nam War intensified
all during the same turbulent year.

Robinson was a product of the times and truly an extension of
the local families and the Winterville, community. Remember, one
of the unique aspects of the union school was the combining of the
elementary and high school grades at one venue. Our family was
completed with the enrollment of "baby sister" Grossie in 1965.
My oldest sister (Evelyn) was a senior, my sister (Emma) became a
sophomore, your author, was a freshman, and my brother (Johnny)
was a sixth-grader. Other families had similar situations with family
enrollment. Accordingly, Robinson fostered a superior closeness and sensitivity for the sharing of common instructional and
extra-curricular experiences through family members which permeated throughout the community.

High School Academics and Interscholastic Athletics

Freshman literature became an area of special interest to me
immediately. Miss Giles was an attractive first-year teacher with
great enthusiasm and instructional skills. I'll never forget the
manner she taught concerning Phillip Pirrip and Ms. Havisham
(the lady who always wore the old wedding gown) from the novel
"Great Expectations" by Dickens. This began my long-held interest
in reading with comprehension for subsequent analysis, discussion, and writing.

I had always liked math, but Algebra was a different way of
understanding math. The idea of transferring words and the use
of symbols into a math problem or expression was a new concept much different from elementary school. There the focus had
been upon basic (arithmetic); grounded in adding, subtracting,
dividing, and multiplication. However, Mr. Ward proved to be a
very insightful and dedicated type of teacher in this regard. Also,

his use of the slide rule and its' placement above the chalkboard gave his classroom a very distinguished feeling for math. His concern and diligence as a teacher made sometimes difficult concepts more easily understood and our success more likely. Being recognized on his bulletin board as an outstanding student for a marking period was an honor cherished by all of us who had that experience.

Mr. Ward was a highly respected contributor to the school and the Winterville community. He not only gave of his time and expertise in the area of academics, but he did so for extra-curricular activities as well. He had a recognized reputation with parents for accurate and thorough feedback for them at PTA meetings concerning their students. In service as Boy Scout Master, he provided adult leadership and supervision to School Troop 88 members. Under his guidance, we held meetings and regularly attended annual Boy Scout Camporee competitions. By the way, he cooked a "mean beef stew" at the camporee. Mr. Ward used his personal car to transport basketball team members to games before the school owned an activity bus. These are some of the reasons all the community seemed pleased when he was promoted to Assistant Principal at Robinson in 1969 our senior year. These are the reasons he had become the quintessential educator and role model for many contemporaries and students alike.

Thankfully, Mr. John Taylor was my very gifted and multi-talented ninth-grade physical science teacher. He was an outstanding academic teacher with an extraordinarily successful manner in making students feel better about themselves partly by assigning names, especially to the girls. He was quite accomplished on the piano playing at commencement and graduation. He helped with the supervision of the boy scouts and coached very successfully for a short period of time. He further established himself as a winner by capturing both the JV Conference Championship and Pitt County Tournament in 1965 at Ayden. He was later appointed as Associate Superintendent of Pitt County Schools.

Mr. Harrell was the industrial arts teacher that required all students to produce a project to demonstrate skills learned in the class. Projects such as corner shelves, small tables, and bookends as I produced were examples. I remember Mr. Harrell for his wit and ability to get students to actualize their projects. He had also been the very successful boy's basketball coach prior to Coach Shelly Marsh.

Our class was the first 9th-grade class taught by Mr. Shelly Marsh. He was a young energetic Health and Physical Education teacher in his first year at Robinson from North Carolina A&T. We enjoyed his class and friendship as he was both teacher and coach for many. Coach Marsh coached both the junior varsity and varsity basketball teams. Making the team was a much-desired accomplishment as a freshman. The following class members accomplished that desire: Linwood and Bobby Crandall, Jeffrey Jones, John Maye, Jr., Kenneth Hammond, Clinton Person, Willie Ward, Kenneth Waller, and me.

A freshman's learning curve is always significant but "all in all" the school year ended with significant optimism. The civil rights movement was seemingly beginning to reap the benefits. Nationally, the Elementary and Secondary Education Act (ESEA) of 1965 provided funding to improve the quality of elementary and secondary education across the nation.

Integration of school faculties and "Freedom of Choice" were employed as early phases of integration in the Pitt County District. Placement of African American and Caucasian staff members in the other respective schools and allowing students to select the school of their choice seemed to be a reasonable approach. Federal programs and mandates allowed a wide spectrum of improvements and new opportunities for Robinson and all district students. For us, this made possible the acquisition of new books, audiovisual equipment, building improvements, and transportation needs including an activity bus.

Additionally, the county implemented a mobile library program through the utility of a "bookmobile" as sort of a neighborhood library on wheels.

Sophomore year began with the news of Ms. Elnora Vines having become our homeroom teacher by her own special request. This was said to have been related to our reputation for having something of a rowdy tendency, and less than conformist behavior. This resulted in a mixed blessing. Ms. Vines, a wonderful and concerned teacher, proved to be very well versed in her subject matter but also possessed an irritating propensity for an inquisition into her student's personal matters.

Integration, Extra-Curricular and Poverty Program

Integration among the faculties of Pitt County Schools was the major change beginning the school year. During homeroom, I became aware that my civics teacher would be Mr. Stephen Westfall a Caucasian and a recent graduate of East Carolina University. All students seemed to be fine with their schedules and the idea of our new faculty members.

The early days of Mr. Westfalls' class proved his personality and teaching style to be one that would be very amenable and successful with his students. He started by giving us something of his personal background. He was from Martinsville, Virginia. We learned he had done a tour of duty in Vietnam as an enlisted Army infantryman. He served directly under an African American sergeant that he had tremendous respect for. Concerning this sergeant, he once stated, *"I would follow him into a burning building with full confidence that his leadership would bring us out safely."* Mr. Westfall taught well with emphasis on the great issues of the day. Never did he provide an uncomfortable moment to the class through his personality, instructions, content, or methods. At the end of the school year knowing he was not returning, Mr. Westfall offered his home address and personal recommendations to class members. He was a 100% class act: and a wonderful role model for the integration of the Robinson faculty.

At Robinson, sophomores usually expanded their participation in school clubs and organizations such as The Debating Society, Future Homemakers of America, The French Club, Drama Club, Student Government, and Athletics. It was well known that usually, our athletes were also among our best academic performers and our "all-around" most prominent students. The idea of the "dumb jock" was a misnomer. We had jocks but they certainly did not fit the title of "dumb". Extra-curricular activities were extremely popular and seemed to provide a balance for all students in the key areas of academics, social development, and school pride. This knowledge was to serve me well later during my career.

The very popular North Carolina Joint Council on Health and Citizenship was an organization founded and facilitated by community leader and icon Dr. Andrew A. Best, MD. The program originally was designed for juniors but later opened to high school students across the board. The purpose was to teach and involve students in productive and participatory hygienic and civic-minded behaviors.

It appeared that support for academic success was often rooted in learned behaviors derived from extra-curricular participation. These include good sportsmanship, proper socialization and activities offered in the development of life skills.

For example, JV basketball our sophomore year did not prove fruitful at least where wins and losses were concerned. However, it became great for the value of learning sportsmanship with a record of 3W and 17L. 1967 was the year that all juniors were required to play varsity. The JV became stuck with only freshmen and inexperienced sophomores. This apparently became part of the rationale for the administration's decision for selection of two sophomores to receive summer tuition for basketball camp. John Maye, Jr. and

I became selectees to attend the N. C. State University Basketball Camp in Raleigh during early summer 1967.

Other school activities included the somewhat newly organized concert and marching band's preparation for concerts and parades. The much anticipated performance at the Wilmington Azalea Festival was a major band undertaking. Much to my regret, I never became a band member, but several classmates and family members became dedicated members and skilled performers under the direction of Mr. Charles D. Wooten (bandmaster) and Mr. T. S. Cooper (Jazz Band Director).

The Neighborhood Youth Corp was part of President Johnson's "War on Poverty" which provided a source of summer employment for "underprivileged" school-aged youth, fourteen and older. I might add that the term underprivileged was not how we recognized ourselves at the time even though the term was probably accurate; relatively speaking. This became the first officially sanctioned employment for me and other qualified schoolmates beginning in the summer of 1966. My job description at the school was primarily that of a grounds-keeper-helper. The program provided employment for about four weeks. We were quite happy with the opportunity to have a legitimate source for pay of any variety at the time. The program timing also made it possible to work harvesting tobacco later during the season. Maybe this was coordinated by design.

By mid-July, very early in the morning, tooting horns could be heard all over town. Farmers were arriving at the homes of town dwellers to transport workers out to farms. Although, these workers (many school-aged students) were not farmers this was their main source of summer employment. "Putting in tobacco" remained the primary source for summer employment even with the emergence of the Neighborhood Youth Corp. A mandatory financial need for students was created for back-to-school clothes, school fees, and summer spending.

It was a well-established tradition at Robinson Union to dress very sharp and neat once having moved up to high school rank. Some of the best examples among the guys known for this tradition and legendary for their style and dress were Henry Knox, the Dancey Brothers, Harvey Hammond, A.C. Edwards, Wiley Edwards, Jarvis Pridgen, and others. So, the idea was to work during the summer in order to purchase the best quality and the most quantity in clothing possible.

This is a short story I am compelled to share at this juncture. Over the years my mother would share her story about me in this regard with my friends and visitors at our home. She would explain how I would work during the summer to buy expensive shirts, sweaters, slacks, etc. from Steinbecks of Greenville, (local fine clothier) but would never purchase sufficient drawers (underwear). I would thereby have a major deficit in that area before Christmas. So, she would say concerning me "no matter what he looked like on the outside", she was always sure what at least one of my Christmas presents would be. You know--Drawers! Now I must admit that my recollection of this matter was not quite in-sync with hers but after all who can dispute Mom? Right?

My sophomore year ended with increased confidence and optimism in the areas of (1) personal growth and opportunity, (2) school and community improvements, and (3) governmental support for improved racial relations through assigned school personnel and federally funded programs.

Classmates, Personalities, Protest and Tragedy

Eleventh graders are often referred to as **dignified juniors**. These acquired attributes made the term applicable to my classmates by the end our junior year. Linda Jones was intellectual and composed. Kenneth (Hamp) Hammond was noble and ambitious. Jeffrey (Juicy) Jones was versatile and gifted. Arthur King was mannerly and light-hearted. Brenda Streeter was honest and reverent. Ronald (Wrench) Ennis was urban and swift. Evelyn (Chet) Patrick was trustworthy and faithful. David Wilkes was thoughtful and dependable. Willie Jean Phillips was decorous and joyful. Peggy Smith was cultured and tactful. Betty Blount was neat and decisive. Joseph Edwards was insightful and friendly. Ada Hooks was trustworthy and consistent. Ophelia (The O) Grimes was impetuous and driven. Donald Cox was easy-going and level-headed. Patricia Mills was family-oriented and softly spoken. Peggy (Bufo) Cox was neat and jovial. Sharon Carmon was introspective and energetic. Ester Hardy was straightforward and goal-oriented. Geneva Ward was bold and steadfast. Lee Barrett was gleeful and strong. Naomi Mooring was perky and endearing. Belinda (Fat Gal) Brock was talented and poetic. Sam Blount was expressive and tireless. Marvin (Chubb) Tyson was cool and dedicated. Willie (Gee) Ward was athletic and stately. Betty Dupree was studious and obedient. Deloris Battle was melodic and meticulous. Cody Cox was witty and outgoing. Belinda Boyd was joyful and spirited. Johnnie Mae Cox was nice and cooperative. Nellie Ebron was pleasant and amenable. Harvey (Cheese) Strong was helpful and thoughtful. Barbara Faye Bryant was inquisitive and resilient. Brenda Lacy was courteous and considerate. Sylvia Bryant was wise and thoughtful. Marvin Blount was hard-working and side-kickish. Frances Worthington was tidy and orderly, and Clint Person was disciplined and cosmopolitan.

Mrs. Doris Lee became our very capable homeroom teacher for both our junior and senior years. It was explained that this decision was made for the purpose of continuity as we approached graduation with all the accompanying required preparations. The choice could not have been better. Mrs. Lee had an outstanding temperament and the patience of a saint, which was very much warranted for our homeroom of students.

The selection of officers and positions of leadership was completed early. Ken Hammond became our class president for the third consecutive year. Other class officers were Jeffery Jones, Evelyn Patrick, Brenda Streeter and me.

Students became eligible for bus driving as juniors. Not only were they paid but their selection was considered a privilege and an honor. Remarkably, there were few bus violations; I do not recall any. Disruptions, fighting, general misbehavior, or disrespect for the drivers' authority was a non-starter. Some of our classmates who qualified as bus drivers were Willie (the Buzz) Ennis, Sam Blount, Linwood Gay, Harvey (Cheese) Strong, Jasper Wright, Joseph Edwards, and Dallas Staton. This level of conformity on the buses is almost unheard of currently even with adult drivers and bus monitors. My! How times have changed.

Ms. Doris Teele taught my favorite subject of my high school study. She was also one of my favorite teachers with an individualized teaching style and a charismatic personality. It was she who helped me understand geometry as the study of shapes and objects compared to the dimensions of space in which they exist. Even though I never asked, I always felt I had been recommended for her student assistant, by Mr. Ward.

Mrs. Leary was our somewhat quiet, and soft-spoken chemistry teacher. Her quiet demeanor was not to be mistaken for incompetence. She was widely respected for knowledge of her subject matter and concern for her students. Whenever she deemed the class not performing at or near their best, we received this warning "class when you get to college everyone will be valedictorians, salutatorians, and honor students". Stated otherwise, the competition only gets greater as you move up the educational ladder. My experience later supported Mrs. Leary's assertion.

Coach Shelly Marsh, as a coach, made a great effort to provide as many opportunities for his student-athletes as possible. Our freshman year having been his first year as a teacher always gave us a special bond. He always seemed to be more than just a teacher/coach for us. For this reason, we were not surprised that he was influential with Mr. Maye (principal) in bringing baseball to Robinson's athletic program. There wasn't a lot of athletic funding at the time. So, our first uniforms were not perfect fits but gleefully received as donations from Camp Lejeune Marines Baseball team.

Losing the best basketball player ever at Robinson to graduation (Raymond Bryant) the previous year had a major impact on the team. Larry Daniels (LD) and Edward (Peter) Farrow were the senior leaders of 1968. The team posted a record of 11W and 12L. We lost both regular-season games and in the tournament finals to South Ayden. The other Pitt County Tournament participants were H.B Suggs of Farmville, G.R. Whitfield of Grimesland, and Bethel Union of Bethel. The tournament was hosted at each of the five-county schools on a rotational basis. It was held at G. R. Whitfield in 1968 and would rotate to W. H. Robinson in 1969.

One of the year's highlights was the first-ever Robinson junior-senior game. There had been a lot of speculation about which class would win if such a game actually occurred. The juniors were easily the winners. This resolved lots of banter and locker room conversation between the "class of 68" and the "class of 69".

Although the big game had generated fun and excitement, our junior year did not end with the abundance of enthusiastic optimism as had the previous two school years. Several students from Robinson had made Winterville High School their "Freedom of Choice" selection. However, none from Winterville High School selected Robinson as their "Freedom of Choice" school. At year's end, many attendees from Robinson at WHS received failing grades in English, which resulted in repeating that grade. This became catastrophic for Robinson students and practically ended "Freedom of Choice" for its short existence in Winterville. After the "Freedom of Choice debacle, integration did not start in earnest until the consolidation of the two schools plus G. R. Whitfield at newly constructed D. H. Conley three years later in1971.

President Lyndon Johnson's Great Society Programs had become the substance of moral and practical hope after the loss of JFK in 1963. His "Great Society" Programs resonated with many African Americans especially in the area(s) of education and public schools. However, the Viet Nam War had become very unpopular and a major political problem for his presidency. Suddenly in March with an approaching election, he announced that he "would not seek nor accept the Democratic Party's nomination for president". To make matters exponentially worse, Martin Luther King was assassinated on a warm spring evening Thursday, April 4th nearing the end of the school year. I recall the news bulletin as our family watched TV together in shock. The next day we received a phone call from my oldest sister Juanita from (North Carolina College at Durham). She was informing our dad that the school was ending classes early and closing due to the assassination. The presence of the National Guard checkpoints and their searches along the way in Raleigh and Durham was a very harrying experience throughout this ordeal. The anger sparked by the death of MLK resulted in immediate protest and riots across much of the country.

Locally, curfew hours were instated merely for precautionary purposes in Greenville. Area public schools did not recess early for summer even though national tensions remained elevated. Then the assassination of Democratic presidential candidate Robert Kennedy on June 6th continued the nightmarish events of 1968 well into the hot (non-air-conditioned) months of summer.

Robinson's class of 1969 began its senior year not unlike most across the nation, especially the seniors at Dudley High School of Greensboro, NC. We all had witnessed a long hot summer of civil unrest, which rendered civil rights protest, political assassinations, opposition to the Viet Nam War, and acquired disillusionment from it all.

For many African Americans, the death of King accelerated the need for new perspectives on how best to address "issues of civil rights." Members of The Student Non-Violent Coordinating Committee (SNCC) and their leadership set forth a persuasive example of transformation away from the King philosophy. Stokely Carmichael and later H. Rap Brown denounced nonviolence and began to pronounce the philosophy of "Black Power" along with the emerging Black Panther Party. This idea was best expressed in Carmichaels' book <u>Black Power</u> of 1968.

The military casualties and the subsequent frequency of funerals were a disturbing reminder of the continued raging war in South East Asia. It brought to mind the question raised by Motown Recording Artist (Edwin Starr) which was War Yeah! What is it Good For? He went on to answer his own question by stating "Absolutely Nothing".

Fortunately, we had Ms. Elnora Vines as our Social Science teacher to help us understand it all and to place it into perspective. One of the most enlightening aspects of her classes was her encouragement for class participation and discussion of critical issues. This illustrates a problem inherent with standards testing requirements currently held in public education. With the required time and emphasis, placement on standards preparations and testing afford precious little time to utilize the successful teaching methods used by Ms. Vines with us. Strictly mandated curriculums and instructional pacing requirements prevent or significantly hamper the use and benefits of such teaching styles presently.

One of the first observations in our return to school was the absence of our classmate and friend John Walter (principal's son). We were informed that he had transferred to Eppes High in Greenville. The other conspicuous school opening detail was further integration of the faculty, which had begun in 1967. Mrs. Margaret James was selected as our English 12 teacher and Mrs. Mildred Still became our new Music Appreciation teacher. Mrs. James sometimes employed the use of a dummy and her considerable ventriloquist skills as an instructional tool. Both teachers demonstrated quality attitudes and amenable teaching styles, which made us as young seniors feel really great early about our new teachers and classification.

The return to school in August was at the height of the presidential election of 1968 between democratic candidate Hubert H. Humphrey and Republican candidate Richard M. Nixon. Nixon ran on the issue of "law and order" which was interpreted as code for placing brakes on "Black Power" and the Viet Nam War protest movement. Needless to say, he was not our "candidate of choice". Regardless of our preference, Nixon was elected as the 37th president of the country on November 5th, 1968. Our class was highly disappointed and nearly on the verge of disgust from these results. I recall Ms. Vines having concerns but immediately became a calming voice. She made clear that the country had challenges in its past and that we would get through the Nixon years. We now know, the outcome of his administration was to become a national catastrophe and considered by many a historical "turning point" in the American Governmental System.

The senior business was high on our agenda after classes and schedules had been resolved. The following officers were elected: Jeffery Jones (president), Danny Smith (vice president), Brenda Streeter (secretary), Bettie Blount, (assistant secretary), Evelyn Patrick (Historian), Ronald Ennis and Kenneth Waller (reporters), Parliamentarians (Ada Hooks and David Wilkes) and Calvin Wilkes (treasurer). Ken Hammond was elected president of the Student Government. Brenda Lacy and Belinda Boyd were elected senior class representatives to the Student Government.

National ethos and trends had moved more toward the youth with less trust in authority and established thought processes. Robinson seniors were about to raise their voices and register legitimate concerns with their school administration.

Basketball season was always highly anticipated with exceptional student and community support. So, by '68-'69 the rivalry between Robinson and South Ayden had become so intense that each team used the others activity bus for transportation to the away game at the others school. Coach Shelly Marsh coached his best game of the season when the Tigers took on the Eagles of South Ayden at Robinson in their first encounter of the season. To aggressively defend South Ayden's best offensive player (Charlie Grimes), he prepared the team around a specific strategy. Robinson won the game. Unfortunately, there was no specific preparation for the next two encounters, South Ayden at Ayden or the Pitt County Tournament Finals played at Robinson. We became Pitt County Co-Conference Champions with South Ayden and Runners-Up in the Pitt County Tournament to South Ayden and Runners-Up in the District Tournament to Conetoe High School of Edgecombe County. The 1968-69 varsity basketball team (16-8) improved its record significantly beyond that of the 1967-68 team (11-12).

The rivalry continued somewhat between D. H. Conley and Ayden-Grifton after full integration/consolidation in 1971. However, that old spirit and rivalry that once existed between Robinson and South Ayden was never to be duplicated again.

Each senior class heretofore had been expected to leave a senior gift upon graduation. Savings were accumulated by maintaining a savings account from freshman through senior year to achieve this goal. Early senior class business meetings revealed a discrepancy in the senior treasury. Unfortunately, our funds did not match our recorded savings. Although there were several minor concerns, the senior class considered this the major immediate problem.

At this point, Principal John Maye was known and revered as a "strict disciplinarian" who ran a very "tight ship". There was a personal experience early on during my senior year, which became instructive to this point. One day during English class I decided to "test the waters" with Mrs. James knowing she was a new teacher at Robinson and didn't know the ropes. I was very aware of the well-established expectation that there was no good reason(s) for being out of class once the bell sounded to be in class. So, I asked for permission to be excused to the restroom anyway. She surprisingly replied, "Yes Danny, hurry". I thought "Wow that was easy" as I left the room. I entered the main building from the opposite end where the school office was located. I immediately noticed that the twin hallway doors were open completely through the building down to the office. I then decided it would probably be best to quickly get water from the fountain near the entrance door and return hastily to class. The hallway was completely empty from end to end as I bent to the fountain to drink. Just as I was completing my drink, I observed "Chief" leaving the office door and heading towards me. Oh, man! Forget the facts that: I was a member of the senior class, vice president of the senior class, captain of the basketball team (soon selected), a member of the Crown and Scepter Honor Society, and had legitimate permission from the teacher to be out of class. It was like a terrible dream; his eyeglasses twinkled a reflection; I panicked and quickly returned to Mrs. James' class before he could reach me. I had barely sat when his voice came over the intercom; "Mrs. James will you send Mr. Danny Carl Smith to the office and tell him to bring his books with him". As soon as I entered the office he stated, "Cat Salad, Suzanna (his favorite expletives substitutes). Mr. Smith, we're not going to run this school, I'm going to run this school". He never asked me, why was I out of class or if I had permission to be out of class. Strangely enough, I really felt that he was right, and I was wrong and in violation to which I admitted. Luckily, when he called to my home, he spoke with my dad who agreed to come immediately to the school. Mr. Maye explained to my what had occurred while I sat quietly.

He then agreed to allow me to remain in school with my s' support for his instructions and my cooperation. I was then permitted to return to class and was never caught out of class again. I often wondered what would have been his response if I had actually been a disruptive type or a genuine disciplinary problem.

Students understood his strict nature and toughness therefore hastily scampered at the sight of him and some teachers' voices trembled at the sound of his voice when called via intercom to their rooms. He was more often than not referred to simply as "Chief" by the student body. He was usually the only security source during after-school activities and basketball games. I recall once at a game three neighborhood rowdies entered the gym thinking Chief was not present and began scribbling (dancing) across the court. He could not be seen, but once he observed their behavior, he ran toward them removing his coat in his approach. Fortunately, the trespassers (not students) hastily retreated out of the gym. I thought as did others, Chief is no joke! In all matters at all times, he was to be taken seriously.

Our senior advisors were clueless, had no explanation for the treasury discrepancy, and even less interest in confronting "Chief" concerning anything. We likewise received no immediate information or clarification from neither "Chief" nor our advisors. Later he decided to meet with the senior class in a special meeting held in the gym. On the morning of the meeting, the gym was arranged such that students were seated on a section of bleachers facing four folding chairs to accommodate Mr. Maye and advisors. When Mr. Maye (Chief) arrived, he found no advisors seated. All decided to stand. I wondered why? Did they know an attack was imminent? He began by attacking individual students. He immediately attacked Ken Hammond by calling him a "black snake". He then alluded to our friendship by stating to me "friendship is thicker than blood". He then scolded Ronald "Wrench" Ennis by stating, "you can't say anything" and you know why, referencing an ongoing legal matter. The meeting did not yield real answers but did produce several unwarranted personal attacks.

We started our boycott of the cafeteria soon thereafter following our command decision. The most surprising outcome of the boycott was the underclassmen's participation without our solicitation for their involvement. As a matter of fact, we had no knowledge of their awareness of our intentions to boycott. On the first day of the boycott, there were only two people in the cafeteria during high school lunch. Those two were Mr. John Maye (Principal) and Willie the Buzz Ennis side by side and all alone. "Chief" appeared angry as he chewed while drinking milk. Willie the Buzz looked content as he sat with "Chief" all by his lonesome. What a sight! The remaining student body had lunch in various places elsewhere mostly on the front lawn. The Boycott could not have made a bigger impact because, with the underclassmen, it was broader and more complete than we had ever imagined.

After the first day of the boycott, students slowly drifted back to the cafeteria; but our point had been made. Years later, we discovered that we had the silent support and admiration of many teachers and staff members throughout the ordeal. At year's end, the class was able to leave a class gift. In our final analysis, we concluded that a portion of our class treasury had been used for a legitimate school purpose, albeit not necessarily as the class had intended.

Another student-driven boycott at Dudley High during the spring of 1969 in Greensboro, N.C. was to have a much greater impact and consequential outcomes than did ours at Robinson.

Willie Grimes (a 1967 Robinson graduate) lost his life at his beloved A&T State College currently (University) in Greensboro during the early evening hours of May 22, 1969. His death came amid racial strife and civil unrest spilling over to the A&T college campus from a boycott on the Dudley High School campus. The horrific death of the Winterville native and Robinson graduate received national news attention. The story was covered on the CBS Evening News anchored by the legendary reporter, and icon Walter Cronkite.

Boy scout Troop 88 of Winterville, NC; 1964

A&T and Dudley students had successfully cooperated previously back in 1960 to force the very historical desegregation of the Greensboro Woolworth's lunch counter. It seemed highly likely the same level of cooperation would be needed again. Many facts surrounding this senseless death remain a public mystery. The primary missing fact became and remains, who actually killed Willie Grimes.

His funeral was held at the Robinson High gym in Winterville, NC. There was overflowing attendance by his grief-stricken family: Joe his father, Ella his mother, older siblings. and younger brother George then a Robinson sophomore. Others within the group of more than 2,000 mourners were college students, Pershing Rifles Fraternity Brothers (pall barriers), Aggie Faculty and Staff; local schoolmates, friends, and media types. Serving as an usher was both an honor and a heart-wrenching experience for me. After watching so many civil rights events on news shows and having related discussions in Ms. Vines' class the idea of experiencing a homeboy lost in the same context was surreal. He and I had been members of Boy Scout Troop 88 together (pictured standing side by side in this 1964 Camporee photo standing 3rd and 4th respectively left to right); basketball teammates, (although he was varsity when I was JV), and schoolmates. Others pictured left to right top: Curtis Lacy, Samuel Holloway, Dalton Knox, Earl Daniels, Lester "Breeze" Patrick; bottom left to right were Douglas McKenzie, Milton Knox, Kenneth Hammond, Willie Fleming, and Lloyd Hooks.

Willie's funeral would be one among five to be held in Robinson's gym my senior year and endured by the Winterville community during "the tragic spring of 1969".

Jimmy Worthington a Robinson graduate and school basketball legend had completed one successful tour in Viet Nam before he unfortunately volunteered and accepted a second tour. Jimmy was wedded to his high school sweetheart and Robinson graduate, the sorrow filled, Theraldine Suggs Worthington. I became especially attentive to the long, dignified family processional as they entered the gym. The line included several military men in uniform who were really striking. One of them was Lyman Cox a '68 graduate and personal friend. He looked as stoic and polished as a sailor could in his dress-white cracker jacks as he entered with his sweetheart, Claudette among the family.

Josephus Daniels was the second Robinsonian Viet Nam casualty, and the third alumnus to be funeralized in the Robinson gym during the spring of 1969. He was the son of Joe and Effie Daniels. After the death of Jimmy Worthington and Josephus, this would become my awakening and breaking point beginning my mental opposition to the Viet Nam War!

David Wilkes a 1969 classmate, basketball teammate, and fun-loving friend, was lost in a car accident after graduation in the late summer of 1969. His death occurred after leaving work en route home early one summer morning. David was senior class parliamentarian, basketball teammate, member of the Crown Scepter Honor Society, and all-around good guy. Among male classmates and teammates, we served as ushers and pallbearers at the funeral in the Robinson gym.

Ella Belle Vance was a 1958 graduate of Robinson and reported to have been killed by her significant other. She resided out of state at the time of her death. My memory of viewing her remains was such an attractive lady and such a tragic death.

Mentioned here are four national events that impacted the country and my worldview at the time in 1969. Richard Nixon became the 37th president of the United States in January of 1969 but resigned office during his second term due to corruption. Fred Hampton and Mark Clark members of the Chicago Chapter of the Black Panther Party were killed in a pre-dawn raid by Police in December 1969. The ongoing Viet Nam War in 1969 claimed the lives of more than 11,000 American Servicemen. There was also the moon landing and "that's one small step for man" one giant leap for mankind"; as proclaimed by Neil Armstrong. The reported moon landing on July 20th, 1969 became that great scientific and techno-logical event of the twentieth century.

Graduation in 1969 became a blend of accomplishment and challenge. The decision for participatory social change was not an option. Our perspectives regarding war, peace, and progress were emerging. The Viet Nam War, the struggle for racial justice, and the explosion of technology had become the canvass for our expres-sion as we gazed towards a future of "broader horizons".

Regional Higher Education

The explosive growth of East Carolina University and the estab-lishment of its Brody School of Medicine and the East Carolina School of Dental Medicine have factored heavily in the advance-ment of Greenville, N.C., and the surrounding area. Since 1969 the area has grown around (education, industry, and agriculture); becoming the tenth largest city in North Carolina.

It has become a major university deserving its' wide-ranging recognition. Institutions of learning and particularly those of higher learning are the products of their governing bodies and the vision and leadership of their administrators. Being reared in the area and having the opportunity to witness the emergence and benefits firsthand has been positively significant and equally inspirational.

Pitt Community College has likewise brought more diverse higher learning opportunities to the area. Established in 1961 it quickly became one of the most popular methods for acquiring associate degrees. Many such degrees offered qualifications for employment in technical and service-related fields. At the time of graduation several Robinson and other area students would take the admittance exam, some quite successfully. One Robinson student, (Willie Lester Jones), was reported to have recorded one of the highest scores on record circa 1966. More recently, the continuing education programs which avail matriculation for a bachelor's degree through four-year university programs have become an extraordinary and highly successful collaboration.

CHAPTER 3

THE MEN OF THE PITT COUNTY SCHOOLS MAINTENANCE DEPARTMENT

Worker's Wisdom 101

As graduation had grown near our guidance counselor made us aware of a federal program called PACE. This program provided summer employment for college-bound students. At this juncture, I had no other probable employment sources. I therefore hurriedly submitted an application and anxiously awaited the response.

My program assignment along with several other local college students was at the Pitt County Schools Maintenance Department located in Winterville, NC. The federally funded program had the unique feature of providing pay for its student employees only after completing their summer work and their return to college. This prevented some non-spend-thrifts from summer spending thereby reserving their much needed funds for tuition and related expenses once they returned to school. It was my privilege to be employed by the PACE program during the summers of 1969, 1970, and 1972 at the (PCSMD).

Among ones' life experiences are varying impactful occurrences often from unexpected sources. My three-year summer employment with the men of the Pitt County Schools Maintenance Department (PCSMD) proved to be a major "case in point". I never had reservations concerning blue-collar work or its values. After all, my parents and much of the community that produced me were instructive in this way. However, the men of the (PCSMD) taught me lessons I have since carried through life. Through the expressions of their words and the demonstrations of their characters, they conveyed to me and the other students in the program how to work, the value of work and the proper respect to have for each other in doing so. A humble reverence for their occupational work; and Mr. Prices' supervision, a healthy respect for each other yielded honorable results for a school district, especially for the students served.

Coordinator William Price

Mr. William Price, Maintenance Coordinator, (a caucasian gentleman) was the highly respected operations leader in charge of all maintenance activity. He set the tone and modeled the proper behavior for a good and productive work environment for all employees. There existed a very fair and amenable atmosphere for all workers: including personnel safety and appreciation for the worker as much, as for the work they performed. Mr. Price persistently sustained his maintenance mission seriously; no matter what the job. As coordinator, he remained mindful that before a building opened, a single child could be seated, or instructions from a curriculum could be taught, the humble but outstanding work of his department and men was required.

In 1969 the (PCSMD) did all school maintenance short of constructing new buildings. Subcontracting was not the order of the day. This included: roofing, bricklaying, grass cutting, landscaping, exterior building repair, framing, electrical, plumbing, drywall, flooring, painting, doors and windows, mobile classroom reloca-tions, coal delivery, vehicle repair, book delivery, janitorial services, the "honey truck" (sewage removal and disposal) and more.

The following is a list of schools that were maintained by his department. Robinson High, Winterville High, South Ayden High, Ayden High, Ayden Elementary, Bethel Union, Bethel High, H. B. Suggs High, Farmville High, G. R. Whitfield High, Grimesland High, Chicod High, Stokes High, Grifton High, Faukland Elementary, Pactolus Elementary, Belvoir Elementary and others.

As can be deduced by the number of schools and repairs needed, often the work list would become quite extensive. The numerous plumbing and roofing jobs, structural work, painting, grass in need of cutting, drywall in disrepair at multiple schools, vehicles needing service, and we always had several mobiles to move during summer months, busy was an understatement. Mr. Price would then become very animated; especially on Mondays in sharing weekly work assignments with the various job specialists. So, the men would be waiting to receive their work details in front of the office with their trucks ready. Mr. Price had a very minor limp, yet he would be walking briskly toward us. We could always discern his level of anxiety by his movement gate and whether or not he was talking as he came out the door. Suddenly, Mr. Price would emerge from his office talking, while glancing at his notes often using the term blank the blank in lure of profanity. He could be heard saying things like, "the plumbers just left Belvoir last week and got to go right back, we have three mobiles to move by Thursday, "the blank the blank book truck needs a new motor, I went to Sunday school yesterday, I don't want to curse but it's hard not to". He would finally settle down and give everyone their "marching orders"! Alas! The men would be cheerfully off to the schools and their respective jobs to begin their work for the week.

Mr. Price will always be remembered and revered for his honesty, fair-mindedness, and his endearing personality by his employees of all persuasions. He was likewise admired by school adminis- trators, central office personnel, and school board members for his dependability, job performance, and his overall dedication to the school district's mission for the well-being and education of all assigned students. There is one final note to Mr. Prices' very fair consideration; he never allowed PACE workers (college students) assignment to the "Honey Truck" (sewage collection and disposal).

Carl Heath

Mr. Carl Heath's job description was primarily that of dis- trict custodian supervisor and second in charge to Mr. Price. This required him to become a rover across the district keeping track of the needs and performances of the custodians at each school. Likewise, he was required to keep track of maintenance crews assigned to various schools for their respective temporary jobs. This meant that no matter what the specific work, Carl was a con- stant threat to suddenly appear at any crew work site and often comment on their work about which he had little knowledge. This area of his responsibilities certainly became a contributing factor to his "popularity deficit".

He seemed to have had some awareness of the general dis- like held for him by the men. I recall once me and another PACE employee needed to assist Carl in the completion of a small job detail. We had embarked his truck before he arrived. This allowed us to observe his stash of solely country music cassettes on his dash. Needless to say, we had a little chuckle concerning his choices in music. When Carl returned to the truck he interestingly and imme- diately selected a tape by Black Country singer Charley Pride for our consumption who had absolutely no appeal to us whatsoever. Later after discussion, we both agreed that this became an "I'm not such a bad guy after all gesture". Maybe to Carl it had even, presented an opportune moment to demonstrate a highly "uncommon liberal side of himself" Ha! Ha! Ha!

John Dorey

Mr. John Dorey (Caucasian) was treated as third in the chain of authority at the PCSMD. He was highly liked by the men but seemed to be the object of much of Carl Heath's distaste and ridicule. He was a decorated veteran of WWII and was respected by most to be very knowledgeable of most things mechanical and maintenance work in general.

Mr. Dorey was always concerned about his workers. Junie Jackson was his main assistant and for Junie he constantly sought pay raises from the superiors. I also remember him as a very pleasant man who constantly considered the human factor as the proper approach in consideration for any maintenance or construction application. Long before the (Americans with Disabilities Act of 1990) became law, Mr. Dorey had such thoughts in mind. For example, if we were constructing steps he might say "ok men let's build that railing "good and strong" for any elderly or handicapped that may have to use it. Mr. Dorey would come in and say "its corn cheese time" this was the cue for *a break*. Corn cheese was a favorite snack among the crew. Mr. Dorey once remarked that one day we would say "I once knew an ole bird that would enter when we were working and say, "it's corn cheese time". I wish he was still here to know; I'm actually writing about it. Here is to you, Mr. Dorey.

Joe Daniels

Little Joe Daniels was an African-American specialized carpenter at the PCSMD. He also operated a small grocery and variety store in North Winterville. Little Joe was effectively a site manager who had the privilege of driving a work truck home. This is some-times known colloquially as a "shirttail boss".

Joe would sometimes come to work with several hundred dol-lars in his shirt pocket and would reveal it to those nearby; often to their annoyance. I personally found it amusing and felt it was something akin to jealousy for the annoyed. Joe was a big cheerful man with little concern or fear of physical challenge and seemingly happy most of the time. However, I always sensed a deep-felt pain he held for the loss of his son Josephus killed in Viet Nam. He had become one of the "tragic five" eulogized at the Robinson Gym during my graduation year of 1969.

Little Joe was most memorable as a carpenter for his method of remembering measurements when framing for a cut. He would make the measurement then say the measurement out loud over and over and over again as not to forget the measurement. For example, if measuring a cut for door framing, he would say out loud: 84" high, 84" high, 84" high that door is 84" high until he actu-ally cut the board. I've used that same method as a self-reminder when doing similar work to the present day. So, it serves as both a practical reminder for the dimensions of the cut and as a memory of my mentor and friend Little Joe Daniels.

Leamon Carmon

Mr. Leamon Carmon was employed by the Pitt County School Maintenance Department during the summer months for campus grass cutting and landscaping. During the winter months he hauled and supplied coal for school boilers.

Mr. Leamon Carmon took great pride in care and beautifica-tion of the school surroundings and had a work ethic second to none. He was known to be very meticulous and a man who took his work very seriously. Due to the nature of his work, he usually worked alone. I remember him as a man who spent very little time socializing or making small talk. He was respected as "a man of action in a very few words". Once at work I recall him making haste to his truck and continuing to his next assigned task.

During the winter months, he kept busy supplying schools that required coal for heating. According to his daughter, Shirley Williams, on one occasion her father came home after work and changed his clothes but forgot to remove the coal dust from his face before leaving home. Such was his focus and intentions to move very timely between jobs or his next activity. Mr. Carmon worked more than one job most of his adult life. Respess James BBQ, Greenville, NC was another place of employment he held while also employed at PCSMD. He was also a lifelong loyal member of Saint Rest Holiness Church, Winterville, NC.

Willie Phillips

Mr. Willie Phillips was a master carpenter who could complete jobs much faster than most. Hence, he was known by his cohorts as "Quick Willie". Often a job would be called into the department requiring immediate structural repair or even construction from scratch. This was known as a job on a *rush card*. Willie would become "the man in demand".

He would receive such assignments and work alone. "Quick Willie" was known to do more work alone than others with assistance. He also seemed to prefer it that way.

I also remember Quick as a great local baseball fan. The local team under the management of Mr. Rufus Clark and such local legends as Red Ingram (Pitcher) of Ayden, N.C. would play games during summer months on the field behind Robinson School. He could be seen there regularly with his neighbor and friend Mr. Les Jones cheering on the team.

Willie's daughter, Willie Jean, was a classmate and a friend from grades one through twelve with me at Robinson. She was known for her great personality and her very keen good, natured sense of humor.

Willizard Edwards

Mr. Willizard Edwards was a dedicated drywall and plasterer maintenance specialist who loved his work. I recall his easy-going and patient manner in the performance of his job. He established himself as a model of how to get along with and have a good relationship with co-workers and those around him.

I also had the pleasure of knowing him and his family before working with him at the PCSMD. We both lived as neighbors in the Newtown area of Winterville. His sons William (Smooth) and Clinton were just a few years older as we grew up together in a close-knit neighborhood.

Mr. Willizard Edwards was a lifelong member of Mount Shiloh Baptist Church located in Winterville, NC.

Junie Jackson

Mr. Junie Jackson worked primarily as a helper and assistant assigned to Mr. John Dorey. Junie was a mild-mannered man and not 100% oriented for this line of work. He and his family lived close to my family at the time in Winterville. Although we never worked together very much, I do recall his and Mr. Dorey's jousting sense of humor the few enjoyable times we did. His favorite joke revolved around Mr. Dorey's unsuccessful attempts to secure him a pay raise. Junie would jokingly state "so far the only raise I received was one from off the floor to upon a ladder". Mr. Dorey would respond jokingly by stating something like "if he sent Junie to make a lumber purchase, he would not return empty-handed". However, if he requested ten 2x4x8, Junie might return with eight 2x4x10 or just about anything he had not ordered all in humorous banter. Although they poked fun at each other, they had a light-hearted but very respectful working relationship that proved entertaining to those of us in observance.

<u>Raymond Bess</u>

Raymond Bess was known by about all in the town of Winterville. The first time I ever recall seeing him was as a young elementary student while walking to school. He was catching baseballs in front of the old Knox Shop in a squat with a mitt. He was, however, catching the balls with his arm behind his back. I thought that was odd and also dangerous.

During this era, just about every town had an area considered to be the town hangout. In Winterville, this area located in North Winterville was known as "the Corner". It could be found at the intersection of Railroad and Tyson Streets. The area consisted of a couple of shops and a pool room. I recall the menacing presence of Raymond Bess often as we walked by the corner towards downtown Winterville.

Raymond Bess at this time was considered to be quite the bully by many. He was known to threaten and fight at the drop of a dime. If you came within close proximity, he may rush towards you feigning bodily harm but pull away at the last moment resulting only in intimidation. Frankly speaking, most people were afraid of the guy. It was widely repeated that in a challenge he once dropped a $20.00 dollar bill on the ground on the Corner and dared anyone to touch it. He then left the Corner with instructions that "no one better touch my money." After being gone for several hours, Raymond returned and retrieved his $20.00 exactly from where he left it. From that peculiar story alone, everyone just accepted the fact that Raymond was a "BAD MAN" and if you didn't know you had better ask somebody!

This was one of the PCSMD employees that I and other PACE workers worked with during the first summer of our employment. I recall the first work with him was the demolition of an old floor in need of replacement. Yes, he was somewhat different and a bit wild but through our work together and conversations, I began to develop a curiously perspective of Raymond Bess. Beneath his reputation, I personally discovered a hardworking, smart, and principled guy who wanted to share ideas but most of all prove that he could perform and do more work than anybody around in which he usually did.

Raymond became the main roofing specialist for tar roof repair. This was the process of overlaying tar-based roofs with layers of tar to prevent water damage. The method required hot tar, which was melted in a cooker and then moved to the roof for mopping. Raymond mopped, as Wayland Garris and I were the tar transporters via five gallon buckets. Even with two five-gallon buckets, we could not keep pace with Raymond's mopping speed when he got on a roll! We would constantly hear him saying things like "tar, tar, tar" or do I have to mop and get my own tar too?

Later after leaving the PCSMD Raymond became self-employed performing roofing contract work. During this period, he was contracted by my parents and many other locals to shingle or repair their roofs. His reputation for good work became impeccable in the community.

So, it can be said, that through his roofing career Raymond Bess was able to elevate his local reputation from that of a misunderstood bully to one of self-reliance, excellent work, and provider of customer satisfaction.

Willie Nicholson

Willie Nicholson began his employment with Pitt County Schools as a G. R. Whitfield janitor. By all accounts, he served as an efficient and loyal custodial provider to the school for many years. However, given the opportunity to trade his custodial position under Carl's supervision for spray painting specialist at the PCSMD became a "no brainer".

I had worked with several maintenance specialists such as framers, roofers, and mobile classroom movers before becoming somewhat of a permanent assistant to Willie.

We worked within a crew of painters, which included him and me as the preliminary (spray painters) and James Daniels (Chicod Custodian) and Arthur Sparkman (South Ayden Custodian) trimmers as the secondary painters (summer employees only). The secondary painters followed Willie trimming the windows and doors. Willie's official responsibilities were to paint the walls of classrooms and the interior of buildings as assigned by the use of the spray painter. My official responsibilities were assisting him in preparation, replenishing, and servicing the painter. My other responsibility was to be on the lookout for the arrival of Carl Heath which I did very effectively. This had been one of my unofficial responsibilities with other work crews previously.

I had been well schooled on being aware of his arrival and reporting to the crew so as to ensure Carl's presence never caught them off guard. It was not an issue of the men attempting to not do their work or skirting responsibility. They liked their jobs and respected Mr. Price's leadership to the point that they wanted to avoid any such appearances as excessive smoke breaks, snack runs, or building wandering. I recall only a couple of occasions when corrective actions were required by crew members. So, by the time Carl made his appearance, all were in place; even me. Carl came in once and stated after observing us "Hot damn" that Danny will work! All the men just shook their heads, yes but they were all smiling inside, especially me.

Mr. James and Mr. Arthur Sparkman took particular pride in not allowing their clothing to be soiled with paint whatsoever while painting. I recall one day at the end of work Mr. Sparkman walked by a mirror and discovered a small drop of paint on the back of his shirt sleeve. He then remarked very regrettably, "hum I got a drop of paint on me today". Such was out of the scope of his personal expectations and below his standards as an expert painter.

Willie always demonstrated gratitude for his employment as the spray painter specialist. He was always meticulous with the details of his painting, especially in the classrooms. He was equally pains-takingly careful with the painter's equipment. He kept that sprayer and those spray tips "clean as a whistle". Willie always made it clear that the sprayer was the key to his paycheck and him being his own shirt-tail boss. I surmised that he remembered firsthand the toll of farm work and the demands of janitorial work. Given the contrast, he easily made the choice for painting with no desire for reversion.

During the two summers we worked together with Mr. Willie Nicholson, his ideas, our work-related interactions, his life stories, perspectives, his joking humor, and last but not least his love for the ladies impressed me in a way that I have never forgotten and will always remember to share with others. He never presented himself to me as having the least desire for distinction of status between us either as employees or men despite our significant age differ-ence. Mutual respect, understanding, and bond were to develop for the remainder of his life as it turned out. He called me Danny and sometimes just Smith and I always called him Willie as he seemed to have preferred. This became the basis of a quickly established working relationship and friendship which never wavered.

Willie was a person you could always depend upon to lighten the atmosphere with humor during a moment of indifference or just from outright boredom. He was a small-framed African American man with the stature and comedic talent of a Don Knotts without the nerdy side like Barney Fife (a character from the old Andy Griffith Show). A good example, I recall one day we were having lunch purchased from a nearby grill. So, I had purchased a couple of hot dogs and a honey bun. We had just started eating when Willie suddenly grabbed my honey bun and feign it as he was tossing it out the truck window. Knowing my mouth was full and could not speak and at the moment, I could only make a muffled sound; as I did. We both had a big laugh from the episode. It then became a source for teasing me as he would occasionally remind me. "Hey Danny, do you remember that day you thought I was going to through your honey bun out the window and you couldn't say a damn thing because your mouth was so full"? "You could only squeal like a little pig"? We would then have a laugh together, which would always lighten the mood.

He was also the type that would share any good fortune he had with those around him. For example, before there was a North Carolina Lottery there were unauthorized numbers played through small-time bookies. People would typically buy dollar tickets, two-dollar tickets etc. The more the ticket cost the larger the payoff would be. Well, Willie would often play the numbers on weekends and sometimes hit (purchase the winning number).

We would know because he would buy lunch for the trimmers and me that Monday. Then while having lunch he would crack a joke by saying something like, "I can't stand a bunch of broke, hungry painters around me at lunchtime". We would all have a laugh together, that's the kind of good, fun, guy, he was!

Sometimes we would have conversations about different issues and ideas concerning current events and everyday life. This was the early 1970's. Civil rights and race relations were prominent news stories and Nixon was president. Willie's perspectives on issues of the day such as The Black Power Movement, Busing for School Equality, and Affirmative Action were exceedingly more conservative than mine. Whatever the issue, he would seemingly take a position like "it takes time and Rome wasn't built in a day". I would always be like, why should we have to wait for something that was due to us years and years ago? Willie would respond generally by stating something like, "you're a pretty smart ole college boy but you're just so dog gone impatient". However, there was something I became keenly aware of from all such conversations we had. Willie never once said to me, Danny you're wrong. I believe this was directly related to the respect and validity he gleaned from my positions and the respect and value we held for each other.

It was also during one such conversation that Willie confided in me the fact of the tragic loss of his only child (a son) found with his girlfriend from a carbon monoxide death in a car.

Willie was born and lived in the small town of Grimesland, North Carolina located in Pitt County. There he resided most of his life. One of his favorite stories and probably the most historically significant was the story of Bryan Grimes, (plantation, slave owner, and decorated Confederate general). He was the person for whom the town was named. Willie explained from his "oral tradition sources" how the Grimes Plantation had been one of the largest and most productive in North Carolina. This plantation had more than 100 slaves and thousands of plantation acreage. On one occasion while working at G. R. Whitfield in Grimesland, he gave me a drive-by tour of the remnants from the old plantation house and the once slave quarters. General Grimes's old antebellum home was in disrepair and the slave quarters appeared to have been converted into livestock shelter.

He also described the strange death of General Grimes after commanding confederates, being wounded several times in battle, and surviving the civil war. Willie told me how General Grimes was shot and killed from ambush while traveling via buggy between Grimesland and Washington, N.C. He stated that he was buried locally in a family cemetery on the plantation.

I must admit that study of confederates was not a major area of personal interest nor a major part of my formal education at the time. This was applicable at both high school and college levels despite my major in history. Willie almost fondly shared aspects of this local history with immense interest, concern, and passion. As we logged more working hours and shared more conversation, so did my interest level and curiosity grow about his General Grimes story.

Later over the years during my career as an educator, I found time to research and verify or dismiss Willie's fascinating claims. My personal research into the life and legacy of General Bryan Grimes substantiated Willies' historical account and provided more compelling details. According to the book <u>The Life and Times of General Grimes, 2010 by</u> Hudson, he never had formal military training. He became the last Major General appointment to the Confederate Army of Northern Virginia Campaign. He fought in battles at Manassas, Chancellorsville, Fredericksburg, Petersburg, Richmond, and Gettysburg and was in support of Robert E. Lee at Appomattox prior to surrender. He had two sons to die as his namesake Bryan after having been born to two different wives. Finally, his assassination was at the hands of one William Parker a local individual who was originally acquitted only later to become the victim of a local lynch mob (Harrell; 1999:282).

There were many conversations and much dialogue we shared for the time we worked together. However, I can't be emphatic enough when I attempt to convey his tremendous attraction and love for the ladies. Remember, by this time Willie was well into his seventies. He would almost become excited merely discussing females including their appearance, fragrance and especially their walk.

A very memorable occasion once occurred when Willie had just returned to the truck after a bank deposit. When I spotted an attractive lady, I pointed her out to Willie by asking him did he see that good-looking lady" just leaving the bank. He quickly responded, "yes I saw her, probably before you did" as he jokingly explained "Hush Boy just be quiet," he said, "they don't even look good to you yet, just wait until you're my age then you'll know, and better truly understand just how good they really look". His point being only when you *surpass maturity* and become virtually able to do little more than just observe them only then will you truly be able to appreciate just *how good* they look.

Willie had a method of explaining and teaching life's lessons making them remarkably clear to me. He accomplished this sometimes through humor, often with history but always with consideration for others and tons of "plain ole common sense". That's why he will forever remain in my memory as *"Good Ole Willie"*.

Conclusions

Lessons learned in life originate from many sources. Those lessons emanating from the Pitt County Schools Maintenance Department were applied throughout my career in Education as well as during my time served in the U.S. Navy. Recognition from their superiors and co-workers alike were highly valued for the quality of work performed. Being acknowledged as a good worker was very important to the maintenance employees. They were knowledgeable and willing to share their expertise. This made it possible for those like me to develop many skills they shared. Equally important I learned their values and the respect they held for each other proving there is dignity in work. The culture permeated at the PCSMD was one of outstanding work ethic, personal and occupational safety concern for each other, and high group morale for the department. Lessons learned here could easily become critical criteria that any goal-oriented entity could benefit from currently.

Finally, I discovered that a successful work environment begins with respect. It continues by cultivating cooperation and teamwork. The work then becomes less difficult as such relationships evolve. It's at the friendship level that the process becomes a self-reinforcing methodology.

The evidence was clear that genuine respect and appreciation for their work and each other among blue-collar workers in an organization goes a long way towards maintaining a cooperative, efficient, and productive work environment.

Ken Hammond my best friend in the world worked PACE one summer at PCSMD. He attended East Carolina University, Shaw University, and N.C. State University acquired a Doctorate Degree and recently retired from a successful career in the ministry. Wayland Garris the valedictorian of Winterville High School Class of 1969 successfully worked one summer in PACE. I haven't since heard of his whereabouts. Lifelong friend Lester "the Breeze" Patrick worked a summer or two. He later graduated from N.C. A&T and relocated with his wife Linda to Los Angeles, CA. where he completed a career with the U.S. Postal Service. A.T. Mills of Grimesland likewise worked as a

PACE employee. He later finished Duke University Law School moved to California and was reported to have been involved with the Patty Hearst case.

CHAPTER 4

LANDING IN THE EAGLES NEST
NCCU
1969- 1973

I t was an early fall morning in September 1969 when I arrived as
a freshman at NCCU Durham. I had received my housing assignment at 109 Chidley Hall Men's Dormitory earlier that summer.
There had only been two serious considerations for higher learning
elsewhere. Campbell College because of their interest in me as a
basketball recruit and N.C A&T because it was the only other college, I ever held an interest in attending. My decision was quickly
swayed after having visited NCCU's homecoming of 1968. Besides
my two older sisters Evelyn, Jean, and a first cousin, Curtis, were
all upperclassmen there already.

Successfully navigating oneself through freshman year especially the first week was not always a simple proposition. Freshman
bashing and forced beanie-wearing was part of "all in good fun"
for many upperclassmen at Central. Beanies had the tendency
to resemble a "dunce cap" and caused freshmen wearers to stick
out like sore thumbs on campus. My status had just changed in a

major way with little regard for any previous academic, athletic, or social accomplishments from my recent high school years. I had just become "a very small fish in a bigger pond" hailing from tiny Winterville, NC. I had just become a newly minted freshman, absent a single semester hour or quality point. Additionally, eastern North Carolina was considered rural ("country"), by those from the piedmont area of the state, although the entire state was mostly viewed similarly by attending students from the large cities of the northeast. The piedmont included the areas of Raleigh, Durham, High Point, Winston Salem, Greensboro, and Charlotte. The urban northeast includes the following but is not limited to Washington, D.C., Baltimore, MD., Philadelphia, PA., New Jersey, New York, NY., and areas of Connecticut.

The first few days of college without the familiarity of familiar faces and places were not easy. My Mom, Dad, Brother Ray, Baby Sister Grossie, Sweetheart Delphia, family and Buddy Ken "Hamp" Hammond (at ECU) were lamentably all back home.

Roommate Culture Shock

The experience of meeting my roommates for the first time became something akin to culture shock. They were both from New York, New York. They were both 100% city boys through and through who seemed beyond arrogant toward both the south and Durham almost to the level of disgust. They constantly ridiculed how other students spoke and dressed but especially complained about bugs as they walked across campus. You would have thought they had never seen a bug in their NY lives. I often wondered why they even bothered to attend college here. Colleges and Universities did exist in the North after all!

Playboys were the stylish shoe they wore at the time. The shoes' distinguishing feature was a thick rubber sole. They also delighted in there matching silk underwear sets. So much so, they constantly kept their sets hanging around the room as to be obviously observed when entering. During most of their conversations they would act as if I wasn't there while chatting and listening to their music. I must admit theirs' became the first stereo component set I had ever experienced. We only had the old console stereo to spin records at home. Isaac Hayes "Hot Buttered Soul" was one of their favorite albums to play. I grew to like it as well especially over the years since.

Back in '69, New York fashions, music, and cultural aspects were generally more out-front and advanced beyond their southern counterparts. Eventually, we would get them but somewhat later and at a slower pace.

Currently, because of the well-dispersed advancements in technology largely due to satellites, internet usage, and global marketing diverse geographical regions of the country often share styles, commodities, and cultural events almost simultaneously. Today, thankfully, more uniform access has become the norm and an antidote to previous disparity of timely access between the large urban northeast city dwellers and southerners.

Within just a few days I discovered my roommates were "dealing". I had observed the number of mostly city guys frequenting the room and the dispensing of small brown envelopes being sold. Finally, during a conversation one day one of my roommates turned to me and asked, "Hey Danny do you smoke man"? I replied not attempting to be sarcastic or a dummy and said, "yes man Winston". He gave me a quick glance and just turned and left the room with a slight smile on his face. I couldn't determine if his reaction was in response to relief from fear, I might attempt to steal his stuff, or that I was such a hick for not knowing he was referring to smoking marijuana. After I was sure he had left the dorm, I checked the box he often accessed from beneath his bed. There I found several dozen of the envelopes. I knew immediately what was up!

This was one of two concerns that my had warned me of before leaving home for college. He was very serious but somewhat comical in his delivery as he expressed them, "don't be up there in Durham messing with no drugs and don't be hanging around any "funny boys" either.

My "weed" discovery was the last straw and my cue to find new roommates immediately. My new roommate became Terry Brown from Washington, NC. The fact that our conversation went great, and our hometowns were in adjoining eastern counties helped seal the deal. It should be noted that my early experience with my first roommates never swayed me to limit my friendships and outlook. I later developed friendships with other students hailing from all over North Carolina, other states, and even international students.

The fourth floor became my new home for the remainder of my freshman year. Here I became acquainted with classmates that I would become close friends with throughout my tenure at N.C. Central. Terry my roommate was on a tennis scholarship and played in the band as well. Terry's older homeboy and Viet Nam Veteran "Boo" lived on the same hall and frequently visited our room. Boo was quite gifted as an artist and had a great personality. Strangely, I would several years' later, work together with his mother as co-teachers at my first school of employment.

Frankie Shaw of Kinston and Larry Guess from Ashville lived next door and became our closest friends on the hallway. Hall Melton and Hubert Sturdivant of Wadesboro likewise became great friends who lived across from us. Hall and Hubert had several homeboys with which we all became freshman buddies. They were James Ratcliff, Alan Clemmons, and their homegirl Margaret Bennett. This group became the core of my friends during my freshman year.

Homeboy

It is a common practice for students from the same town and often a common area to reference each other as homeboys and homegirls. Some of many freshman classmates and friends hailing from nearby eastern Carolina towns included: Lureta (Shoot) Allen, Bettie Harp, and Hilda Payton of Ayden, NC; Claude and Edward Lyons of Battleboro, NC; Velma Wilson of Murfreesboro, NC; Jacquelyn Vann of Ahoskie, NC; Pansey Taft and Juanita Bullock of Greenville, NC; Michael Slade, Alice Slade, Larry Slade of Williamston, NC; Patricia White and Joyce Jordan of Farmville, NC; John Hill of Snow Hill, NC, Earline Wilson and Anita Beasley of Washington, N.C. and of course my three wonderful Robinson High School classmates Connie Tucker, Frances Worthington and Evelyn Patrick of Winterville, N.C. These are but a few of my freshman classmates from eastern N.C. that survived our freshman experience together.

The preparation for the academic semester began with class registration. In 1969, this was a non-automated and very time-consuming procedure. We often stood in lines for hours to complete our semester schedules by attaining class cards.

NCCU remains a liberal arts school (The first such HBCU in the nation). The idea is to provide a well-rounded collegiate educational foundation. The applicable 101 courses in the liberal Arts and Sciences were required for most major areas of study. A 101 course is usually an introduction, basic elements, or fundamentals within an area of study or discipline. So, although I was a history major, I was required to take classes of English Literature 101, Biology 101, Music, Art, etc. during my freshman year.

Student Orientation was a required non-academic course designed to provide new arrivals with school history, relevant information, and perspective. The freshman class of '69 was especially excited and proud for becoming the first to attend North Carolina

College's newly advancement to North Carolina Central University at Durham.

Most of my time during the first semester was consumed familiarizing myself with college classes, campus life, and nightly discussions with dorm mates. Men dormitories were strictly for men and ladies' strictly for ladies. During this time, there were neither co-ed dorms nor room visitation.

We sat up many nights discussing various issues important to us. The ones most prominent were those involving racial inequality, civil rights, the Viet Nam War, and the draft. We began to develop a bond from our conversations and a degree of camaraderie as we traversed together up and down the steep and challenging Chidley Hall hill to classes and the cafeteria.

Marches and Militancy

Howard Fuller was a prolific human rights advocate, educator, community activist, and founder of Malcolm X University in Durham. His school and center of activity were located on Pettigrew Street a few blocks from NC Central. Frankie Shaw, Larry Guess, and I marched in protest with Fuller once concerning local educational issues related to public school and higher learning funding.

Recently Dr. Fuller has "come under fire" and been labeled by some as "a turncoat" and currently leaning right on political issues involving education. These include support for charter schools and Betsy Devos as Trump's appointee as Secretary of Education. Currently, I would be interested to hear Fullers' rationale for his support for Devos and other right-wing education positions taken. However, he remains in support of African-Centered-Schools as a useful component in addressing diversity needs.

Ms. Brenda Berryhill was a self-described activist and newly graduate of Sociology from Howard University. She was a tall, and very attractive young African American woman styling a beautiful Afro reminiscent of Angela Davis. During the very first-class meeting, Ms. Berryhill entered and surveyed the class of students. She then responded immediately to the presence of several Caucasian students by stating, "if you're white you can leave now because I'm not teaching you what I know." The "white" students rose immediately and left the room. When we returned to class the next day Ms. Berryhill was no longer there. We discovered later she had been dismissed, by the university.

It was also during my freshman year that we had presentations from two well known Black leaders with very contrasting prospectives. Stokely Carmichael (Kwame Toure) spoke to an enthusiastic audience of mostly Central students at B. N. Duke Auditorium on campus. On another occasion Ralph Abernathy a follower and protégé of Dr. Martin Luther King was a guest speaker.

I recall Stokely being impressively flanked by Black Panthers on both sides as he spoke. His subject was "The Differences between a Guerrilla and a Gorilla". His message seems to have suggested the need and possibilities of armed warfare in the country related to systemic racism and oppression. Although I had admiration for Carmichaels' courage, confidence, and clarity, I never saw the feasibility of a "guerrilla warfare strategy". I likewise never doubted that I was not a "gorilla" helpless and afraid as defined by Stokely. Later he converted to a more practical plan of organizing people and resources to combat global racism and oppression through the strategic application of Pan Africanism.

Ralph Abernathy had been ostensibly a protégé of King who had been killed in Memphis a year before. His visit and presentation at NCCU was centered on the merits of non-violence as a civil rights methodology. He painstakingly enumerated and emphasized the gains having been realized from its usage. Abernathy's reception was respected by students albeit with less enthusiasm than had Carmichael's rousing visit earlier.

My freshman year was by recollection a time of major change and life trajectory. Meeting peers from across the state and those from elsewhere helped to broaden my viewpoints and personal outlook. Campus life, sports, socializing including entertainment from national recording artist such and Percy Sledge and the Temptations were sources of much fun and enjoyment.

Central sports were a major source of school spirit and Eagle Pride. NCC was known nationally for its Track and Field Program under legendary coach Dr. Leroy Walker. The long-standing competitive rivalry with NC A&T has well been documented over the years. The rivalry came clearly into focus again during the '69 football season with the game ending as an epic gridiron classic 28-28 tie in Greensboro.

Finally, the impressions made by my instructors, professors and visiting national leaders would be the ideas imprinted on me for life.

My freshman year was now finally over. I had made my return home with the experience thankfully behind me. My summer would consist mostly of employment at the PCSMD and activities at the Robinson High Recreation Center.

During the summer of 1970, it seemed to have been a typical early evening at the Robinson Recreation Center. A group of us college students' home for summer recess became involved in conversation as we often did. On this occasion, the topic concerned the deficits so pervasive in North Winterville. Someone questioned why we had so few streetlights on this side of town? Another asked why there were so many streets unpaved? Another questioned the lack of sidewalks. Then there was a boisterous yell don't we pay taxes on this side of town? Calvin Henderson mentioned to us at that point there would be a town meeting that afternoon at 4:00 pm. The decision was made. We would march downtown, enter the meeting, and protest our concerns to an all-Caucasian city council at the time. They were completely caught off guard with the demonstration. This seemed to be a strange and curious event in tiny Winterville at the time, but these were the signs of the time.

This event became the first and only such protest in the Town of Winterville from the citizens of North Winterville. The event was covered by The Daily Reflector Newspaper and WNCT Channel 9 of Greenville, NC, and reported on the evening news. Most participants consisted of Robinson graduates, current high school and college students, and responsible adults. This is not a completed list: Calvin Henderson, Clinton Ray Anderson Sr., Margaret Hammond, Rander Harris, Josh Crandall, Lewis Crandall, Clinton Person, Jeffrey Jones, Elmer Corbett, Nina Wilson Blount, and Danny Smith your (author) were participants. Local media reports alluded to the event as mostly resulting from college student mischief and unrest and all would return to normal once they returned to school.

Sophomore Year

The end to summer 1970 came quickly after the March on Winterville. It was back to NCCU with my college friends and newly acquired lifestyle. Most of those in our circle had contemplated acquiring wheels during summer break. We would then find housing living off campus our sophomore year.

Remarkably, Frankie, Alan, Hall, and I all returned to school with our much desired, "set of wheels". We celebrated by taking an excursion to Raleigh each of us sporting our newly acquired rides.

Living Off-Campus

A car made it more convenient to live off-campus. This became our next objective. My friends from Wadesboro found housing with a family near campus. Frankie, Larry Guess, and I were able to get a two-bedroom apartment in the College Plaza Complex located on

Fayetteville Street just a few blocks from the NCCU Campus. Terry Brown moved into the apartment adjacent to ours with his cousin Rayvon (tennis player) and a friend from Grimesland, N.C., Ron Pridgen. Terry visited often, especially when we had food that was not always plentiful. His nickname was the "waffle wiffer" for his knack of timing his arrival with food availability.

The College Plaza Apartments were located in close proximity to Durham Business College which was 95% female. Needless to say, the ratio of 6 females to 1 man at Central lead to there not being a shortage of parties at the Plaza.

My sophomore schedule was mostly composed of courses in my major (history) and my minor (sociology). Corbett Jones became my favorite instructor immediately. He demonstrated his photographic and highly unusual memory during the first day of class. Mr. Jones had every student in the very large class write their names and hometowns on a strip of paper then placed it in a small box. He then had each student give their names and hometowns vocally. A randomly selected student read the hometowns of each student from the paper in the box. Mr. Jones then gave the name of the student merely from the hometown cited by the reader show casing his remarkable memory.

Pledging Puzzle

College fraternities and sororities called (Greeks), fellowships, and sisterhoods are usually of college origin sharing a professional or social interest. These groups for men and women were mostly founded to promote academics, community service, character, leadership, and/or social activities. During the fall of 1970, my friend Terry Brown of Washington, N.C. and Paul Stroud of Durham (deceased) and I decided to pledge the Groove Social Fellowship. The initiation was about seven weeks. The process referred to as "being online" included learning the history, details, and rituals of the organization to which one pledged. There unfortunately was a considerable amount of unwarranted hazing in the old days. I'm pleased to note that presently this aspect of pledging has been all but eliminated by most colleges and universities. Terry Brown, Robert Braswell, Daryl McFadden, Clarence (Satch) Stafford, Mike Spears, Billy (Wild Bill) Bryson, Ron Draper, Gary (Gee Baby) Garrison, Garvin Stone, Duke Freeland, Roger Washington, Gary Wall and "Sweet Sug" Huff were among many of my brothers during my time at Central.

My sister Jean had pledged Zeta Phi Beta the previous year and served on the Greek Pan Hellenic Council. At the time I was "online", she crafted and presented a pillow for me commemorating my pledging and induction into the Groove Fellowship. Evelyn Patrick and Juanita Bullock (my home girls) were "online" for Alpha Kappa Alpha during the same time period as me.

My sophomore year was mostly a period of growth in familiarity with the peripherals of college life, and the greater surroundings of Durham, minus proper growth in academics or consciousness. Thankfully, Corbett Jones and similar professors played a major role in helping begin the process of redirecting my focus. My interest was helped to be skewed back toward academic areas, of historiography, historical perspective, and the generation of a relevant worldview.

Junior Year

The major surprise in returning to Central our junior year was the no-show of our roommate and good friend Larry Guess from Ashville, some of his home people indicated he had opted to join the military. This, however, seemed an out-of-character choice from views previously expressed by him from our many rap sessions and conversations. Needless to say, we were all shocked and disappointed by the revelations.

Growing Through Changes

With Guess's absence, Frankie Shaw and I needed at least one more roommate in order to make rent at the College Plaza ($120.00) plausible. So, we happened stance upon Sweet Cakes one of my Groove Brothers, and Vanzell Woodard his homeboy.

We learned that Vanzell was a Viet Nam veteran and later discovered him to be a victim of posttraumatic stress disorder (PTSD). Sometimes he would walk up to a street crossing and snap to attention standing motionless until prompted to move forward by one of us. He would also while casually sitting often just go into shivers (as if severely frighten).

The Groove Fellowship was to consume much of my time as I was elected president and Robert Braswell (Sweet Cakes) as treasurer for the school year. In 1972, the newly formed Division 1 Mid-Eastern Athletic Conference Basketball Tournament was hosted by NCCU. The Grooves and several fraternal groups sponsored balls and dances during the week. We did so in collaboration with the Roy Southerland and the Aggie Chapter from N.C. A & T., it proved to be a successful venture and bolstered our recognition and treasury. Later some "fellowship brothers" were to refer to our apartment as "the White House" because of our unwillingness to acquiesce with any attempts to spend money on a whim without proper protocol and a sound purpose. I sometimes pondered why I was voted president as a neophyte with so many other members available to serve. I finally concluded it to be ambivalence, apathy, and a perplexed state within the organization. The next year brother Daryl McFadden returned to Central with the desire to become president of the chapter. His vision was to implement organizational changes through the improvement of chapter goals and image. Some of his ideas included: cooperative efforts with other campus organizations, greater dedication to unity and purpose, and establishing viable community outreach programs. This seemed to be exactly "what the doctor ordered" from my vantage point. He thereby landed my immediate assistance for his efforts. Unfortunately, he was confronted with indifferent attitudes and remarks like, "we don't want to be a bunch of welfare-providing social workers". Eventually, insufficient support from the majority resulted in his disillusionment for his progressive agenda.

Back to academics, one summer school enrollment of at least six semester hours was usually recommended by the various Schools/Departments of Arts and Sciences. This was encouraged to comfortably complete a four-year degree program without schedule overload. I, therefore, attended summer school following my sophomore year. My selected six hours were Social Psychology and Russia under the Monarchy. The summer of 1972 was also the time of nuptials for my middle sister Emma Jean Smith and Creft Haggins, Jr. both N.C. Central alumnus. The wedding proved to be "the event of the summer" for both families.

Senior Year

Full Court Press

Summer School thereafter ended quickly, and thoughts of my senior year rapidly grew with intensity. My junior year helped me finally realize my purpose for being at Central. Party time and useless games were over. I had finally sensibly decided to properly matriculate and complete my field of study as part of the Class of 1973.

Sweet Cakes had graduated, and Frankie did not return senior year initially. This, therefore, required me to find new roommates. I met a couple of seniors living a few blocks off Fayetteville Street and became roommates with them. Harold McCullough from Rockhill, South Carolina was one and the other was from Goldsboro, NC. This living arrangement did not work very well. I managed to tolerate our many differences during the first semester but knew doing so the second semester would be virtually impossible.

It was early during the second semester that Larry Slade and I became roommates. All went well for my housing after that decision. He and I became roommates and interacted like brothers. We soon discovered we had likeability in sports, similar taste in music, could wear each other's clothes and even had similar viewpoints on issues of the day.

By this time, I knew lots of people and had several options for social affiliations. I frequented St. Augustine in Raleigh often to visit my home girl and sweetheart Delphia.

Henry Suggs, my homeboy, a Central graduate, and history professor at Clemson University would stop by when in town. He would treat me to dinner, mention his work on his book (P. B. Young Newspaper Man -- Race, Politics, and Journalism in the New South 1910-62), and give me all kinds of school advice. I always thoroughly enjoyed his visits. I was also kept busy by part-time employment and the major emphasis I was placing on academics with my senior semester looming large for graduation.

Money was never a plentiful commodity during my college years, and this certainly included my senior year. I would sometimes sell a pint of blood for $15 to the Red Cross even with my parents doing all they could as providers for my support. My senior semester part-time employment consisted of loading tractor trailers at night for an Overnight Trucking Company which lasted for about a month. I was quickly reminded why I had become a college student; and made the choice to seek a white-collar career.

Professor Corbett Jones was something of an icon and legend in the history department and the entire university generally. He was an extremely impressive and proud man being a graduate of Howard University and having been taught and tutored by the renowned historian and Africanist, Dr. Leo Hansberry. He explained to the class that those students at Howard who failed to achieve academically would find their possessions placed outside not by the academic dean but by other students. Such was their personal high regard for academic compliance and performance.

Professor Corbett Jones (Pride and Principle)

During the late '60s and '70s, Black Studies Professors came into great demand at the predominately White colleges and universities across the nation. Professor Jones and others became in great demand from many such schools. He made it clear we need not worry about losing him, since his services were not needed before at such institutions. Professor Jones decided accordingly, he saw no need to leave N.C. Central then. We were thrilled with his decision!

Dr. David Bishop and Mr. William Smith (Interpretation and Motivation)

Dr. David Bishop had a remarkably similar appeal as did Professor Jones and became my undoubted favorite instructor this semester. He introduced his U. S. Diplomatic History course in a manner that greatly aroused and captivated my interest from the very beginning.

The first assigned task was to read and submit a book report on The Prince by 16th-century philosopher Nicolo Machiavelli. Dr. Bishop introduced his course with this opening statement "The United States was born and matured in a Machiavellian world and learned her lesson well". The book The Prince was written by Machiavelli during the sixteenth century in medieval Europe. He expressed his crafty ideas of how a leader could gain power, maintain rule over his constituents, and be feared by his enemies both foreign and domestic. This work is considered by many to be the foundation of modern western politics.

I was always impressed in a major way how Dr. David Bishop could articulate a position then allow our discovery of the facts to support that position. He displayed a certain mastery in his inter-pretation of history much to our benefit. He also would enter the classroom, peer through the window, and look back at the class as to say, *"I know lots that you do not."* He would do this in a non-ar-rogant way suggesting we had a lot to learn which served as moti-vation for me and other class members. No matter if it was the XYZ Affair, the Monroe Doctrine, or the Spanish American War it never failed. He taught and fostered an extremely high level of com-prehension among his students. Dr. David Bishop was a master conveyer of historical facts but more importantly, he taught his-toriography (an interpretation of history) through context and perspective.

Likewise, Mr. William Smith was very impressive as a math instructor of Math 101 for Education Majors. This was a required basic math course for all seeking a Bachelor of Arts in the certifi-cation areas for teachers. The course included mostly the general areas of arithmetic, algebra, and geometry. It was obvious that Mr. Smith had been a high school teacher at Durham Hillside before coming to N. C. Central. He was excellent in his delivery and had the patience of a saint with students having difficulty with the gen-eral concepts and postulates of mathematics. He was known to have great concern for the success of every student and demon-strated this with every learning objective.

There are undoubtedly instructors and professors not men-tioned here but could have been. I am exceedingly grateful to so many who contributed to my educational preparation and world-view at N. C. Central. For this reason, placing the appropriate value on liberal arts education is so exceedingly relevant.

The development of a well-rounded learned individual is the basic rationale of a liberal arts education. The goal is to provide general knowledge across the academic spectrum along with

specific and detailed studies. So, even with a major in home economics, reading or foreign language a certain level of competency
and balance in both the arts and sciences is relevant.

Graduation for me in the spring of 1973 was not a complete
certainty. Primarily due to some misplaced priorities and lack of
required focus during the three preceding years. My Mom had
emphasized the importance of these very points to me all along the
way, and thereafter often alluded to the fact that I, unfortunately,
didn't apply myself properly until I began to mature and come to
my senses by my senior year. You know Mom was right again. So
as one might imagine, I was happily relieved to receive my letter of
completion of all requirements and graduation date clearly without
any version of Laude near my name. Rather, graduation requirements having been validated were received with a giant exhale, and
"Thank You Laude". So, there I was, although barely, I had the great
fortune to have survived the gauntlet of many potentially detri-
mental distractions over the past four years. Many of my friends
had not been so fortunate.

HBCU Relevance

In summation, North Carolina College at Durham was founded
in 1910 to originally provide a liberal higher education for African
American students. Today as North Carolina Central University, it
serves the educational needs of all groups with the specialized care
of a Historical Black College or University like more than two dozen
others across the nation. I found the uniquely tailored methods
and experiences at North Carolina Central (HBCU) motivating and
all-out inspiring. Academically and instructionally, professors and
instructors understood the urgency of the African American issues
and dilemma which infused greater energy and emotions into the
educational formula.

Likewise, an elevated level of school spirit was generated from non-academic aspects of the HBCU. Step Shows and other activities sponsored by the fraternities, fellowships, sororities, and sisterhoods were usually inspirational and entertaining. Sporting events such as football and basketball games were and remain venues for student cohesion and group expression. The bands often generate as much competition between themselves as did the teams. The HBCU's unique band sound, precision rhythms, and stepping is always a crowd favorite. Their accompaniments of a high stepping drum major with majorettes and dance girls who can really "shake it down" became the "cherry on top".

Academic areas involving literature and reading for cultural enrichment were made relevant. Required readings along the way such as Before the Mayflower by Bennett 1964, From Slavery to Freedom by Franklin 1947, Jubilee by Walker 1966, The Naked Soul by Iceberg Slim 1971, and Blood in my Eye by Jackson 1971 may have never occurred at a non-HBCU. The motivation that I incurred when Dr. Bishop momentarily stared out the window and quickly turned back to the class to give us his unmistaken look of "if you only knew", became invaluable to me throughout my career. The thought of the exuberance I received during a halftime performance when the NCCU Eagle Sound Machine (Band) took the field followed by the NC A&T Marching Band was and remains beyond exhilarating. Most importantly, the nexus of rivalry coupled with the shared legacy of racial struggle is common among Historical Black Colleges and Universities and should never be taken for granted nor underappreciated.

Chapter 5

Local Profiles in Courage

I n every community large and small throughout the nation, and presumably around the globe, there are those who distinguish themselves by virtue of their service to others. This is a brief list of such individuals of my "small town of origin".

Janice King Smith (1927-2014)

My mother and first teacher Janice King Smith was the first born of Henry King and Ida Pugh King on September 29, 1927. Her siblings were Lester, Osborne, and Juanita.

She grew to be a stoic woman who spoke softly but always with foresight and wisdom. She usually had a philosophical rationale to explain or justify her decisions and/or directives for her children.

As an elementary student, I often expressed good feelings for my new found friends of kindness, respect, admiration, and a desire to share with them. We called ourselves the Fifty-Fifty Gang. She listened intently before saying without explanation "charity starts at home then spread abroad". Her statement seemed to indicate that we should practice those feelings at home because anything worth doing elsewhere was worth cultivating and implementing at home initially then to those on the outside and elsewhere. Much later as a neophyte educator I shared with her the enjoyment for and dedication to my new profession. She stated to me "a new broom sweeps clean," always leaving her philosophical statement open to my interpretation. My understanding of her implication was as novelty decreases so did the potential for ones' level of interest or success. She seemed to have been saying that it would be a personal effort not to allow loss of novelty to decrease my effectiveness or performance as a teacher.

She was a faithful member at Piney Grove Free Will Baptist Church in Craven County, N.C. I distinctly and fondly remember the closeness of her Cousin Ruby Grimes, and Mrs. George Anna Patrick riding there together on third Sundays. Her lifelong dedication and service as a Church Mother was resolute for all to witness.

She taught me self-discipline and standards by modeling the behaviors she so demanded from me and my siblings. She maintained a home, and environment conducive for a clean healthy, lifestyle while working every day without uttering a single complaint even when ill. Mrs. Janice was typical of other mothers in the community as a working Mom, homemaker, and active community participant. She delighted in her membership of the local Home Demonstration Club where community homemakers shared arts, crafts, and quilting skills, and as a member of the Eastern Star Lodge.

There were days I recall her coming in from work and immediately finding something in the kitchen to prepare after my personal surveillance had determined no food or subsistence at all to be found in the cupboard.

My mother along with my father established and enforced family order through a chain of authority among our siblings. This disposition was based upon our respective ages, and the oldest was given authority in their absence. The arrangement took an unexpected turn on one occasion. The oldest once received a *"whipping"[1]

---

[1] "*Whipping" is/was a pejorative term carried over from slavery to reference spanking or physical discipline and is not recommended as a useful term related to contemporary discipline.

for misbehavior and the next two of us received the same for not informing our Mom of the eldest's behavior.

Janice Smith and other local mothers were the major disciplinarians at home as well as ardent supporters of discipline at school. She would check our report cards each six weeks and write her comments on the back always paying strict attention to our conduct as well as academic assessments. She likewise discussed with teachers our classroom behaviors and academic performances at the very well attended Parent Teacher Association Meetings at Robinson.

Her encouragement and support for participation in extracurricular activities at school helped establish a sense of well-rounded balance and an edge of confidence among my peers. Whether it was fees for sports or club activities, the purchase of band instruments, her attendance at a basketball game, or May Day Celebration we could rest assured of her full commitment.

Once while reading and discovering the life and teachings of Malcolm X, I came upon an album with one of his speeches entitled "Message to the Grass Roots". The only source to play an album at home was the stereo console located in the living room near my parents' bedroom. So, the first time I played it she came out immediately scolded, and admonished me to "stop playing that mess in her house". So as not to be "hardheaded" (disobedient) although I disagreed internally, I immediately complied with my mothers' demand. After a few days, I would quietly lie down on the floor close to the console and play it on an exceptionally low volume. Little did I know she had some very sharp ears and continued to hear it. Finally, one night she came out of her room and said, "Danny Carl you know the more I listen to Malcolm X the more sense he makes". I just shook my head up and down acknowledging my agreement. She turned and went back into her room and never discussed it again. I became aware from that moment my mother was a lifelong learner and certainly nobody's fool.

The incident concerning Malcolm by no means was the sole proof of this fact. It confirmed what I already knew. For as long as I could remember my Mom like so many other parents in this tiny community, tirelessly endeavored with minuscule material means to increase, enhance, and enrich the learning experiences for their children. Fortunately, she had the wisdom not to exclude herself.

Emanuel Smith Sr. (1924-2018)

My father was the last born of Reverend Emanuel Smith Sr. and Charlotte Hardy Smith on November 6, 1924. His siblings were Sam, McKinley, Marybelle, Dewey, Martha, Janie, Mark, and Baby. He was reared in rural Pitt and Green Counties near Ayden, N.C. share cropping on a (neo plantation) owned by Clara Spear. His early life was also centered on the activities of nearby Little Creek Free Will Baptist. Later as an adult, he would take prominent leadership roles there on the finance committee and as a member of the deacon board.

My father attended high school at South Ayden H.S. Ayden, N.C. where he was a good academic student. His father Emanuel Smith, Sr. died when he was just a young lad. This left the responsibility of farm work to the remaining sons living at home (Dewey, Mark, Emanuel) and Baby had died as a young school-aged boy. Emanuel was allowed to attend school much to the chagrin of older brother Dewey who could not. He felt Emanuel should have been required to do likewise. However, mother, Charlotte was not having it. She insisted that her youngest son should and would have the benefit of a formal education.

South Ayden High School is where he met Janice King and later married her during the fall of 1945. They lived in Raleigh soon thereafter while Dad attended Barber College. According to my mother, he chose a profession that suited his very placid personality well. Through the years he always had a primary source of employment during the week and did his barbering at his shop on Saturday. His primary employment of greatest significance during his years of employment was as a shipping clerk at Cox Trailers of Grifton, N.C. for more than 25 years.

Little Creek FWB Church had for several generations been largely a church of extended related families. The families consisted of Joyner, Smiths, Darden's, and a few prominent others. During different periods, Little Creek was controlled by various, different families. My earliest memories had our relatives the Joyners in the key leadership positions there.

When my Dad evolved to prominence, he moved quickly to full throttle. After becoming chairman of the financial board, along with church leaders and membership he pursued a vision for structural restorations and improvements. Also, very prominent in this period of growth and improvement were deacons John Waters, Caleb Forbes (brothers in law), Mark Smith Financial Board Member (brother), Willie Cannon (cousin), Anninas (nephew), and others.

My father's congenial personality allowed him to be pleasant and get along with others very well both at church, civically, and on his job. I recall during many heated conversations at his barber ship he would never be on one side or the other during the many conversational fracases. He was a Worshipful Master of the Prince Hall Masons, Ayden, N.C., Member of the Odd Fellow Lodge, Ayden, N.C. and Proprietor and manager of Smith Barber Shop of Ayden, N.C. for over 35 years. He was known to be nicely dressed and a well-groomed man. He also took meticulous care of his cars and later trucks he owned.

I recall asking him questions concerning my interest in his perspectives. A couple of such questions were: (1) which leader did he like most among the 1960's and 70's Black Movement? (2) And what would he like to have pursued as a profession if he had his choice and equal opportunity? Without citing a specific name in response to the question (1) he replied" the one who best get along with all people". His response to the second question after thinking for a moment was, a court judge. My first thought was, what an excellent choice since he was so balanced, and fair-minded in his thought processes.

Learning obedience and discipline via corporal punishment was a prevalent method for our generation. My mother dished out most of the corporal punishment at our home. This made the few times that my Dad did so much more memorable. Only on two occasions did he get my attention in this manner. My sister Jean and I once received "whippings" (see the previous footnote) for striking matches under the bed while Mom and Dad were away. The other occasion resulted from an act of personal disobedience and a potentially deadly violation of safety. During the early 1960s, there were no swimming pools for black youth in Pitt County. Kids would therefore locate irrigation ponds to attempt learning to swim. Almost invariably, every summer some kid would be drowned as a result. I once became a potential tragedy of such an incident. My father discovered this and exacted the most convincing corporal punishment ever. This act on my father's part was a vital lesson and may have been a literal lifesaver for me.

My father transitioned during the writing of this book. I attempted to express his major impact on me as a father at his eulogy. His lifelong centrist and judicious perspectives were maintained in his thinking and decision-making throughout. This quality I admired and utilized in assessing both sides of issues even if my determinations did not always result centrist as did his. Secondly, his pervasive attribute to problem-solving was a constant source for me, and my siblings' youthful admiration and benefit. For family members, church members, and friends they could always depend on him to stay the course until he converted a negative trajectory into a positive one for all concerned.

David Henderson (1910-1980)
Robinson PTA Organizer
and Local Civil Rights Pioneer

Mr. David Henderson, of Winterville during the 1940s, became the first Parents Teachers Association president of Robinson School. He was likewise one of the founding members of the Ayden, Grifton, Winterville Original NAACP Charter (National Association for the Advancement of Colored People). This is substantiated by documents currently held by the current Pitt County chapter of the NAACP.

Mr. Henderson joined forces with other community parents and Mr. John W. Maye, principal, in establishing a school grounded in student discipline and academic achievement. According to attending parents, participation was extremely high as indicated by attendance and dedication to the school's goals and mission.

He valued education as one of the indispensable triads of pillars serving as the foundation of the Winterville community. The three pillars being home, church, and a good school. According to Calvin Henderson (son), his father encouraged a cooperative and continuous relationship with teachers and Mr. John Maye, in order to establish and maintain their support for and trust in Robinson School. Activities such as plays, May Day Performances, Science Fairs, sports, NCJCHC Activities (North Carolina Joint Council of Health and Citizenship) sponsored by Dr. Andrew Best and others gave parents opportunities to visit and experience both curricular and extra-curricular school events regularly.

Among some of Mr. Henderson's most ardent PTA supporters were Mr. John Waters known to be an industrious and "self-made man"; Mr. Fat Bryant assistant and vice president of PTA; Mrs. Mary Hammond (mother of eight students) who served as a PTA officer at various times, Mr. Buck Bryant dedicated Boy Scout Master of charter Boy Scout Troop 88 of North Winterville, NC., and many others. Mr. David Henderson in his role as first Robinson PTA President, is remembered as a highly successful one that set the tone for active parental involvement and community cooperation with school administration. His early performance and dedication have created a legacy of successful collaboration for which I and many other Robinson graduates are extremely appreciative.

Calvin Henderson
Civic Leader and Pitt County NAACP Chairman (2003-Current)

Calvin Henderson known to family and friends as (C.C.) is the son of Lizzy and David Henderson. He is a Robinson graduate and a lifelong citizen of Winterville, NC. Calvin's work can be viewed as a continuation of his father's. This perspective may be easily documented through the life work of both.

I first became aware of Calvin as a civic-minded person when during the mid-1960's he became instrumental in organizing The Winterville Boys Club. Mostly School-Aged boys would meet on Saturdays for games, sports, and youth activities. There would also be personal counseling, short trips, and motivational activities for participants. It was a much needed big brother/mentorship-like opportunity for the young men of that era in Winterville, NC.

In the summer of 1970, Calvin, your author, and others were participants in the spontaneous March on the Winterville Board of Alderman (city council meeting). Calvin as a very capable activist emerged as a spokesman. It was not until 1974, when he became the first African American Winterville Alderman thereby integrating said Board. He likewise later became the first African American to become a candidate for mayor in the town of Winterville.

During our more than three-hour interview, I received the impression that the NAACP chairman of the county was not a position he actively sought. It was more a call to duty from which he understood and refused to shrink from 2003 to current. He shared a few of the misconceptions and challenges of his experiences. He expressed his being inaccurately labeled by media types and others as "a troublemaker, and user of divisive tactics". This does not deter him but becomes a nuisance requiring a constant response. He also stated that his home had been targeted in 2008 by vandals throwing a cement block through a window. He cited NAACP's diligence led to the construction of Hillcrest Park in North Winterville in response to the resistance of Black Youth usage of recreation facility at A. G. Cox School downtown. Henderson also effectively sought the building of Winterville Court which provided more affordable housing for the elderly and qualifiers. His efforts along with those of the NAACP and HUD brought a much-appreciated change in housing standards for many citizens of Winterville.

NAACP Chairman Henderson indicated current recruitment efforts among county youth and a reinvigoration of activism are among top agenda items. He says, "time is of the essence as much so today as ever before."

Dr. Leo Jenkins (1913-1989)
East Carolina Chancellor (1960-1978)
Educator and Visionary

The wisdom and perseverance of Dr. Leo Jenkins were immeasurably rewarding for the people of eastern North Carolina. He tirelessly worked to transform East Carolina College into one of the major institutions of higher learning across the nation. My earliest memories of Dr. Jenkins were the regularity of his voice and image stressing the needs of East Carolina College on local news stations. These were primarily WNCT and WITN broadcasts of Greenville, NC, and Washington, NC respectfully. He would consistently cite the needs and rationale for a medical school or university status for ECC and likewise concerns for other budgetary issues. There were many articles in the local Daily Reflector Newspaper with accounts of appeals to political leaders and/or the state legislature. This was during a time when his efforts were met by some across the state with less than enthusiastic support. He eventually thereby became more than just an advocate for East Carolina College but a leader and spokesperson for the educational, health, and economic interests of the eastern region and some would argue for the entire state. His tireless work began to be rewarded in 1967 when the college was granted university status, which pioneered a pathway for other state colleges to do the same. In 1974, the legislature approved funding for the ECU School of Medicine and the ECU School of Dental Medicine was added in 2006, after his retirement.

Once the Medical School was established this became an "existential game-changer" for Pitt County and all Eastern North Carolina.

Heretofore, treatment for the more serious and rare medical cases was rendered primarily at either Duke Hospital at Durham or UNC Medical Facilities at Chapel Hill.

I recall a personal family hardship regarding Uncle Dewey Smith who was inflicted with a rare leg disease. My father would sometimes transport him the lengthy distances to Durham or Chapel Hill because of local medical inadequacies. I and other children's family members would often remain in the car for extended periods of time waiting as my uncle received care. Thankfully, such hardships and inconveniences ended after the establishment of the ECU Medical School and its networks throughout the region. Additionally, like so many other locals my parents were able to receive the highly professional medical care and life sustaining emergency care resulting from the ECU Medical Schools' existence. For this, I'm exceedingly grateful.

Donald McKinley Smith (1953- Present)

He was born the second child of Mark and Vergie Strong-Smith on September 21, 1953. Mark Smith was the late elder brother of my late father Emanuel Smith Sr. As the offspring of hardworking sharecroppers and a God-fearing family, Donald understood early the virtues of respect and the differences between right and wrong. Donald enjoyed an early life among his six siblings and loving parents. Also, his family visits with other extended families after church services were a common occurrence. They included numerous aunts and uncles, cousins and both grandmothers one of which (Charlotte) resided with his family for a period early in his life.

Donald attended school at segregated South Ayden High until integration and the consolidation of South Ayden, Grifton High, and Ayden High School into the new Ayden-Grifton High School in 1971.

Existing tension from the integration of all public schools in the area was heightened when a young African American farm worker was killed in handcuffs by a state trooper under very suspicious conditions. William Murphy was shot and killed by Billy Day (Caucasian state trooper) during the evening hours of August 6, 1971, near Ayden, N.C. The accounts of events by Trooper Day leading to Murphy's death were in sharp contrast with those of Murphy's family and the Black Community.

Resentment and anger intensified in the area with each protest and demonstration as school opening grew near. It happened the first morning of school on the opening of the newly consolidated Ayden-Grifton High School. Dynamite exploded in a bathroom near the auditorium and shocked the entire region.

The family received word that Cousin Donald Smith and Cousin Jerry Bissell were among the several young activists sought after by authorities. The remaining accounts of this segment are written according to details obtained via a personal interview held with Donald Smith on April 21, 2018.

He originally left the area and relocated to Philadelphia, PA; only to discover there was a warrant for his arrest back home. He remained there for about a month before he decided to return home and answer the warrant. He called the local police once in Greenville to be taken into custody from a store on 5th street. At the bond hearing, he was placed under a 50,000 bond and was detained at a juvenile facility in Fayetteville, NC, after not being able to make such a large bond.

At the beginning of the trial, there was an initial attempt by the court to adjudicate all the Ayden juveniles together. This procedure ended abruptly when the sheriff spoke before the court with what was believed to be false information. Cousin Jerry Bissell spontaneously yelled out loudly "you're a goddamn lie." According to Donald, although Jerry's outburst "tore the courtroom up" and ended the court's attempt to try the defendants together, it helped in unifying the group and made them stronger as individuals. The group became known as the Ayden 11. Thusly they were identified and affiliated with similar prisoners of the day as Ben Chavis and The Wilmington 10, Huey Newton, Bobby Seale, Angela Davis, and George Jackson as political prisoners across the country.

The individualization of the cases required Donald to employ the services of attorney Frank Ballard. Attorney Ballard sought a plea bargain with district attorney Eli Bloom after becoming aware his client was facing 40 years. The plea bargain reduced his charge and reduced his exposure to 20-40 years before being found guilty. Donald stated that the court was harsher on him after the district attorney presented evidence of his alleged cavorting with an affiliate of the Wilmington Ten prior to the explosion at Ayden Grifton.

His first assigned place of incarceration within the North Carolina Department of Corrections was at the Pope Youth Center in Raleigh due to his under 18 juvenile status. I asked Donald was he afraid after being sentenced to 20-40 years in prison. He responded, "not as much as he should have been because "I HAD NO IDEA WHAT I WAS UP AGAINST AT THE TIME".

He began to learn quickly at Pope that prison was a much different reality than the everyday civilian life he had before. He stated that the guys from the western area of the state like Raleigh, Durham, and Charlotte hung together. Likewise, the guys from the smaller areas of eastern North Carolina were forced to do the same in order to avoid victimization.

He had been at Pope for about two years when he became eighteen and considered an adult by corrections. He said that one of the officers came to him and remarked, "hey nigger I've got a birthday present for you, Caledonia Prison". A general understanding of the prison system is the larger the number of inmates incarcerated at a facility, the worse the prison. Donald made clear, this proved to be true since Caledonia was the second largest prison in North Carolina at the time. Only Central Prison in Raleigh was considered worse at the time. His one consolation at Caledonia was the job he was given as a shop mechanic, changing the oil in the compound vehicles. This type of work was considered by the inmates as a "pie job".

He remained at Caledonia for about two years before his transfer. Other unit assignments included Gates County, Warrenton, Maury, and Central Youth Center. No matter where he was assigned, he said usually there was someone from a previous place of incarceration with him that would "show him the ropes".

He stated there were many lessons learned from his experience of incarceration but the following three were among the most important:

1. Some inmates that he met didn't deserve a day of their sentence and others deserved all that they received and more

2. It would be his goal to establish and operate his own business and advise others to do the same once released

3. Never would he allow himself to be distracted by irrelevant attention stealers (pacifiers), those things such as television and fashion which serve to diminish valuable time, and desire for the truly important aspects of life and well-being.

Donald was released during the fall of 1977 after serving nearly 7 years of a potential 20–40-year sentence. He speculates that his early release resulted from the facts of good behavior; prison overcrowding, and the steady drumbeat of support that he and other "political prisoners received during the 1970s. This included his parents and family, international leaders, and politicians such as President Nelson Mandela of South Africa; Congressman Walter B. Jones; probation officers such as Samuel Cooper, and organizations such as The National Alliance Against Racist and Political Repression.

Presently Donald McKinley Smith lives a quiet life in Eastern North Carolina and is viewed by friends and family as a freedom fighter and a local civil rights hero. He owns a small business and assists in the care of two cherished grandsons.

John Walter Maye, Sr. (1912-1970)
(Principal Extraordinaire)

Robinson Union School located in Winterville, N.C. of Pitt County had at least sixteen principals during its existence. None more accomplished respected or revered than Mr. John Maye, Sr. He came to Robinson in 1943 from Pitt County Training School of Grimesland, NC to serve a 27-year career there.

Mr. Maye was a graduate of North Carolina A&T Greensboro. There he was prepared as an educator in the areas of math, social studies, and education administration. He also became a celebrated athlete in the sports of football and boxing. He seemed to be immediately accepted as an authority figure not to be challenged by students or staff as principal. Maybe this is the reason he was respectfully referred to as, "Chief" behind closed doors but certainly not publicly.

School safety, instructions, and student learning were always at the forefront of his leadership concerns.

Robinson was located just a couple of scores of yards beyond train tracks. The school's proximity to the Atlantic Coast Line Train tracks and the frequency of the passing train and stops were the best example of a major safety concern. Amazingly, the safety procedures and practices implemented and enforced by Mr. Maye and his staff prevented even a single related incident/accident over the years.

Just below the importance of safety was the importance of teaching and student learning. Teachers entered their classrooms prepared to teach and students arrived at their classes with required materials prepared to learn.

Discipline could have easily been mistaken for Mr. Maye's middle name. "Woe be unto the student perpetrator" that attempted to violate this effort. Mr. "Chief" Maye had absolutely zero understanding or tolerance for such "acts or attitudes". It was seldom to never that a student was referred to his office due to his well-established, reputation, and intolerance for indifference or misconduct. Principal Maye would sometimes physically visit classrooms to observe or listen to classes via intercom. Occasionally, he would decide the need to speak via intercom, and the teacher's voices would often tremble attempting to respond to him.

Some of the advancements at Robinson during his 27-year tenure include: (1) a rapid growth in student population and faculty of nearly 400%. (2) a major increase in square footage of the physical plant through additional classrooms, a gymnasium, cafeteria, and a new library. (3) increased focus on academic excellence with the founding of the honor group (The Crown and Scepter Club). (4) successfully promoted an athletic program including basketball and baseball which "excelled" with winning records and championship seasons through the years in the annual Pitt County Schools Conference games and tournaments. (5) establishing a health and hygiene organization called (The North Carolina Joint Council of Health and Citizenship facilitated by Dr. Andrew Best). (6) and by gaining full accreditation status with the N. C. State Department of Public Instruction in 1959.

In retrospect as a career educator, I value John "Chief" Maye today more than ever. Principal John Maye Sr. respected and teamed with parents, community leaders, and central office personnel to make the best of scarce and limited resources. Through his educational leadership, Principal John Maye Sr. became a legendary icon within the local community and is properly credited for the production of well-prepared students equipped for a demanding world that takes few prisoners.

Chapter 6

Teacher/Coach
Aurora High School 1973-1981

Small Town "Big Hearts"

The summer of 1973 brought prospects for my professional employment that was both daunting and exciting. Fortunately, my sister Evelyn (Juanita) likewise a teacher had recently returned home from Connecticut, which allowed us to collaborate in our search for teaching positions together.

We immediately began traversing the state, especially the eastern school districts seeking those in need of English teachers in her case and Social Studies in mine. After being interviewed she would inquire on my behalf for any district needs for social studies teachers and me for English teachers on her behalf. Finally, upon arrival for an interview at South Lenoir High School while entering the building my sister looked down and found a penny on the ground. She at once proclaimed "good luck D.C." from the finding. As fate would have it, she was phoned and offered a position teaching tenth grade English during the same week. Amazingly, later the next week I was called by Mr. Paul Comegys, the principal, at Aurora High School for a scheduled interview. On the day of the interview, my sister accompanied me to the school. As we disembarked the car, she at once looked down and found a penny on the ground, again. She was certain this was a sign of good things to follow for me.

Upon entering the office, I was met and greeted by, Mr. Paul Comegys, a friendly and well-mannered man, whom I discovered quite prepared to conduct an interview with me. He shared a modest amount concerning his own background, educational philosophy, and his HBCU experience at Shaw University. The interview lasted about 30 minutes and went well from my perspective. I particularly liked Mr. Comegys as his career had been anchored in coaching as well as that of a classroom teacher. At this point, the best opportunity for my first professional employment became even more exciting since my first principal's career path would parallel my intentions as an educator. His experience, tutelage, and mentoring would become invaluable.

Juanita's prediction for good fortune "from the penny find" became true. I received the phone call from Mr. Comegys early the next week. He offered me employment at Aurora High School as a teacher and coach for the 1973-74 school year.

Since my contract included a coaching component, I was required to report in early August for the start of football practice. My first official meeting with other school employees was with the football staff. Here, Mr. Comegys introduced me to head Coach Bobby Christopher and assistant coach Jim Close. I was briefed on our respective coaching assignments, responsibilities, schedules, and player rosters. I left this introduction and briefing exhilarated and ecstatic about finally having arrived at this employment opportunity. My coaching assignment was for the defensive backs and wide receivers. The other two coaches and I continued making acquaintances and discussing the upcoming season at lunch at a diner in downtown Aurora.

Finding housing in this small community became my next objective. Here it had become common practice for new teachers to rent living space in the homes of locals. Mr. Comegys recommended Mrs. Anna Parker an elderly widow with long standings in the nearby community of Idalia. She took me in and made me feel perfectly comfortable as a tenant living in her home. She had daughters that lived out of state. One of her sons James, Sr. owned and operated a small convenience store nearby.

I soon discovered that Aurora High School was composed of students from the town of Aurora as well as several small surrounding communities. The following regional areas were contributors: Idalia, Blounts Creek, Bonnerton, South Creek, Royal, and Lowlands. The racial composition of this small rural eastern North Carolina town during 1970's was about 50% Caucasian, about 40% African American, and about 10% other according to my observations from student demographics.

Local Business Support for School

Texas Gulf Corporation (Phosphate Excavation) had become the largest employer for locals and one of the largest for all of Beaufort County. TG was a high-profile and greatly valued international company. Their local support for recreation and Aurora High School Athletics was well known and envied throughout the school district. By all accounts, Mr. Comegys had played a key role in cultivating and promoting this very beneficial partnership. Such was the prevailing factors contributing to my good fortune having become an Aurora High School teacher/coach during this time.

With this backdrop, School opening became a time of excitement, exhilaration, and euphoria for me. After all, by now I had become familiar with the administrative team, coaching staff, and most teachers. I had received my classroom, teaching and duty assignments, class schedules, books, and supplies. Desks, tables, and bulletin boards were all in place. The only missing piece by now was the students.

Classes, Teaching and Learning

My classes on the master schedule included Civics and U.S. History. Although out of my area of certification, Mr. Comegys requested that I teach a class of challenged freshmen in basic general math. My answer was a resounding yes. It was a challenge I gladly accepted because it immediately became my goal to improve student deficits wherever they existed.

In reflecting upon my own high school experience, early fall return to school stirred my personal memories of reuniting with classmates and friends. This included academics, sports, and social events. During the opening week, we were always interested in the new clothes, hairstyles, and other changes in appearances that happened over the summer months.

My perspective as a first-year teacher had appropriately altered my focus. My role within the domain of education had changed into a more professional and financial matter. The entry into my lifelong career goals had begun. I was no longer the student but now the teacher. I was no longer the athlete but now the coach. I was no longer the recipient but now the giver and facilitator for every student and athlete that I had the privilege to instruct at Aurora High School beginning in the fall of 1973. However, there were many learning experiences I had along the way as a neophyte teacher.

It was during an early faculty meeting that I "stuck the proverbial foot in mouth". The subject was related to the politics of school funding in North Carolina. The fact that further east of the piedmont one found themselves in the state, the fewer school funds were availed. So, this was the point at which I made the comment that "any area east of Raleigh was considered scum and since Aurora was very distant from Raleigh, it made "Aurora the scum of the scum" as it related to school funding. My desire to appear knowledgeable overmatched my ability to think clearly before speaking. Following the meeting, Mr. Comegys very professionally addressed the comment to me in his office. His major concern was if I was aware that I was actually calling the people who lived there scum? I realized in a desire to appear informed and bright in the meeting I had done the opposite. This became a valuable lesson from that point forward. Important lessons learned from this experience were: simply think well before speaking, better to say nothing than the wrong thing, and always be reminded of who your audience consists of.

Once I progressed beyond my early blunders, my initial year as a teacher/coach was every bit as interesting, challenging, and rewarding as I had anticipated. Although most of the staff proved to be cordial and professional, there were several faculty members who became my trusted cohorts over the years. They were Ms. Blanche Downing (English teacher), Mrs. Peggy Simpson (English teacher), Mrs. Gloria Bryant (eighth grade teacher), Mrs. Ann Freeman (counselor) and Mr. Wayne Morris (drafting teacher).

Student cooperation and school spirit were evident. High levels of participation in student council elections and activities, club affiliations, and support for school sports were at a premium. Community activities and interests often made the crossover into school-related ones such as performances from the local 5th Street Gang musical performing group. The performers included Clevester Speight, Pam Ham, Curfew Speight (facilitator), and others. They were all students. The community-based Aurora High School Booster Club was dedicated supporters of school sports placing the greatest emphasis on football.

I was fortunate as a teacher/coach to have the opportunity to work with students and groups from the full spectrum of academic and extra-curricular areas. This made the school year pass quickly with few instances of boredom.

111

My strategy from the beginning with the challenged math class was to assess their math skills and start as fundamental as warranted. I discovered major deficits in basic arithmetic skills such as multiplication tables, division; fractions, decimals, conversion of measurements, and rate-time-distance problems. I attacked these areas by prioritizing my areas of instruction. We maximized in-class work directly under my supervision. We employed the use of kinesthetic, visual, and auditory instructional methods. Some applications of these methods were creating fraction pies and making cutouts, by comparing visual units of measurement such as quarts, pints, and ounces, and having students explain concepts verbally in their own words. Homework was utilized primarily for practice but not for the introduction of new concepts. In this way, students had an immediate opportunity to have underlying rules and postulates explained during class in order to avoid initial confusion and lack of comprehension. They began developing skills with understanding and confidence in areas of math never achieved before. Lessons learned from this early experience as a teacher: teachers must believe that barring a cognitive abnormality all students can learn, all students want to learn (have success) and the employment of appropriate instructional methods yields positive results. The feedback and memory from this class of students have become one of the most rewarding and memorable of my career.

In contrast, another freshman class of Civics students were quite prepared academically and thereby began at an elevated level of performance. This group of students in large numbers had virtually no difficulty in mastering the course content and their class discussions were always a joy.

School sports in my first year were highlighted by a successful football season; posting as runner-up in the Beaufort-Martin-Hyde Conference with a record of 5 wins, 2 losses, and a first-round loss in the State 1-A Playoffs. Eli Tatum (Running Back), Randy Potter (Quarter Back), Winfred Hamilton (Defensive Back), and Terry

Moore (Lineman) were among the most outstanding players of the season. My assignment was the assistant coach for receivers and defensive backs. I mostly enjoyed this first and only season coaching Aurora High Football with Head Coach Bobby Christopher.

The beginning of basketball season became an opportunity to demonstrate my independent skills as a coach. By this time, my life-long dream to coach basketball burned inside me to make the most of this opportunity. Our season started with some disappointment with a couple of early losses but began to assume momentum with every game thereafter. This proceeded until the end of the season as we found ourselves crowned Conference Co-Champions. Some of the key student athletes in our success as first-year JV coach were Keith Holmes, Ervin Chapman, Clevester Speight, Sampson Moore, Dexter Moore, Dennis Hamilton, Ken Sadler, Clarence Peed, Edmond J. Moore, William Bell, Darrel Fuller, and Alphonso Moore.

The varsity basketball team posted a record of 11-10 under Coach Ray Hall. Rodney Moore was the outstanding varsity player and Edith Moore was the outstanding varsity girls' player. Neither girl's basketball nor boys' varsity baseball records were found for the 1973-74 season.

My first year as a teacher/coach at Aurora High School had been a wonderful entry-level experience. Some of my most intro-spective and joyous moments occurred when regularly on my drive to work I would be reminded of my good fortune. I could observe instructional materials beside me, check my shirt and tie in the rearview mirror and glance into the back seat and see bas-ketballs all over. Exuberance could have been my middle name as I thought to myself "and I am actually being paid for doing this". Life is wonderful.

The contract assignments for my second year included an increase in assignments and additional responsibilities. Classes taught were U.S. History, Civics, Study Hall, and African American Studies, which replaced General Math. Additionally, I received responsibility for Junior Class Advisor and was appointed head basketball coach with responsibilities for coaching both junior varsity and varsity teams. I later volunteered to serve as Monogram Club advisor.

My marital status changed as I relocated back to Greenville, N.C. with my wife Delphia and newborn son Byron. Since my new domicile became a 55-minute commute, I was fortunate to share a carpool with William Blalock of Raleigh, a newly hired teacher.

My classes went well, and we managed a Varsity record of 11 and 9 that season having lost four starters and five seniors during this rebuilding year. At the conclusion of the second school year (1974-75), it had proved to be equally enjoyable as my first.

Texas Gulf provided funding for a summer recreation program at the Aurora High Gymnasium. The program provided a salary for coaches which was very timely since the district was on a ten-month pay schedule.

The start of my third year at Aurora brought excitement for the new school under construction. It was being built, just a short distance behind the old one which was more than fifty years old.

Recently and contemporaneously academic scrutiny has become a much greater focal point across the nation. During the seventies, teachers in the Beaufort County School District were provided a basic curriculum, textbooks, with an occasional visit from an instructional supervisor but left mostly to their own wits as to the how, when, and overall methodology regarding instructions.

The African American Studies Class with little district input was designed to study history roles and contributions of African Americans to American culture. An example of student demonstrated application of acquired knowledge, was by strengthening bonds between the youth and "Elders" in the Black Community. During the Christmas season, the class prepared and delivered Christmas Trays to the elderly for the purpose of demonstrating the following behaviors: "respect, reverence and knowledge of self".

Conflict Following African American History Month Program

The early seventies had been a period of transition involving civil rights and the integration of schools. How these changes would evolve and what the process would look like was an uncertainty and a tender box at best. This was the reality in North Carolina as well as many other places across the nation both North and South. Whether in Hillsborough Schools of Orange County, Charlotte-Mecklenburg Schools, Rose High of Greenville City Schools, or Ayden-Grifton High School of Pitt County Schools, the tender box of school integration had been accompanied by conflict and confrontation before the semblance of resolution occurred. Aurora High was no different in this regard although somewhat belated. During the 1979-80 school year, the conflict resulted after a well-intentioned program commemorating African American History Week. This first-ever at Aurora High School was being sponsored by the Black Studies Class and its' teacher (Your Author). Black students became upset when Caucasian students refused to stand during the singing of Lift Every Voice and Sing "The Black National Anthem". There had been no request for anyone to stand. However, upon recognizing the time-honored song by some of our African American staff, they quickly rose to their feet. Black students quite naturally followed their lead and did likewise while "White" students remained seated.

Because I was behind the curtains on stage prepping students for the program, I was oblivious to what was happening in the audience. There was absolutely no verbal outburst or confrontations whatsoever in the auditorium during the program. It was after the program and during the next exchange of class that the verbal confrontation and any physical exchange occurred. Several students suddenly entered my classroom and loudly exclaimed "they're out here fighting Mr. Smith". At that moment, I was totally unaware that it was related to the program at all. The school did not have security officers as most do currently. It was reported that some students had left school after the confrontation between several Black and White students. However, as I walked around, I didn't see any students fighting or engaged in arguments. It was reported that someone had thrown a bloody deer onto Mr. Comegy's vehicle. Before school was dismissed, there were news reporters from TV stations Channel 12 WCTI New Bern, NC, and Channel 7 WITN Washington, NC were on the scene doing stories. The Washington Daily News and the New Bern Sun Journal published articles for several days in their newspapers. Mr. Comegys was constantly called and hounded, contacted, and interviewed for the next several weeks. Surprisingly, I was never called or sought after in any way concerning the Black History Program or the incident that followed, not even from the **locals or school officials.** Although the Aurora community located in the most eastern region of North Carolina remains a very small, and remote community it has produced many outstanding graduates.

I had the privilege and honor of teaching, coaching, and mentoring many such students and athletes. Among A.H.S. alumni there are medical doctors, attorneys at law, accountants, career educators, engineers, corporate executives, airline pilots, and professional athletes among other successful career selections. The aforementioned students are but a partial list of outstanding classes and individuals who were outstanding.

Outstanding Classes
1977-1981
(African American Studies Students 1977-81)

Laverne Tripp Essie Hill Gerald Mattocks Sheila Dudley
Leslie Hil Vernessa Taylor Pamela Parker Bern Pritchett
Valerie Hill Doris Grimes Willie Jennette John Adams
Barry Tripp Sandra Moore Carl Thompson Olif Tyre.

(Civics Class 1977)

This was my highest achieving class as freshmen. Some of the students were:
Rita Broome Delilah Cooper Lorraine Edwards Pam Gegg
Sheryl Gillikin Jose Hardy Wanda Herwig Iris Moore
Brenda Tyre Shirley Schat April Smith Welton Turner
Adele Moore Ken Sadler Percy Moore Edmond Moore

(U.S. History Class of 1978)

This was my highest achieving U.S. History Class, some of the students were:
Sheila Dudley Vernessa Taylor Garland Guion Pamela Parker
Bern Pritchett Gerald Mattocks Kevin Tripp Richard Ives
Derell Oden Faith Edward Mary Hardy.

Monogram Club

Prior to my acceptance as Monogram Club advisor, it had been a club composed of select varsity athletes only. We opened membership to all students willing to accept the oath of dedication to the support of all Aurora High School Athletics. Club membership more than quadrupled to become the largest school club immediately.

Club members were actively motivated to participate in activities such as creating signs and posters for sports events, selling jackets labeled with the school logo to increase school visibility and pride. Fundraisers were held to purchase athletic equipment; club trips were sponsored for members to the beach and yearly cookouts were facilitated with food often in excess. There was one occasion in which non-students were sought from the streets to help consume it all.

Chess Club

Chess has always been a game of interest and challenge once I became a player. Also, I've never learned any game or sport that I wasn't interested in sharing or teaching others. The Aurora High Chess Club began with the motto "Learn, Play, and Teach Others to Play". We began during "Study Hall" and as interest grew, we expanded to an after-school activity. The first players and club members were: Eddie Andrews, Richard Ives, Allen Shepherd, Michael Mattocks, and others. They not only played chess but would often discuss and debate other issues important to them. These young chess players had become philosophical thinkers as well as good checkmaters.

The Sportsman Club

My idea of a Sportsman Club grew from the booster club concept with emphasis on support of all school athletics and not merely football. It also provided a source for the bonding of a group of local young African American Men for the support of younger ones in the form of mentorship. Founders and initial membership included: Danny Smith (your author) Thomas Coffey, Avon Moore, Carson Wright, John Ship, and Dalton Tyre. Community support for the Aurora basketball program, at my request, added an external spark to the basketball program. Often club members would act as ushers/security at games since we had no official security or police presence.

Later club members added a social affiliation to our membership by opening a social establishment called the "Utopia". The Utopia offered music, dancing, cards, and wholesome community entertainment for ages eighteen and over.

The first opportunity to occupy the space of a lifelong dream was not taken lightly by me. I was thrilled and appreciated the chance to coach all the young men I was given the opportunity to work with at Aurora High School. These are the names and short descriptions of some of the most outstanding chronologically.

A.H.S. Outstanding Athletes and Support Staff

Keith Holmes from the Aurora High Class of 1976 was a four-sport athlete during his time there. He participated in four different varsity sports including football, basketball, baseball, and track & field. After graduation, he attended N.C. A&T. Here he excelled as a standout member of the A&T Track Team. He became the 1978 MEAC Triple Jump Champion and the most valuable trackman at the MEAC Track & Field Championship.

Robert Williams was an outstanding varsity basketball player in the Aurora High Class of 1978. He was among the leading scorers and rebounders in the region his senior year. Robert was a leader on and off the court with a great attitude as a student and role model. He constantly received compliments from other coaches and was highly recruited by several colleges and universities. Robert became the first Aurora athlete to receive a basketball scholarship after my arrival at AHS.

Edwin Moore of the Class of 1980 was one of the most inspiring and gifted players in attitude and performance that I had the privilege to coach. His work ethic was second to none. Edwin was the type of player our program desperately needed during the transitional period in which he played. His contribution to the Aurora High Basketball Program was both timely and outstanding. He was likewise widely sought after by colleges and universities for his extraordinary talent.

Willie Jennette, a graduate of the Class of 1981 was the most versatile and sought-after player I had the privilege to coach. He was indicated to me to be a future star at AHS by Keith Holmes (a fellow Fifth Streeter). "Willie Earl" was just a little guy at the time.

As a senior, he led the team to the BHM Runner-Up Conference and Tournament Championships. He was the leading scorer in the conference and among the top scorers in the state. A recruiter approached me at our District Playoff game discussing Willies' talent and accomplishments. So at the end of our brief conversation, he alluded to Willie's scoring average by stating "Willie is the second-leading scorer in the state about 24 ppg" (points per game). I was not aware of that statistical fact. I knew he was the conference leader and a regional leader but not second in the state. Then checking his notes, the recruiter said *"yes* second to some guy from Wilmington named *Jordan".* At the time I had no idea who Michael Jordan was and certainly nothing of the megastar he would become, and the rest is history. Later Jennette and Jordan would meet and ball together, and even make a commercial with Jordan while both were players at NCCU and UNC respectively (true story). Among all his recruiters, East Carolina University and North Carolina Central were the two finalists for his selection. After school and home visits by several schools, Willie and his family decided NCCU would be their choice.

While at N. C. Central, he led the CIAA in scoring his senior year and opted to play professionally overseas in Italy before settling in Australia. There he played his career and became known as "No Net Jennette" for his sharpshooting skills.

Richard Coffey graduated in the Class of 1983. I had the privilege of coaching the mild-mannered young man for two years before leaving Aurora High School. Richard was a wonderful young man from a wonderful home and family. By the time Richard came along Thomas, Ray, and Cynthia, his siblings, had been among my previous students. His older brother Thomas had been a good player and participated as a very dedicated member of the Sportsman Club as well. I at once became aware of Richard's good-natured personality and great heart. One day while in conversation he mentioned he had some new puppies and he wanted to give me one.

I must say that at the time I really didn't need a puppy because of my being constantly on the go. As it turned out, Mutt became an excellent pet and very reliable watchdog. Richard was a player that started quite small as a J.V. player, but grew tall and full when it came time for varsity. He came along with a good group of team-mates such as Jeffrey Blango and Bruce Jackson. They successfully captured the Junior Varsity BHM Championship in 1981, which was my last year at Aurora.

I continued to follow his career after my departure. The team did very well as a varsity. After graduation, Richard joined the Army and played on successful teams during his enlistment. He received the accolade of *"All Army"*. After his enlistment, he was awarded a basketball scholarship to the University of Minnesota. Following his time at the University of Minnesota, he was drafted by the newly franchised Minnesota Timberwolves, where he played in the **National Basketball Association** for several years becoming a bonafide hometown hero and local basketball legend. Whenever I had the opportunity of watching him on TV, and if there were other ears around, I would always say, "I coached that kid as a JV player at Aurora High School. I would then finish by saying very, very proudly "and just look at him now; YES".

Support Staff (1974-1981)

Our official scorers, statisticians, bus drivers, and coach's assis-tants were completely loyal and 100% reliable, in support of our program through the years. They were Sharon Midgette, Derrell Oden, Theresa Hill, Valerie Hill, Miranda Parker, Welton Turner, W.C. Boyd, and Yulonda Moore.

Tragedy and Grief at A.H.S.

Unfortunately, in reflecting upon the most enjoyable and rewarding times experienced at Aurora High School I can't help but recall the ones of greatest tragedy and grief. The sudden death of Daphene Robinson, the auto wreck death of Richard Ives, and the dual drowning deaths of cousins Richard and Timothy Stilley. These were among the most heart-wrenching moments of my career.

Daphene Robinson was a quiet and demure young lady seemingly liked by everyone. When she suddenly and inexplicably died, schoolmates and staff alike became prolonged grief-stricken. It was a case of an entire school being in mourning for an extended period of time. I was personally moved to write an article in the school newspaper entitled "The Death of a Student".

Richard Ives was an unassuming caucasian young man and a member of the Chess Club of which I sponsored. During his junior year, he tragically lost his young life in an auto accident. He had become a good chess player and a great sport.

The tragic summer drowning deaths of cousins **Timothy** and **Richard Stilley** and their subsequent dual funerals was a most difficult time. The funerals were held in the school gym where I had coached Timothy as a J.V. basketball player. He loved the game and was so willing to work and do what I asked of him to improve. I along with many others was heartbroken. I couldn't help but sob contemplating thoughts of these young lives ending just as they were beginning to find themselves.

It was reported that one jumped in to save the other, even though neither could swim.

I believe some of the best life lessons and great stories emerge from small-town America. If this is true, the small town of Aurora, North Carolina fits very well within that group. I have never regretted one day I spent there. There I was given an opportunity to obtain the foundations upon which a career evolved. Other career educators and community support were at the core of my success with students and athletics emanating from my Aurora High School employment experience.

Mr. Paul Comegys, (principal) willingness to demonstrate patience and administrative guidance within which I could successfully nurture and develop was invaluable. Ms. Blanche Downing, Mrs. Peggy Simpson, Mrs. Ann Freeman, Mrs. Mary Peele and Mr. Wayne Morris became my valued co-workers upon whose professional friendships I could always depend.

The community of support received from the following individuals and others: Mrs. Anna Parker, Ms. Johnne Ann Bullock, Mrs. Gloria Peacock Jennette, Mrs. Pearlie Moore, and Mr. James Parker, Sr. provided much needed housing, local knowledge, and moral support as needed. The small rural town of Aurora, North Carolina, its community, people, and especially students served me well; and is one I will always remember and cherish.

Concurring Events in Greenville, NC

I lived in Greenville for a portion of the period while employed at Aurora High School. There were two impactful community-related events which occurred during the time my young family (Delphia, Byron, and I) lived at Eastbrook Apartments between the years of 1976-1978.

Greenville Tennis Association (GTA)

First was the founding of the **Greenville Tennis Association**. During the 1970s with increased television exposure to such youthful and colorful athletes as Chris Everett, Arthur Ashe, and Jimmy Connors tennis popularity had dramatically increased across the country. In 1977 a group of African American men, tennis enthusiasts, in the Greenville, N.C. area planned and organized a much-desired community-based Tennis Club. Although Arthur Ashe was a noted exception heretofore tennis had been viewed more as a Caucasian and an elitist sport by many especially within the African American community. An increase in recreational funding during the 1970's made possible more public courts and facilities for practice and play of the sport by the general public. This became an opportunity for more of those not able to afford the country club lifestyle to learn and enjoy the sport as well.

Recently we have become very cognizant of two very accomplished sisters who have currently benefited mightily from learning tennis on the public courts of Los Angeles, CA. The sisters Venus and Serena Williams have broken most records and established themselves as household names and icons in the wonderful sport of tennis.

Founding Members of the **Greenville Tennis Association (GTA)** and first Executive Board included: Howard (1st President), Danny Smith (Your Author, 1st Secretary), Bobby Short (Greenville Recreation), Leon Johnson, Robert Johnson, Don Ensley (ECU, P.E. Instructor) and Thomas Midgette (Pitt Community College Counselor).

Racial Incident at Eastbrook

The second event was an unexpected incident that occurred on a Fall Sunday afternoon in 1978 as my bother-in-law (Creft Haggins) and I left the apartment en route to purchase beer before a football game began on television. It was almost dark as a car sped by us and yelled the slur "nigger" from the vehicle. My brother-in-law threw the bottle towards the vehicle, instantly. The vehicle abruptly stopped and began to back. A bottle was hurled towards me as I heard the bottle whistle by my head. The car then quickly accelerated. I began running towards the car as the driver again abruptly stopped again. The driver opened the door and stood there hitting his leg exclaiming, "I have my roscoe right here" (meaning a gun) as I approached him. Creft then said, "let's go". We then went to my car and left for the store. While turning into the store area the car from our previous encounter approached and threw another bottle towards our car. This bottle hit the top of the car and skidded off causing not even so much as a scratch, despite their intent. The car then made a U-turn in the middle of the street fortunately avoiding a serious accident.

We then entered the store and made our purchase before returning home with our beer. As we approached the apartment complex, we observed at least ten or more police cars all with flashing lights scrolling and beaming. We were shocked by the commotion and wondered verbally what it was all about. We had no idea it was related to our previous incident. Just as we began to disembark the car several police rushed towards me and stated, "you're the one out here trying to fight white boys', right?" By this time, the parking area had become full of others who resided in the complex (mostly Caucasian students attending East Carolina University). They emphatically explained to the police that I did not start the confrontation. Rather, I lived there very quietly and had never caused any problems. They explained that the white individuals in conflict with us were the "troublemakers" and didn't even live there. It was only after their explanation that the police reduced their aggression toward me. They then began to pull back and express a different tone and tenor. They finally stated, "if they return notify us immediately".

About two months later, I had a visitor from the State Bureau of Investigation. There was a knock at my door on that remarkably interesting night. There stood a tall, and athletic looking Caucasian male as he presented me his badge/credentials. I knew immediately what it was about. I was neither intimidated nor impressed. I very politely invited him in and offered him a seat. He continued introducing himself by giving a few more details of his educational and professional background. I recall he revealed he had attended Michigan State University. He asked about the school of my undergraduate study. I informed him of my having attended a small HBCU in Durham, N.C. with which he was probably not familiar. He didn't disagree or correct me on that point. As our conversation progressed, it became clear my assumption was that the visit was a follow-up to the Sunday evening confrontation with the "white hooligans" from a couple of months prior. It seemed that the query was more an assessment of my disposition and state of mind than the incident itself. He asked probing questions like did I intend to increase my formal education or seek a higher degree. Another question was something along the lines of my level of interest in politics. I responded by informing him, "I couldn't imagine a person in America not wanting to better prepare themselves through education, if possible, to do so". I also pointed out that as far as I could discern politics control all our lives. Now any person who understands this fact would necessarily have no choice but at minimum be interested in it (politics). The interrogation went on for about thirty minutes before he left never to be seen again.

Through the years, I have often wondered about that encounter. Questions lingered such as: Did they ever seek to locate or investigate those who were clearly at fault as implicated by my Caucasian neighbors? Did they create some type of file on me related to this as a racial incident? If so, has such a file ever been reviewed and adversely used against me?

CHAPTER 7

NAVY ENLISTMENT & OLD DOMINION UNIVERSITY

A fter eight years at Aurora, all my instincts indicated it was time to move on. I knew for certain travel, an accumulation of savings, a master's degree, and pursuit of a karate black belt were among my immediate goals. The Viet Nam War and civil rights considerations held heretofore had basically kept military service low on my desired list of employment options. These issues had become much less relevant by the fall of 1981. I now realized all immediate goals were achievable with a single tour of military duty with Uncle Sam.

Carolina Company and Navy Boot Camp

I officially became an active-duty member in the U.S. Navy on October 16, 1981. The entire group of inductees with me at this time had become a special company (The North Carolina Company). Usually, company members don't know who their fellow members are until arrival at the Recruit Training Command because they are usually from different areas of the United States and territories. We met immediately. The entire company attended the

127

Raleigh State Fair together the day before departure as a company of recruits. However, we were no longer civilians. We wore T-shirts lettered U. S. Navy Recruits Carolina Company accompanied by our commanders.

That night we left Raleigh-Durham Airport on our flight to Orlando, Florida, our Company soon discovered that we were the only such state-designated recruits upon arrival at Recruit Training Command. We were issued uniforms, a Sea Bag, and The Bluejacket Manuel (a sailor's guide to everything navy); then given our individual assignments on 1-1 day. One-one day was designated as such because it was the first day of the first week of training. Each subsequent day was named accordingly through the eighth week and our day of graduation (8-3 days). We also learned quickly that our special company status carried extremely high expectations from our two company commanders. They had the lofty goal of achieving "Hall of Fame Company" for us. Later I discovered our special designation placed something of a target on our backs from the other companies. I was selected as the second recruit in charge by the company commanders. Other Officers were as follows: (1) Recruit Chief Petty Officer (RCPO), (2) Master at Arms (MAA), (3) Port and Starboard Watch Leading Petty Officers, and (4) Yeoman. The RCPO was the company leader and formation caller when in company formation. The Master at Arms (my title) was in charge of in-house activities. The Port and Starboard Watch Leading Petty Officers supported the RCPO in formations and the MAA on their respective sides of formation in-house.

Each day of recruit training was a day of intense learning some aspect of our new Navy lives.

Daily Routine: Reveille –All hands up and prepare for the day, Breakfast –0545, Morning Muster – headcount 0730, Classes/ instructional periods 0730—1300, Noon Meal—1300-1330, Fitness and Recreation—1330-1650, Evening Meal 1650-1700, Use of telephone, Study, Free period 1700-1900, Showers and Radio

--1900-2100, Taps, Lights-out, and Bed check –2130. Note that use of telephone, purchases of snack items (gee dunk), and radio listening were all earned privileges. The Plan of the Day (POD) activities kept the company thoroughly occupied and completely focused all day every day.

One concept internalized early in navy preparation was always give your 100%, undivided attention to the instructor whether lecture, demonstration, or participatory activity. If you've ever heard the term "curse like a sailor" you would well know the meaning if you ever made the mistake of losing focus during instructional or training sessions. The instructor would give you a not-so-subtle warning like, "I'll rip of your head and defecate down your throat". Only, another word that you can easily imagine was used instead of "*defecate*". Inadequate and misunderstood training in critical activities such as weapons movement, firefighting, underway replenishment, and especially general quarters (prep for battle) made clear the possibility of loss of your life and your role in those of shipmates; more likely.

The Navy's goal was to keep each recruit engaged and focused while developing his/her acute ability for "attention to detail". Also, to impress upon each recruit an extreme understanding of "the right way, the wrong way and the Navy's way" and which was most important. Superb physical preparation and training would be required to successfully manage what would be encountered in the fleet. "The fleet" was often referred to as the "real navy" while boot camp was merely the place of training for this eventuality.

The North Carolina Company quickly gained notoriety for its winning ways in the competitions among the other companies. Areas of competition were Academics, Inspections of Barracks, Lockers, Infantry, Personnel, and Physical Fitness. A company was required to win in all categories for both competitions to become a "Hall of Fame Company".

By 8-3 day 73 of the original 74 Navy recruits of the North Carolina Company had successfully completed the required training and accordingly received their school assignments. The company had successfully won all competitions twice except locker competition; won just once. We thereby fell short of achieving Hall of Fame status by losing 1 of 12 competitions. Likewise, there was the loss of one recruit after not meeting the required swimming qualifications.

Despite minor disappointments, this was a time of pride with strong feelings of accomplishment for most of the company. It was late December and an early Christmas present. We were finally off to "The Real Navy" with RTC Orlando in the rearview mirror.

Tour of Duty

Personnelman-A-School was my choice for enlisted technical training following boot camp. Naval Training Command at Meridian, Mississippi became the second stop on my navy tour of duty. There I received specialized training in the maintenance of enlisted service records and naval administrative procedures.

A-School seemed almost a breeze following boot camp and two weeks of leave for Christmas. Class work was not a problem since Ms. Doris Lee had taught and tutored me well in typing and office practices while attending RHS. After eight weeks of Personnelman School, my orders arrived to report to PCO Stephen W. Groves (pre-commissioned ship under construction) at Bath Iron Works Bath, Maine.

The Groves was a Perry Class frigate (FFG) with a small crew of about 80 crew members. It was approximately 95% completed before the crew manned the ship. We took the maiden sea trial about two months later and arrived at homeport Mayport, Florida during early spring 1982. Mayport is a relatively small port within the Jacksonville, Florida metro area. Naval Air Station Jacksonville is also located in the region. Naval Air Stations (NAS) are numerous in the Navy primarily because of the air wing affiliated with the numerous aircraft carriers in the fleet. When the ship was in port, shipboard work was much like a regular 9 to 5 unless you had duty. If you had no duty, then you could leave the ship and go as you please until muster the next day or after Friday until morning muster Monday. If you had duty during the week, you were required to remain shipboard for duty day and night and for Friday, Saturday, and Sunday in the case of weekend duty. This required quarterdeck or safety and security duty for four-hour watches and any required departmental duties.

Because The Groves was a newly commissioned ship it was required to meet all ship specifications and crew requirements before officially becoming sea and battle worthy. Some of our most intense training occurred at Guantanamo Bay, Cuba, and Roosevelt Roads, Puerto Rico. After about seven weeks of successful shipboard training in these places, we returned to Mayport with great relief.

It was after our return that I received a duty assignment that was customary for every shipboard junior enlisted person. "Mess cranking" was galley or kitchen support for the Cooks. Basically, the work included about three or four months of the worst aspects of the meal preparation and cleanup process. Specifically, the cranks' jobs were: humping boxes and bags of food; cleaning and washing equipment, sweeping and swabbing galley floors, removing trash and garbage from the ship and worst of all taking orders from the MS's (cooks). Believe me; they (cooks) had no problem in writing cranks up at any time if they felt you to be inadequate or disrespectful in any way. This assignment was not a bag of laughs or fun for all by any stretch! Thoughts at once began to creep into my head like, why did I join the navy, and was I a glutton for punishment?

I had taken a pretest for pilot school before enlisting and unfortunately discovered that my lack of background in physics and calculus did not adequately support my ambition. Likewise, my vision (eyesight acuity) was not up to the required specifications. It was explained that if interested in surface officer school, I could apply once I arrived at my first permanent duty station. A short time with mess cranking very quickly intensified and speeded my interest in changing my situation.

By virtue of my job designation as a personnelman (pencil pusher), I had access to most administrative and instructional manuals. Unless there has been a significant change in attitude, precious few shipmates are willing to help when the goal of an enlisted sailor is seeking advancement from enlisted to officer status. So, it was left to my own personal motivation and willpower to explore, research, and acquire that which was needed. The necessary and properly prepared forms (about 20 pages) along with supporting documents were merely the first steps. Remember anything missing or incorrectly entered was immediately sent to file 13. As always in the fleet, there was the right way, the wrong way, and the navy way, which was the only way. Since none of the senior enlisted types on The Groves would help me, finally I befriended a First Class at a nearby PSD. He assisted me with the completion of the remaining outstanding forms, which I then submitted as required.

One morning during the middle of routine cleanup after morning meal there was an abrupt commotion as a shipmate yelled: "attention on deck"! Everyone quickly jumped to attention. It was Captain Bozzelli whom you rarely laid eyes upon any place on the ship let alone in the Galley. He spoke authoritatively as he briskly stated, Seaman Danny Smith front and center.

Not thinking of my OCS application, I was thinking, what have I done? He read from a letter, "you have been selected to attend Officer Candidate School Newport, Rhode Island, report for duty no later than October 14, 1982. That is all". He then gave the order "As you were". He then invited me up to the pilothouse, where he placed his cover (hat) on my head and exclaimed to all around "he will someday be your boss". My good fortune became documented Navy news in the local Jacksonville newspaper.

Captain Bozzelli recognizing OCS candidate
for OCS candidate school

I often had cause to reflect on the treatment I received on the Stephen W. Groves under the very fair-minded and upright leadership of Captain Bozzelli. I would discover later this would be in sharp contrast to much of the remainder of my Naval career.

Missing Ship's movement is an egregious charge for any sailor attached to a sea-going command. Such behavior usually results in serious consequences regarding loss of pay and pay grade, restriction, and extra duty. To be able to do so in compliance with regulations was a great, great feeling. This is why I made it a point to be on the pier to actually watch the Groves "get underway" without me for the first time after receiving my orders to OCS Newport. I waved to my shipmates manning the deck as the Groves released mooring and set sail. Only this time my name did not appear on "the sailing diary".

I spent a short period of leave with my family and sweetheart Valerie. I also purchased modest transportation in the form of a used but well-maintained Chevrolet Impala. This proved to be a great decision once in Newport.

I arrived at NTC Newport, R.I. on or about October 14, 1982. Officer candidates were divided into companies and named with an International Radiotelephony Spelling (Alpha, Beta, Charlie, etc.). My assignment was to Echo Company. Each company was separated into junior and senior candidates.

At the time, an officer's commission could be acquired through the Naval Academy, College NROTC Programs, and Officer Candidate School. The officer candidate variety was referred to as "a 90-day wonder" because they were required to learn in just ninety days what the other two had four years to accomplish. An OC was also required to possess a bachelor's degree as a program prerequisite. Likewise, all required degrees and certifications were required standards for nurses, doctors, chaplains, and other commission seekers. However, I must admit with something of humorous memory these groups as being the least precise and accurate companies in marching formation and infantry skills (marching, saluting, and military bearing). As I recall, passing such a company of OC's always provoked an internal smile or two or three.

Major courses and class work included naval history and tradition, engineering, ship navigation, sailing, celestial and GPS, military strategy, combined branch warfare, chain of command, personnel administration, and discipline.

Weekend liberty was granted to us only after we had become seniors. This was my first personal experience of the military adage "rank has its privileges". I was able to sightsee or visit local places of interest such as Martha's Vineyard, the Kennedy Estate, and the National Tennis Museum. Weekend-get-away became my stress-relieving opportunity to visit relatives in Providence, Hartford, New Haven, and New York. I most often visited New Haven among these cities. Here two of my favorite cousins resided Eddie Smith, a cousin with which I grew up very closely because of our similarity in age. The other was Martin King Smith because he was always like a big brother and never failed to help me through all manner of adversity. These two beloved relatives insisted that New Haven become my "home away from home" and provided me with local support during this incredibly challenging period of my life.

After about six months of unfairness and consternation with administration, I left NTC Newport during the spring of 1982 with less than two and a half years left on my enlistment. My assignment was to naval ship U.SS. Ainsworth DDG 1090 home ported at Naval Station, Norfolk, Virginia. Here I reported to my second sea-going assignment. This ship had a record of dubious reputation and even worse outcomes. The Ainsworth had a history for constant propulsion problems and general bad luck as a crew. It once had the unfortunate outcome of falling from its platform while in dry dock repair. On another occasion, during a night return to home-port Navy Station Norfolk, it went (DIW) dead in the water. Even more traumatic was the death of the former Ainsworth Captain at his newly assigned ship. Soon after his arrival, he became ill and died suddenly.

My own transfer later from the Ainsworth was a relief from calamity or so I thought! At Commander in Chief Atlantic Fleet (CINCLANTFLT) was considered a great duty and excellent for farewell duty according to detailers (those who assigned duty). Often before accepting new duty assignments, members would make contacts and speak with a member currently at that command.

At least two assigned members advised me to avoid accepting an assignment at CINCLANFLT. I understood their message but felt it couldn't be as bad as they expressed. I was wrong! This command had lots of brass (high-ranking officers) with lots of subservience from enlisted and junior officers.

One day upon reporting to work without pretext our Department Head made the announcement that we would receive a required inoculation. When my name was called, I reported to the designated place and received a shot for which there was no explanation then and none later. It was strange then and even stranger now in review of the manner in which it was done.

Primarily because of a lack of rank advancement and a pervasive attitude of disrespect most of the "brothers" I knew had a serious distaste for the place and wanted transfers or separation as soon as possible. An excellent example was an African American shipmate stationed at CINCLANFLT who often expressed his problems of subjection to unfairness and ridicule. He continued communicating even after I separated. He forwarded documentation of formal complaints all the way up to the Chief of Naval Operations.

Although I never made a formal complaint, my experience had been similar, but I had specific goals and was determined to make the most educational opportunity while assigned there. I discovered a Navy-funded program called tuition assistance. The Navy would fund up to nine hours per semester if a sailor maintained the required grade point average. I promptly enrolled in the Education Administration Program at Old Dominion University to begin taking advantage of the opportunity. Grades had to be submitted to my command each semester to continue funding. Disingenuous complimentary comments of surprise of how well I was doing were quite annoying, but I knew my goals and therefore remained focused.

Montel Williams (future TV talk show host) was a commissioned Naval Officer at the time and some since my release date claimed to have seen him at CINCLANTFLT during the mid to late 1980s. I can't attest to

the claim. They indicated, he was already known as one of high morale and as a motivational and inspirational speaker. We know that he later hosted an extremely popular TV talk show, which bared his name. If this was true, I and several others may have sought the counsel of the very capable future talk show host.

Early during the spring of 1987, a notice was circulated explaining the details of an early-out program. After familiarizing myself with all the provisions and reviewing personal financial matters, I submitted my application. In early July of 1987, I was honorably discharged from the U.S. Navy; with six-plus years of military service.

As a result of my Navy enlistment I was able to achieve three of the four definitive goals I had set for myself initially: (1) save money (2) travel (3) Earn a Master's Degree (4) and obtain a Karate Black Belt. "That ole Black Belt proved to be most elusive".

Old Dominion University Study

Once separated from the Navy I began using my Veterans Assistance Educational Program (VEAP) to continue working towards my masters. I will always remember Dr. Petra Snowden, as my advisor, for writing my problems paper at Old Dominion. She never allowed me to have a "dull moment". She required me to meet her for course-related instructions no matter where she would be found whether at the mall, beauty parlor, or her home. I selected "Alternative Education" as a topic for research. An authentic experience was a requirement with the topic I had chosen. My authentic research was on a special program implemented in areas of southeastern Virginia. It was designed for emotionally disturbed children (ED). The program design was to teach them, monitor them, and encourage their appropriate behavior through a systematic use of rewards and sanctions (SECEP). The program afforded ED designated students unable to function in the regular education setting an opportunity to develop better decision-making and controlled response skills. This was accomplished within the SECEP environment, which provided more immediate rewards and reinforcement for their learning, cooperation, and appropriate behavior.

My Masters in Education Administration at ODU was completed in the spring of 1988. I had also completed a course in Virginia Real Estate as a plan B for employment coming out of the Navy.

My sisters Evelyn, Jean, and other career educators convincingly made the case to me concerning the critical need for more African American males in the public school system. Having been successfully encouraged to reenter public education, I heeded the challenge.

My SECEP experience helped me land a contract to teach behavior-challenged eighth graders at Knapp Junior High in Currituck County, N. C. in 1988. This, my first year back into education following almost six years of navy life seemed quite slow and uneventful. I did meet some very nice people there and thoroughly enjoyed working with the students as always.

CHAPTER 8

PORTSMOUTH PUBLIC SCHOOLS
1989-2013

Waters Middle School
1989-2000

During the spring of 1989, I interviewed for a social studies teachers position in Portsmouth, Virginia. After the interview as I departed the building, I recall the thrill of adventure in the potentiality of departing Currituck County, N. C. in order to take employment in Portsmouth.

New System and Methods

There was much to like at Waters Middle School. Their instructional model featured teacher clusters (instructional teams) which utilized a collaborating team approach to address the instructional, emotional, and behavioral needs of their assigned students. The single consolidated building structure would be an advantage over the multiple building plant of Knapp Junior High (Currituck County). Even what I was able to observe of the Cavalier Manor community seemed to be a clean and progressive community to live or work.

Appreciatively, about two weeks before the end of the current school year at Knapp I was offered the position at Waters Middle. The day that I signed the contract and returned to my car the radio was playing "It's a Beautiful Morning" a song by the Rascals that I enjoy even to this day. I thought. How appropriate is this? The continuance of nine years of public education after six years of Navy life would now begin in Portsmouth Public Schools. All of which would be complete with personal and professional desire to teach, mentor, and motivate intently every student within my domain of influence.

During orientation week for new teachers, I discovered somewhat to my disappointment that the Principal who interviewed and hired me had been replaced by newly assigned principal Michael Spencer. Another discovery was some of the key instructional personnel in the district. I was extremely impressed with Dr. Daisy Murphy who seemed so very skilled and thorough in her explanations and visions for district programs. Later, Dr. Patricia Fisher established herself as a very equitable "nuts and bolts" instructional specialist with the skills and patience to provide instructional leadership for the district.

No one loved their subject matter more than Ms. Rosa Wells; the Social Studies Specialist for the district. She always seemed genuinely excited each time she presented before us, which in turn became infectious to our delivery in the classrooms.

With the start of school, I began to experience the cluster system and middle school methods that I was so impressed with during my interview. The five-member teams for seventh graders consisted of, Science, Social Studies, Language Arts, Math, and Reading teachers. Daily interdisciplinary planning gave each teacher the opportunity to share, compare, cooperate, and plan across their respective areas of subject matter. With this approach, learning objectives could be sometimes combined, and fused for a more comprehensive and colorful learning experience for the middle school learner. Additionally, individual emotional or behavioral issues could be addressed as a team measured response for support and resolution. Another strategy was the very thoughtful utilization of movement of class changes without the distractions of bells ending and beginning classes.

The one Middle School concept of major disagreement in Portsmouth at the time for me was the exclusion of middle school sports. There was a total of four middle schools in the school district at the time. All were void of middle school sports. Currently, elsewhere there had been a near-total movement away from this conceptual practice. It begs the question, why was this idea ever seriously considered and practiced? More information related to middle school sports in Portsmouth will be presented later in this chapter.

One suggestion and compensation for the lack of school-based sports was my recommendation to Mr. Spencer for an "activity day" set aside monthly for student participation. It was a challenge, for scheduling, but with the help of a small committee and staff cooperation, we were able to facilitate the activities for one bell monthly. Some of the activities included: gym sports, basketball, badminton, board games, music, listening, needlepoint, and club formations. One such club was the Leadership Club, which consisted of a group of students that assisted me and the committee in the planning and facilitation of Activity Day. What many of us thought was something of a relief from the mundane was ended abruptly soon after about three or four months, by Principal Mike Spencer, without prior notice.

Honestly, from the outset one of my goals upon employment in Portsmouth Schools was to establish myself as a leading candidate for administrative promotion. My concept was never to be placed or given anything professionally. I only wanted that which resulted from my service, dedication to students, school, and community.

Summer School Principal

The first clear opportunity was summer school principal. My selection occurred during the first summer of employment. I was very excited but soon discovered my enthusiasm was not shared by the senior administrator in the building. The current principal seemed indifferent to my selection.

He did much to deny access to school-based materials, especially books; and a cooperative demeanor for summer school-related needs. His tactics would have become more problematic had it not been for helpful career administrators such as Preston Harts and Deforrest Mapp who were part of the summer school rotation of administrators. Mr. Harts was currently on the administrative team at Waters and used his keys to allow access to books related to summer school needs. Mr. Mapp was likewise helpful with his advice, and expertise with bus logistics and management. They likewise shared any other valuable tips concerning summer school practices and procedures. We had the help of a great staff and a supportive community as well. We were obviously financially sound because Mrs. Norcom (summer school bookkeeper) informed me, "you have submitted more summer school funds than any summer school principal during my tenure". Likewise, my staff conveyed how much they had enjoyed working with me and assured me that soon I must be selected for a permanent position. It did not "pan out" that way. This would be the first of four times I would serve as summer school principal without pay or compensation in the district.

After what I and many others thought was an extraordinarily successful debut as a summer school principal, I was assigned Summer School Principal at Churchland Middle thereafter three years which continued as a payless and mostly thankless assignment by Central Office.

Following my first stint as Summer School principal at Waters, I found myself assigned to a mobile classroom outside the main building for the following school year.

I never indicated my concern about this decision to Mike Spencer (principal), cluster members, or anyone. My students never complained during inclement weather or about being referred to as the "outdoors cluster" nor the general inconvenience of it all. They just continued with great attitudes.

I recall during the holiday season a door decoration contest was held for homerooms. This was early during the introduction of Kwanzaa as a holiday. Our homeroom decided to decorate our door for Kwanzaa and won the Blue Ribbon. Student confidence and attitude towards the mobile soared as we continued about the business of learning, intellectual application, and cultural growth.

I was fortunate to have had Dr. Ella Ward as an assistant principal and administrator at this point during my tenure in Portsmouth Schools. She always had words of encouragement about my career in administration. She likewise allowed me to gain experience administratively under her advisement. As a career educator, she was a role model for many. She very professionally did not allow herself to become discouraged by the inconsiderate and unfair actions of some gatekeepers in her career path. Despite the obstacles, Dr. Ward very astutely and honorably navigated her way by proving herself as a professional educator of a high order, a local political office holder, and a statewide education official senior to many who refused her promotion and attempted to thwart her career.

Community Involvement

The first community activist I met from the Cavalier Manor community was Mr. Joe Wright. I easily remembered his last name because after our first conversation and learning of his dedication and service to the community I thought of him as "Joe Righteous". I have always had a good healthy admiration and respect for dedicated community activists and Joe Wright was such a beloved citizen. We met for the first time at the Portsmouth Municipal Courthouse in downtown Portsmouth. I had taken a group of seventh-grade Civics students on a field trip there. Some of the students recognized him as their once little league coach. After court adjournment, this gave me the opportunity to introduce myself and explain our purpose for being there. I explained that the class was on a field trip making observations of "authentic court proceedings". He then described his purpose as a member of the Civic League in observation for fairness to a fellow citizen of the Cavalier Manor Community on trial. During our brief conversation, he extended to me an invitation to visit their next scheduled meeting. I accepted his invitation and shared my perspective on several school-related issues on the meeting agenda. I returned to other meetings, at their invitation during my time at Waters.

Later, I learned that he and others had established a roving watch team complete with automobile and community monitoring for its safety and well-being. They had similarly organized a team of crossing guards for helping Waters' Middle students traversing the very traffic-busy Cavalier Boulevard in route to school. Later, the much-needed safety service was taken over by the school district after having been shown the way by "Mr. Righteous".

Waters Mentorship Program

Later Mr. Joe (Righteous) Wright would be instrumental in assisting Mr. Otha Collins, William Elliott, and me in founding the first school-based mentorship program at Waters Middle (Waters Mentorship Program). Later in 2005, he would help Quentin Jones and me in founding a much needed mentorship program at Norcom High School.

Nathan McCall would probably be the first to admit that he could have benefited from a well-organized mentorship program while attending Waters Middle School. He chronicled much of his early troubled life in Portsmouth, Virginia in his book ("Makes Me Wanna Holler, Random Press 1994). Concerning choices in life, Nathan McCall states, "I wish there were more successes...I wish that somehow, brothers everywhere would reach down deep and summon the will to defy the inner hatred driving them to self-destruct" (McCall: 1994). Nate's conclusion resulted from an early lifestyle, which resulted in many hard knocks and his own youthful incarceration. The later discovery of his literary talent as a student at Norfolk State University and employment at the Virginian Pilot-Ledger Star, The Washington Post, and the Atlanta Journal-Constitution illustrated his extraordinary journalistic ability. He has been a guest on several nationally syndicated television shows including the Oprah Winfrey Show and currently speaks across the country informing, motivating, and inspiring.

McCall has become a role model for Black Youth as a reformed success story and a special voice for analysis of race relations. He has been placed in the conversation with such writers as Claude Brown and Richard Wright after writing at least three other major books involving socio-economic and political implications for the country. His visit to his middle school alma mater (W. E. Waters) during his first book tour during the '90s, was both enlightening and inspirational to students and staff alike.

As Student Council advisor, I had the opportunity to collaborate with council members, in preparation for his visit to Waters. Mr. Spencer (principal) had stated it was the preference of Nate to be in a small setting for his presentation thusly we found ourselves confined to the small band room area with limited space. Maybe that was Nate's request. I'm not sure. I do know for a fact that the band room decision seemed only convenient for minimal student attendance. At the end of the program, the SCA and I presented Mr.

McCall with an autographed and framed T-shirt imprinted with his book cover on behalf of the student body. For this, he seemed genuinely surprised and greatly appreciative. There were a few fleeting moments before his departure for a book autographing session. We exchanged a few words and a feeling of strong mutual respect seemed to emerge with a solid handshake upon his departure.

Waters Middle School Student Government Officers presenting award to writer Nathan McCall

A group of counselors out of a special program under the district-wide supervision of Dr. Daisy Murphy included a mentoring program. It lasted for a brief period after my tenure at Portsmouth Schools began. The counselor assigned to Waters, and I had become friends through our conversations from visits to the building. He was found dead in a ditch in Portsmouth, and I was always suspicious about his death. In my mind, the best way to honor him and his work was to try and continue it. This among other reasons was the immediate impetus for my involvement with mentorship in Portsmouth Public Schools.

Mr. Otha Collins, a well-respected and long-standing art teacher, became the first mentoring recruit. Mr. William Elliott an educational assistant was likewise there from the start. Mr. Edward Glover a city-based counselor took part for a short period before his departure. The major focuses of our activities were: to enhance self-esteem and personal growth; through self-knowledge, respect for self and others, and development of greater value for learning and achievement. We had speakers and presenters such as community leader Mr. Joe (Righteous) Wright, Football players from Norcoms' State Championship Team, city leaders, and fundraisers. We also developed activities for self-esteem held during our meetings. I recall one of the more memorable self-esteem activities we conducted. This was based around the challenge for mentees to take seriously the good and positive things concerning themselves despite how others might feel, think, or react to them. I explained that each mentee would be expected to look in the face of fellow mentees as they moved around the circle of mentees and state three positive things about themselves and not play or laugh despite the response of other mentees. If he successfully made it through the entire group, he would receive ten dollars, which I placed on a centered table. None made it through successfully without laughing. We discussed the outcome and agreed they had "work to do".

Dr. Marie Shepard became principal after Mrs. Rosa Wells-Garris accepted a principalship elsewhere in the district. Mrs. Garris had been assigned to Waters after Mike Spencer departed Waters for a different assignment in the city. Wells-Garris was supportive of the program during her tenure at Waters. The newly assigned principal, Dr. Sheppard, likewise became supportive of the mentoring concept. She, however, indicated the need for a name change more specific to the "mentoring mission". This request at the time seemed a bit puzzling but the rationale given seemed logical, so I didn't spend much time pondering the request. Soon thereafter, her request would be rendered less bewildering. Brian McNeil and another Coach hired from Manor High School also became new members on the staff along with Dr. Sheppard. The coaches immediately joined Mr. Collins and me as program mentors. Mr. Elliott and Mr. Glover had taken positions in districts elsewhere by the start of the new school term. Soon it became clear to Mr. Collins and me what was happening, and I wasn't interested in establishing animus with the new principal. For whatever reason, she wanted new leadership with the program and her Omega Brothers were a convenient asset. Brian came to me and asked would I oppose his advisor ship of the Mentorship program this year. After a conversation with Mr. Collins, I told him "Not a problem" we would both remain in the program committed to the students as always.

After pondering Dr. Sheppard's request for a new name, Mr. Collins and I developed the name CAP (Cavaliers Achieving their Potential). This became the change from our original name (Waters Middle School Mentorship Program). The change in leadership also resulted in a major change of focus. The new program was more focused on lessons learned from teaming and stepping as a step team and less of a program of mentorship. Surely, cooperation, discipline, and even character growth can be gleaned from such activity; which is not to be besmirched; however, this change of emphasis became vastly different from our original mentoring methods and purpose.

I have always felt it imperative to address some of the shortcomings of the curriculum-based history of African Americans during the designated month of February only. The need was originally chronicled and introduced by Virginia native Dr. Carter G. Woodson dating back to 1926.

Mrs. Veronica Evans (social studies department chair) received Dr. Sheppard's reluctant permission to move forward with our 1997 departmental version commemorating African American History Week. There had been some administrative apprehension concerning students' inability or unwillingness to conduct themselves appropriately for such a program. Especially, since it would be presented in the gymnasium. I expressed my doubt about the necessity of such a concern. I then at once volunteered my services as program facilitator and master of ceremony for the event. Since the focus was appropriately directed on "the Celebration of Youth" our Waters' students thusly became the presenters and stars of the program. I took special pride in support of the students for their earnest program participation and discipline in making the concerns of predicted misbehavior unfounded. This activity now (a treasure) was video recorded. Fortunately, there remains a documented account of this event.

I had the privilege to work with eighth graders during my last few years at Waters Middle. At the time there was no eighth-grade graduation. This situation was a topic of interest and was often discussed during our team/cluster meetings.

Although, completion of eighth grade and middle school is but a small step towards the successful completion of scholastic studies some official recognition is proper and warranted. To prevent any erroneous and premature thoughts of actual graduation we recommended it not be called graduation but a *"Farewell Ceremony".* This was under the advisement of assistant principal Mr. Alan Canassa.

This marked the beginning of an incredibly special occasion recognizing the eighth grader's academic accomplishments and their cooperative student citizenship. This was a moment to properly direct their attention towards high school with expectations for greater maturity, academic growth, and development of improved social skills. The high school experience likewise would become a growth opportunity to participate/take part in all manner of sports (not then offered at middle schools) and the availability of extra-curricular activities would be available there for students in much greater quantity and diversity.

The *Farewell Ceremony* proved to be a very well attended event with total cooperation from students, staff, and parents. It was attended regularly by the district superintendent who was quite complimentary of the activities. I was always pleased as director/

advisor when all "farewellers" had proceeded from the gym, into the cafeteria, consumed refreshments, and departed with Mom and Dad. We coveted the idea that each eighth grader concluded their middle school experience with a feeling of youthful accomplishment in the ceremony of their middle school departure.

Churchland Middle School
2000-2005

Administrative Debut

The summer of 2000 brought a promotion to middle school assistant principal at Churchland Middle School; for me. Somehow Churchland located in the predominantly white, and affluent vicinity was viewed by many as a cut above other areas of the city. The schools there were held in similar regard. At the time, I had been held in waiting for an administrative position since the summer of 1989. I had been fully certified for more than ten years with numerous interviews and summer school principal experience under my belt. Thankfully, interim superintendent Dr. Wilbert Hawkins, School Board Chairman Ray Smith, and Principal Darnell Johnson gave me the opportunity to finally advance on the professional ladder in the Portsmouth Schools System.

I knew my learning curve was steep and fraught with potential missteps and pitfalls, especially in Churchland. A relative and recently retired principal from Fairfax County shared this advice at the start of my administrative tenure in 2000, which I found very useful. He stated: (1) *if you are not already you must become a good listener*; (2) *you must never make any decision that you can't defend from your desk all the way to the school board* and (3) *lastly, get yourself at least one pair of good orthopedic shoes because you will be doing lots of walking.* Unfortunately, I did not heed the last item of advice soon enough. Before the completion of less than a month, my feet were pain stricken, and I was diagnosed with plantar fasciitis. Since I certainly didn't want to lose time at work, I was forced to resort to a pair of thick-soled tennis shoes I owned at the time. I was teased quite a bit about the suit, tie, and tennis shoe combination so as soon as financially able I replaced the sneakers with a good pair of Rockport's. They were not cheap but proved to be worth every dime. The investment in a great pair of Rockport's made constant walking sustainable and life in my new AP position feel much better to the size thirteen's.

Dr. Darnell Johnson the principal at Churchland Middle School had been the assistant principal at Waters Middle at the time of my initial employment. I will long remember Dr. Johnson for being great for motivational stories and long on good advice for a rookie administrator. I was resolutely determined to demonstrate my appreciation by way of commitment to his leadership and his vision for Churchland Middle School.

Mrs. Betty Parent was senior assistant principal assigned to Churchland Middle. She had been the librarian at Waters Middle before becoming an AP there. My arrival became something of a reunion of once fellow Waters' employees. It seemed as if Churchland Middle in some weird way had become the promotion- connection for the three of us. I recall Mrs. Parent as being very enjoyable to work with. She had a much better sense of humor than I had been aware of when she was a librarian at Waters. I always got a kick out of a phrase she often used when things sometimes became frantic. She would repeat a line from a popular song during the 1950s. "It was fun, fun, fun before Daddy took to the T-Bird Away".

The assistant principal's assignments were initially divided between us accordingly. Mrs. Parent's main responsibilities were master schedule and bells, eighth-grade academic supervision, and eighth-grade and half the sixth-grade discipline; third floor and lunch monitoring. My main responsibilities were seventh-grade academic supervision, seventh-grade, and half the six-grade discipline, seventh-grade lunch monitoring, fire drills, school bus monitoring, and discipline and supervision for school and security staff. Mr. Garris was the lead security officer. He was prior military and always a dependable security force in the building.

Teacher Expectations and Parental Factors

Having experienced the classroom both as a high school and a middle school teacher gave me valuable insight into the mindset and concerns of teachers. I soon discovered that different teachers had their own expectations for support from their immediate administrator. However, there was one attribute I discovered to be true for all teachers under my supervision. Each individual teacher's issue was important to them no matter what others felt about it. This was the case whether their concern was student-related, academic, or behavioral, parental, or a staff issue. I concluded incredibly early teachers sought administrative supervision for answers and solutions, not for head scratches or thumb twittering. This was very instructive and quickly incorporated into my modus operandi. I had to become a good listener just as my family mentor had so correctly impressed upon me. Yet there remained the critical transition from my old teacher mode of being the giver, facilitator, instructor, etc. to the administrator who first listened well, then asked probing questions about the teacher(s) concern became a very relevant strategy. My tactic was to enhance my understanding of the problem then encourage their participation and combine our efforts in finding the answer(s) or solution(s).

A joint cooperative solution seemed to always be a more permanent solution, especially with the middle school student and parent.

Many educators find middle school students more difficult mostly because of their behaviors and challenges of early adolescence. Their age range is roughly (11-13) in grades (6-8). Although it was during my time at Churchland Middle that Superintendant Stuckwich placed sixth graders back into the elementary school.

A major experience as an administrator in the Middle School setting was that parents in many ways showed more problematic adjustments than the student. This is not a criticism nor difficult to understand. However, since I have had been on both sides of this issue, I mostly understood this parental behavior. Their behavior is kin to a "don't mess with my baby syndrome". Within the elementary school community, there is a reasonable expectation that elementary teachers will cater as Mom and Dad, to the kind of "babying-mentality". Somehow, most parents are not ready to detach the proverbial umbilical cord even by the middle school years. The question fully unresolved in their mind seems to be "is my child still just my helpless little baby? Or is he/she slowly maturing into adolescence? Which? It's back and forth. We would often receive responses similar to the following upon informing many such parents of their child's wrongdoings. They would often respond something like this. He/she didn't mean to do that, or she is just a child, or the way we handle it at home is, or that child seated beside my child is always provoking and bothering my child.

After being subjected to many such parental responses as these, I was certain that more time was required to assist parents in preparation for the middle school parenting experience. Orientation worships, which should include activities during summer months as needed were included. This process may include seminars and workshops if warranted. This may even prove insufficient! The need for improved preparation for the challenge of the middle school parent should not be understated.

Student Discipline

Student discipline was never difficult for me as a teacher or administrator. The school board provides a manual (The Student

Code of Conduct). In this manual were guidelines for behavioral expectations and consequences when there were deviations. Our role as teachers and administrators was simply to demonstrate the "will" to enforce them. I steadfastly believe that all students' desire structured behavioral guidelines, and relevant instructions in their background in order to appreciate the value of learning. Their interest level will undoubtedly vary accordingly until this realization occurs. Some students certainly will require more and different instructional and especially emotional support. Once the proper values are discerned then daylight or "morning time" is the reward. Even students who are the worse discipline problems almost invariably grow to respect those educators and staff members who consistently demonstrate an authentic commitment to their well-being and belief in the value of each child's education. Mentorship Programs, Special Designed School-Based Behavior Systems, and even Alternative Education Programs can be quite useful in this way. Therein lies the continued or restored need for a variety of academic, vocational, and technical education options for students. Likewise, clearly, the need exists for a robust set of extra-curricular activities. Such structured activities would be most effective if trended from the general in the elementary grades toward the more specific as one advanced through the middle and into the high school years.

A common theme often heard in Portsmouth Public Schools was "students don't care how much you know until they know how much you care." This I feel is a universal truism among most students. It is my personal view and professional perspective that "Every child is a student, and every student is a child" no matter what their academic ability or behavior. Educators don't have the individual right to give up on any child (student). A thorough workshop designed to present data, points, and best practices are definitely warranted.

Dr. David Stuckwisch had been the division superintendent for less than a year in 2004 when he visited all schools and held a separate meeting with the principal and the assistant principals. His visit to Churchland Middle was a very strange exchange mostly between him and Mrs. Betty Parent. My inclination was to yield to Mrs. Parents' seniority as the most experienced administrator in most instances anyway. So after patiently waiting to participate/take part in the conversation and finally attempting to contribute to the dialogue the superintendent began to speak directly over me. I respectfully stopped then listened. At the next opening, I attempted once again to express my viewpoint or ask a question with the very same results. This went on a couple more times until it became clear that I was being shut out of the conversation and not by Mrs. Parent. By the end of the meeting, I was thoroughly confused as to why he didn't just meet with Mrs. Parent alone since he obviously was not interested in any issues or concerns held by me.

Several days later, I had the opportunity to share the results of this curious meeting with Dr. Johnson (principal). He indicated to me that he had been privy to some interesting background on the "good doctor" and it was not all good. Later that year Dr. Johnson went on leave before retiring from Portsmouth Schools. He later accepted a department chair at a regional university. Although, the Churchland Middle faculty was saddened by his departure we were quite joyous for his career move. Ms. Lynn Briley became his immediate replacement.

Selection of Teacher of the Year was a highly anticipated event in recognition of exemplary teaching and professionalism annually at each school within the district. This was one of several reasons I was appreciative, and somewhat awed when Dr. Johnson approached me with the directive to assume responsibility for the selection process. This new responsibility became an annual event I held both at Churchland Middle and later at Norcom High with outstanding results.

The process was conducted like so. Central office would forward selection procedures to each school, which were required to use their own selection process within district guidelines. Every school wanted to select a teacher of the year who would be the best candidate for city- wide selection. The city-wide choice produced an elementary, middle school and high school teacher of the year. Finally, one of which would become the overall teacher of the year for the city.

Once this became my responsibility, I was determined to decipher a method that would yield the best candidates. Candidates were recommended by a certified colleague. We would inform the teacher of their recommendation and request they complete the teacher of the year form. Each teacher who desired my assistance with the form could receive the same upon request. Committee members consisted of prior teachers of the year. We then developed a worksheet that identified areas of the application and assigned a range of points to each area that equaled a maximum of 100 points.

Once the date of application submission arrived the selection process was simple. I would make the forms anonymous by removing the identifying personal information from the application then make copies. Committee members would then assess each application independently according to the point system prescribed for each area of the application. I never was a part of the assessment of a candidate. The candidate which ended with the largest total combined score from committee members became the winner. During my period of responsibility for the selection of Teacher of the Year at Churchland Middle and Norcom all our selections at both schools except one advanced to either city-wide (Toy) for Middle School in the case of Churchland Middle and either High School or City-wide (TOY) in the case of Norcom.

Churchland Middle School Teachers of the Year were:

Alice Brower and Jerri Phibbs. Both advanced to city-wide Portsmouth Middle School Teachers of the Year.

Middle School Sports Revisited

I entered the Portsmouth School District in 1989 during the districts' adopted policy of no middle school sports. This was a part of middle school philosophy by some districts. I never thought this to be a good idea. The thought process seemed to have been premised around the view that competition associated with sports at the middle school juncture was not conducive for their academic and emotional development. Then consistent with this logic, the existence of academic competition would seem to be a detriment as well if mere competition is a "bad thing". Why was competition a bad thing for athletics but for a good thing for other aspects of school academic activity? The best examples are honor roll, academic awards, and honor societies likewise writing competitions, college bowls, debating, etc. All are excellent and very much called for, but they do represent competition. Thirdly, there were never complaints about the competition of this age group taking part in neighborhood sports such as little leagues, Pop Warner Football or AAU. Lastly all school districts never bought into the "no sports" for middle school concept even in this region. The athletes in school districts that didn't restrict middle school sports usually proved more competitive and successful in regional and statewide competition once on the high school level. There must have been another underlying reason!

City athletic advisor Jimmy Williford demonstrated great wisdom as he finally convinced the superintendent that middle school sports should no longer be restricted in this manner within Portsmouth Schools. This was absolutely the view I held all along.

In the spring of 2005, he selected a five-member advisory committee which consisted of himself, the athletic directors from the three high schools (Norcom, Churchland, and Wilson), and me (Assistant Principal Churchland Middle School). The committee initially consisted of Mr. Williford and the three athletic directors from the high schools. After Mr. Williford reviewed my list of submitted recommendations, he decided to add me to the committee. The committee's recommendation was to begin the program with a cost-efficient plan that did not include the pricey purchase of football uniforms and equipment. Our suggestion to the School Board was to start the program with minimal cost sports such as basketball, track, and field, wrestling, and volleyball. We also decided to begin by restricting competition to within the district and crown seventh and eighth-grade champions for both girls and boys. The decision to invest in middle school sports proved to be a great decision for the city. Middle school students became able to develop their athletic talents in Portsmouth at this stage as many others were doing previously within the region. Middle school morale increased among the student bodies of the city's middle schools and fan support bloomed with enthusiasm and pride.

The high school athletic programs may have benefited the most, as they embarked upon a new era of competitive success throughout the region, state, and even nationally. This became especially true at Norcom High School.

After School Board approval of our plan for middle school sports, Mr. Williford offered me his recommendation for athletic director at Churchland Middle as he explained that I could hold both Assistant Principal and AD positions. I respectfully declined his offer and recommended physical education teacher Russell instead. The choice of Coach Russell as Athletic Director proved to be a good one. At the end of the school term, I was off to Norcom High, and Coach Russell began to produce the most winning program among the middle schools in Portsmouth.

Dr. Darnell Johnson (principal at CMS) retired from Portsmouth Public Schools during the 2005 school year and was replaced by Ms. Lynn Briley. As fate would have it Ms. Briley and I would be employed at our next school together as well.

Norcom High School
2005-2014

Norcom High School Legacy

Even before separation from the Navy in 1987, I had become interested in the happenings in Portsmouth and especially at Norcom High School. My Uncle Lester King had planted a seed of interest through his visits from Norfolk while enlisted and stationed there early in his career. He often spent time with our numerous relatives living in what is today Cavalier Manor. When visiting us in Carolina Uncle Lester would share stories of Navy adventures but he would often speak of Norcom High Schools' popularity and its rivalry with Booker T. Washington of Norfolk. So even while living in Carolina as a youngster I had admiringly heard of Norcom High School of Portsmouth, Virginia. My mother was born in Portsmouth and currently has relatives living in Cavalier Manor. This I learned firsthand while teaching at Waters Middle. In 1997, I was spotted and approached by one of my students at the Madison King reunion hosted in Kinston, N.C. Neither one of us knew we were related before this strange occurrence many miles away from Portsmouth at our mutual family reunion.

During my transition from the Navy in 1986, my interest in employment in the area school systems intensified and so did my concern for regional politics. Portsmouth seemed to be one of the tender boxes of Hampton Roads social, economic, and political upheaval. Racial discrimination issues related to the use of Bid-a-wee Golf Course, economic issues regarding and resulting from the closing of The Portsmouth Mall, and the necessity for more African American elected officials were a few of the relevant matters of the day.

Then there was the struggle for a new Norcom High School. During the eighties, much of the African American community in Portsmouth was contesting with the city and school district to fund the building for a new Norcom High. A ribbon-cutting for a new Churchland High School in 1992 was the result of previous plans and funding to replace the old Churchland High by city officials. Churchland High School had historically serviced the white community of Portsmouth in that area of the city prior to school consolidation.

The African American community and the formidable Norcom Alumni were the major impetus supporting the relentless effort for a new Norcom during the '80s and early '90s. Norcom had been the school that serviced the historical African American community in Portsmouth prior to consolidation. Their requests and desire for a New Norcom was never a mere desire for new construction based upon the Churchland decision. Rather, the request was founded in the practical need for replacing an antiquated building design and structure in extreme disrepair. Historically, this was a school steeped in pride, tradition, and scholastic excellence throughout its' long existence. The new Norcom (1801 London Boulevard) became a reality in 1997 after much public inquisition, demonstrating and political discourse.

Needless to say, when I was informed by Mr. Joe Wiggins (Superintendant Administrative Assistant), that I would receive a recommendation during the spring of 2005 to become assistant principal at Norcom I was elated. However, these had become challenging times for educators stemming from stagnated school funding and salaries, emerging governmental mandates, and restrictive guidelines.

Governmental Initiatives and Mandates

The late 1990s into the early 2000s saw a major increase by state and federal government roles in public school education often without related funding. Additionally, oversight and demand for more detailed accounting typically became a by-product of the process. These top-down changes, unfortunately, came as pay raises were very rare in the city. Although the state had not given pay raises in several years some other local school districts found funding within their systems. These circumstances created a retention problem in Portsmouth at a time of greatest need for veteran educators.

No Child Left Behind Law (NCLB) of 2001 quickly became wildly unpopular because of its' inadequately funded mandates and unreasonable requirements on federal programs such as Title I. Additionally, The Standards of Learning (SOL's) became the required content-based expectations at course completion for academic courses at all grade levels in Virginia. Testing began in 1998.

Since the introduction of NCLB and SOLs as mandatory criteria, curriculum and instructional focus shifted sharply to test results. SOL scores, Benchmarks, and Annual Yearly Progress (AYP) quickly became the criteria by which principals, teachers, and schools were evaluated. Students could possibly pass the course but fail the class by failing the standards test. Public schools could lose state accreditation through failure rates on standards tests. Students could be assigned to other schools if their present school did not meet the criteria. Administrators and teachers could be reassigned, or in some cases fired for not meeting required standards in schools and or departments.

Fortunately, the Norcom administration, teachers, and staff had been working cooperatively, diligently, and successfully towards accreditation prior to our arrival. As a new administrative team, we understood our goal was to sustain the successes and continue the path of standards improvement. Thankfully, the No Child Left Behind Law was replaced by Every Student Succeeds Act (ESSA) of 2015. The ESSA afforded more testing flexibility and released greater responsibility to the states.

Significant changes were occurring, and implementation was mandatory. These were often arduous for school districts and their administrators in Virginia and across the nation.

Meanwhile locally important was the fact that the highly influential Norcom Alumni and other supporting school affiliates had become quite dissatisfied and somewhat disgruntled with the school's athletic program. This was especially true in the area of the major revenue sports of football and basketball. Most were "chopping at the bit for change".

We were part of a shuffle of several administrative promotions and changes that year. The sudden death of the previous principal, Mr. Walter Taylor, and the reassignment of his assistant principal and interim replacement (Mr. Tim Johnson) necessitated the changes. Within the context of this educational milieu, Ms. Lynn Briley and I became principal and assistant principal respectively at Norcom High School in the summer of 2005.

Principal Briley was departing Churchland Middle about six months after her assignment there. She informed me of her unexpected ascension to principal at Norcom for the coming school year (2005-2006) one day during lunch in the cafeteria. She then remarked, "I know it was politics". I wasn't quite sure what she meant. I had an idea but didn't question her statement. It was during early spring that she mentioned she would be leaving for Norcom.

I had first met her, interestingly enough, at a training activity held at Norcom about three years prior to our working together at Churchland Middle. I recall distinctly a brief conversation we had about tennis. We discovered our mutual interest in the sport and our enthusiasm for the Williams sisters. Little did we know that in just a couple of years we would work together first at Churchland Middle and then Norcom High School as principal and assistant.

Upon her arrival, Ms. Briley as a Norcom alumnus endeavored to establish a mandate to restore some of the traditions of the old Norcom during her school years. This would be done through striving to match or exceed the overall academic and athletic excellence of the past. She likewise evoked greater school pride by singing the school song at all school programs and events. This often-expressed desire by Ms. Briley was something I personally felt overwhelmingly fortunate to be a part of. The two other administrators assigned to Norcom at the time were Mr. William Saunders and Mr. Todd Neil. Two years later, Mr. Neil would be replaced by Mr. Erskine Morgan after his departure.

Norcom in many ways brought my old high school (Robinson Union) smaller as it was to mind with its school spirit and high morale. For these reasons any responsibility, duty, or assignment given to me was considered an opportunity and a privilege. I wanted to do all I possibly could in support of students, staff, community, and the city.

Portsmouth is a small city of roughly one hundred thousand. Norcom High is located downtown in the heart of the city. I soon discovered that it had most if not all the problems of the major urban schools if only on a smaller scale.

My Administrative Assignments and Responsibilities

Academics and Special Assignments

Initially, my major academic responsibilities included academic supervision for the science and math departments during my first two years at Norcom. I was assigned academic and discipline administrator for the *Greyhound Academy* during the time of its existence (2005-2007). The Academy made use of a strategy utilizing the "school within a school concept" for a group of freshmen students requiring various levels of remedial academic work and often behavior redirection before entrance into regular classes. We were fortunate to have had an excellent core of teachers for this challenging program. It's no wonder that one among this group (Veronica Williams) went on to become Norcom High School Teacher of the Year and Portsmouth City Schools Teacher of Year later. I was also given the responsibility and privilege to announce the names of diploma recipients at the commencement exercise for graduation.

EXCEL (Night School) at Wilson H.S.

A major factor in change to my availability status for after school programs at Norcom was an additional administrative offer at the beginning of the next school term. I was informed by Dr. David Stuckwich (superintendent) that I would receive an offer for an administrative assignment to night school and would receive more details later from Mr. Timothy Johnson (Wilson High School and Night School Principal). A meeting was held with Mr. Johnson and the other night school assistant, Horace Lambert, who incidentally was a former teacher and basketball coach at Norcom. He was assigned assistant principal at Churchland High during the same wave of assignments that I was assigned to Norcom. The job description required me to be one of two assistant principals with administrative responsibility for the night school program held at Wilson High School under Wilson High School principal Tim Johnson. Classes initially were held four nights weekly with the two assistants accepting two nights of responsibility each.

Honestly, at the time I was not thrilled and had serious reservations concerning the offer and the arrangement. I felt that my full attention was warranted towards the administrative challenges at Norcom. These included: academic, athletic and those related to the success of BOYZIIMEN (Mentorship Program). Conversely, I suspected this may have been a career opportunity and if not taken could serve as a rationale for dismissal from consideration towards the next round of promotions.

The problem was that my compulsory evening requirements with night school ended my availability for most Norcom events and activities held at concurring times including mentorship and athletic events. My issues with EXCEL were resolved when at the beginning of the third year Mr. Johnson informed me that there would be a reduction in staff for the coming year and that my position would be terminated.

Life experiences have wisely instructed me that all which has the appearance of gold, is not. That is to say that what appears to be an excellent opportunity could be mere fool's gold being dangled as a lure for a nefarious agenda. Once employed at night school I never experienced a feeling of appreciation for my contributions nor prospects for administrative advancement elsewhere in the district.

The gratifying exceptions were student responses, especially Norcom students, staff cooperation, and aspiring administrative trainees.

My major non-academic responsibilities were senior discipline, supervision for guidance; buses, band (two years), athletics, mentorship programs, behavior review (school-wide discipline plan), and panel and placement hearings.

Teacher of the Year Selection Facilitator

I relished the yearly coordination of teacher of the year selection first at Churchland Middle then at Norcom. I utilized the same selection procedure for both. Teaching and instruction is at the core of what good schools do. Therefore, acknowledging those best among their ranks is a befitting recognition. This process, I felt should be fairly conceived and meticulously executed.

Nominations were made by full time staff members. The selection committee consisted of former teachers of the year. I devised a scoring system of numbers corresponding to values 1-10 for the qualities and attributes set forth by central office. The names and other identifying information were removed from the teachers' profile. Once tallies were completed, the teacher with the highest average among the judges became the winner.

All teachers of the year from the various elementary, middle, and high school levels competed on the city level for elementary city-wide teacher of the year, middle school city wide teacher of the year, high school city wide teacher of the year, and overall Portsmouth Public Schools Teacher of the Year. During the entire period of coordinating this activity at both schools, I only had one case of a selectee not winning at least the next level beyond teacher of the year at their respective building. The one exception teacher did not follow the prescribed procedure and was not present at the city-wide teacher of the year selection ceremony. Why were we so successful? These outcomes prevailed for two prime reasons: (1) we had outstanding teachers at both schools and (2) we devised a very fair and thorough selection process that consistently yielded the best candidates.

Teachers of the Year selected at Norcom that advanced to high school teacher of the year or Portsmouth Schools teacher of the year. They were as follows: Nancy Bell, Donna Dixon, Arlene Woods, and (high school TOY) Veronica Williams (Portsmouth Schools TOY).

All Norcom teachers except one advanced to high school teacher of the year across the city. Veronica Williams advanced to the very top of all participants by becoming Teacher of the Year for the city and division. The selection and official announcement for city-wide selections were held in a banquet format. Most school selectees and officials were present for the commemoration. There was concern among the Norcom flock when Veronica had not been among the selectees when the high school teacher of the year winner was announced. Then finally with great suspense the announcement was made "Veronica Williams is our Division Wide Teacher of the Year" for the city. There was sought of a soft clapping

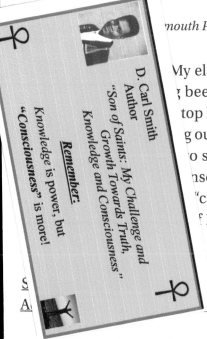

My elation and glee were beyond this mea-
been involved in the process for several
top honors was beyond exciting for me!
g our nominee selected as overall teacher
o stand and fist pump a few times. This
se and comment to me was shocking.
"calm down and be seated". This to me,
Norcom staff. Why not exemplify our

eges and Schools Council on
rovement Coordinator

Traditional accreditation institutions such as the Southern
Association of Colleges and Schools and Council on Accreditation
and School Improvement have been rendered less significant
because of state sponsored standardized testing such as Virginias'
Standards of Learning. SACS-CASI is attempting to maintain its'
relevance through: (a) conventional review assessments (b) its contemporary SOL related instructional recommendations and (c) by
continuous use and monitoring of the subsequent school improvement plan resulting from their review. Norcom became due for its
periodic SACS-CASI review during the spring of 2010. Although the
SACS review did not carry the significance for accreditation it once
did, no school wanted to fail a review from such an established
educational assessment organization. So, once the announcement
for the review was made Norcom much like other schools began to
experience the immediate anxiety and trepidation associated with
the SACS visit. The preparation for and actual review would require
participation by the entire faculty and staff on some level. This
required advanced training accordingly. Key aspects for training
the faculty for a SACS revisit were understanding the *Purpose of
the visit, The Process of Self Study* and *the Procedure for Establishing*

Quality Assurance. The bulk of the work was done in committee consisting of collection and analysis of documented evidence for drafting the mandatory Standards Assessment Report (SAR). The school SACS Coordinator became the person tasked with faculty training and coordinating them with the SACS Accreditation Team. The troubling aspect for me was not that I would be given the assignment as school SACS Coordinator. It was the fact that I did not receive this information directly from Ms. Briley (principal); rather I was made aware in casual conversation from a co-worker who did not realize she was "spilling the beans". Frankly, inwardly I was quite please with the appointment. This was an opportunity to demonstrate leadership in a critical area of educational fitness. I just never understood why I didn't receive the information directly from the proverbial "horse's mouth".

With the support of the audio-visual production coordinator and facility, I was able to produce a school-based video documentary. The product was shown as an introduction to the SACS Team on the starting day of the review. The video content of the school and its stakeholders was well received by the SACS Assessment Team. Norcom Committee chairpersons presented and submitted clear documentary evidence (artifacts) supporting their Standards Assessment Report (SAR). On the final day of the SACS Team visit, school observations and interviews were taken. Several exterior stakeholders gave individualized assessments and other criteria met or exceeded the requirements set forth by SACS-CASI assessment.

The committee chairpersons and staff had cooperatively succeeded in our performance and preparation for our SACS review. As mentioned previously accreditation is currently determined to the greatest extent by state Standards of Learning. None the less, SACS-CASI remains a significant player in the accreditation domain. The superintendants' annual faculty briefing the very same week offered no reference and certainly no congratulations regarding the recent successful SACS visit despite months of preparation and participation from the entire staff.

Soon after the visit, I was invited by AdvancED to train and participate on SACS-CASI Review Teams for review of other schools. After participation as a member on two review teams, I was similarly invited to train as a SACS Team Chairperson for leading teams in review of schools planning for SACS accreditation. During evaluations with SACS-CASI I was placed on teams of accreditation for: Maury High, Norfolk, VA. as a committee member; George Washington High School, Danville, VA. as committee chairperson and others.

<u>Grandparents Club Administrative Supervisor</u>

For a variety of reasons and circumstance responsibility for and even custody of grandchildren often begins with or revert to grandparents. Such was the case with a group at Norcom with which I encouraged and had the privilege and honor to work with called The Grandparents' Club. They were in most cases head of household for students (grandchildren) living in their homes and attending Norcom. For this group of highly motivated and proactive nurturers nothing seemed more important than the education and well being of there grands.

This group of committed caregivers were quick to express any concerns they had for the behavior of their own child, with a teacher(s) or a school policy. The Grandparent's Club was equally prepared to demonstrate commitment to school-sponsored activities, programs, or projects. They shared problems and solutions among themselves; experienced with their grandchildren encountered in the home, school, and elsewhere. This was never done as a complaint or exhaustion but more for informational purposes and a desire for cooperative problem-solving.

Norcom HS Grandparents Club

I regularly presented the administrative brief along with all the encouragement and appreciation for their school support and collective efforts.

The group provided their own finger-foods and refreshments with which they always shared and often left extras in my office. Each grandparent at those meetings became motivation and inspiration for me each time they entered the building. I state unequivocally that my work with this selfless and dedicated group of grandparents provided one of the most rewarding and gratifying administrative experiences ever during my tenure at Norcom High School.

Athletics Administrator

Although Norcom High School had been well documented and remembered for its' successful sports and athletic program it had recently fallen on challenging times. They had won a football state championship during the early nineties during the era of legendary

170

coach Joe Langston. The basketball team had been competitive with the outstanding play of the Norcom big man (Vernon Macklin) in the early 2000's but just didn't seem to be able to discipline themselves into championship status under Coach Horace Lambert. By 2005 at the time of the start of the Briley Administration; Norcom alumni, fans and supporters were famished for a return to that old greyhound championship tradition. Both the football and basketball teams were hovering around a 500% status from the previous seasons. The girls track program seemed to have been the bright spot of Norcom Athletics at the time.

My interest in scholastic sports had not faded from the time early in my career when coaching football and later both J.V. and Varsity basketball teams. Also, my participation on the Portsmouth District Committee for the Revival of Middle School Athletics had sparked my desire and enthusiasm once again. Soon after our arrival at Norcom, I mentioned to Ms. Briley I would be more than pleased to take administrative responsibility for the school's athletic program. She responded in the affirmative, stating "then take it, I don't know very much about sports, but I do know that my concern for ("SOL scores and accreditation") will be enough to keep me busy".

I responded with a hardy "thank you" to Ms. Briley and did a strong fist pump and yes once I returned to my office. It was my clear understanding that this experience would be different. My role here would not involve coaching or directing as an athletic director (AD). Rather at this "level of involvement," I would have the latitude and responsibility to "set the tone and ambiance" of excellence for the entire athletic program. This became both a challenge and a personal goal from this point forward.

High school sports by now had become quite popular locally and nationally, especially with supporting media such as Friday Night Flights (highlight clips on local sports reports). The national syndicated ESPN sports stations had made a significant mark on contemporary sports culture nationally. This increased the familiarity and interest of sports at all levels. There were also online reports from high school sports national authority Maxpreps.Com and others. Any athlete could post and promote their scholastic athletic exploits of themselves via YOUTUBE. It was most definitely an exciting time to be involved with high school athletics.

Football and basketball had become the two major revenue sports, which essentially sustained the other team programs beyond the minimal funds provided by the city and district. Most other sports were dependent upon the two primary moneymakers. It, therefore, became imperative to have success with football and or the basketball program(s).

Mr. P. Moreno was the reigning athletic director at the time of our arrival. He had been a former soccer coach at Wilson High School. Unfortunately, he had precious little background in the two major revenue sports despite his conscientious attitude and work ethic as athletic/activities director. Mrs. Gayle Buckley worked closely with Mr. Moreno as the secretary for the athletic program and special events bookkeeping. She consistently ran a "tight ship" with a "no-nonsense" approach to her work.

Unlike the basketball coaching position, the football position had not been vacated upon our arrival and the contracted season had already begun. Yet there was nearly a stampede to Ms. Brileys' office with a similar chorus. "We must replace the football coach". At the time, I had firsthand knowledge of only one football coach on the staff and that was Coach Danny Hill. He had bus-monitoring responsibility, during my first assignment as Churchland Middle School summer school principal. Coach Hill had impressed me as a very dependable employee with an outstanding rapport with students.

Ms. Briley being a person of patience tolerated a considerable amount before directing the most persistent advocates to my office. Most were reasonable in expressing their perspective on their desire for change in football staffing. They would usually share their point of view with a rational approach then depart my office. However, there was at least one alumnus that especially at the end of the school day, would appear at my office and seemed glued to his chair thereafter. One major aspect to his misunderstanding was that we (administrators) could not arbitrarily fire a coach without justifiable cause once the season started.

Unfortunately, for the coach, he made the error of giving us such cause early into the season. The related cause occurred when a lack of sportsmanship was allowed by not ending a game with the customary handshake. The aforementioned coach was terminated immediately and the remainder of the 2005 season was completed by interim head coach Stanley Edmonds. Coach Edmonds had been former Junior Varsity Head coach at Norcom.

The basketball coach position had been posted and the J.V. coach from Churchland was selected for Boys Varsity Coach at Norcom for the 2005-2006 school year.

During tennis season, I observed the fact that many of the team players were very weak with their basic groundstrokes. Therefore, they were in possession of weak tennis games. I knew firsthand from my own tennis experience that no practice method improved tennis ground-strokes better than hitting off a wall/backboard. Coach Leroy Williams seemed surprised but appreciative and totally in agreement with my assessment and decision. The backboard was erected, and the tennis team was quite excited about its usage for the 2006-2007 season. Unfortunately, construction dysfunction and my exclusion from the financial and decision-making aspects of athletics significantly affected the tennis program and all others. The backboard was never repaired and never given the opportunity to improve the program.

The approaching sports season (2006-2007) required a change from interim coach status for the football program. The basketball coaches' position was back on the table since issues developed from both instructional and coaching-related issues.

The most pressing of the two was to promptly begin the process of a broad and thorough search for a permanent football coach. A search group consisting of mostly relevant stakeholders comprised the committee. They were school officials Ms. Lynn Briley-Principal, Danny Smith- Assistant Principal (this Author), P. Moreno (Athletic Director), Joe Langston-Legendary Norcom Coach, Mr. Preston Harts-Norcom Alumnus and Hall of Fame Representative, Mr. Buxton, Dr. Horace Savage (Former Norcom Head Football Coach/ Former Portsmouth Schools Associate Superintendant).

Interviews were conducted at scheduled times after school hours at the availability of the panel and interviewees. The process became a lengthy one as we approached the end of the search/ interview window for candidates.

Often after an interview, some of us would remain absorbed in conversation concerning the interview and even share stories about past experiences in sports. Joe Langston shared some of his best experiences as a coach. One of which was from the night of a game when his team was trailing at half time due to lethargic play and lack of team concentration. Coach Langston said he became so outraged with his team he broke the locker room window with his fist cutting himself and began to bleed profusely. His team took the message and responded the second half by destroying the competition on the field. Preston Harts shared a memorable account of how a Norcom championship team, of which he was a member, never allowed any team beyond their forty-yard line in route to a state championship.

The process resulted in even more firsthand revelations of accounts of Norcom's legacy. In addition, new friendships resulting from a common interest for athletic excellence emerged.

At least eight good interviews were completed with the final selection being made from the best group of three. This group was given a second interview. The candidate ultimately receiving the second-highest number of votes was best prepared. He very professionally presented a multiplicity of supporting personalized training illustrations, documented coaching strategies, and a playbook with context. Finally, most impressive were his responses to interview questions, which implied and suggested all the qualities for championship results.

I recall his response to my question. Sir, why would you be a successful coach here at Norcom? He responded, thank you for the question. I've done my homework on Norcom, I know that this is a historically African American High School; I know that it has been successful through the years in sports and has a very proud tradition. He went on to say, look at me, I'm not a big guy, as a football player I always had to work harder, and I learned my lesson well. I would apply that lesson here at Norcom with preparation, dedication, and a very "strong willpower" if you allow me the opportunity. In the end, he did not receive sufficient votes to be selected at the time of the decision, but he did receive mine, and Dr. Savage's vote.

Most felt the selected candidate was the better choice for the following reasons. I must say I did not. A few of the stated reasons were due to his local familiarity and coaching background, the success of the program to which he was currently affiliated, and his overall demeanor and personality were a good fit for our students. The final vote was two and one-half votes to four and one-half votes. The athletic director split his vote between the two candidates. Coach Larry Archie quickly proved himself as a very likable coach by his players and coaching staff. He likewise became a highly valuable and popular member within the guidance department.

A special note here to Dr. Patton, a former city employee, who gave many hours of volunteer participation in support of our football program and school during the Coach Archie years. Her untiring contributions were appreciated by players, coaches, and the administration team alike. She also volunteered for monitoring cafeteria lunches, hall duty and made herself available for counseling athletes and other students' needs.

The next coaching need would be to select a new basketball coach. By the time we completed the hiring of Coach Archie the search committee was burned out from the interview process in search of a football coach. This occurrence left only athletic director P. Moreno and Assistant Principal Smith (your author). I was not disappointed by the outcome.

The pool of interested applicants was fairly large. I knew this scenario would most likely allow me to make the choice for the next basketball coach at Norcom High School.

Mr. P. Moreno scheduled the interviews with the candidates we accepted for Head Basketball Coach. Only Moreno and I were involved with the choice and interviewing of the candidates. I was personally keeping Ms. Briley informed of the candidates and our progress with the selection process. This person would have to fill a critical academic math position on the staff. So, I knew the selection of a good coach necessarily required the selection of a good teacher as well. This was not an easy task. This person in my mind had to possess at minimum four mandatory attributes. He had to be academically astute, able to discipline himself, demand the same of students and athletes, and possess the required technical knowledge of the sport of basketball.

There were several good candidates that met most of the required criteria. None as much so as Leon Goolsby employed at Woodside High School of Newport News, VA. The interview revealed he was a North Carolina A&T University alumnus, the son of educators and a math major. He was a coaching staff member of a championship basketball program at Woodside having won consecutive state championships. He seemed comfortable, confident and his responses proved him to be deeply knowledgeable of the sport and a "student of the game." I felt we had our man. I shared the same with Ms. Briley. She responded, "then call him and offer him the position". I made the phone call, he accepted, and the rest is history.

Regional and National Athletic Achievements

Coach Goolsby demonstrated a remarkable aptitude for success from the start of his first season at Norcom. The boy's varsity from his inaugural year (2006) through the year of reclassification and district rearrangements of (2012) he won either the Eastern District Championship, the regional championship, the AAA state championship; one, two, or all of the above.

Worth mentioning here is the fact that as much excitement, exhilaration, and local pride which emanated from the first state basketball championship in 2010 Dr. David Stuckwisch (division superintendent) without consideration for seniors, the championship team, or supporting fans decreed to Ms. Briley no one was to mention the state championship win at year's end graduation. This directive Ms. Briley shared with me in her office several days prior to graduation.

Success slowly emerged for the football program. The challenge in the city initially was Churchland High School but was eventually overtaken by the ascension of the Norcom football program. However, Lake Taylor of Norfolk proved to be a much more stubborn adversary. It was after the first Norcom state basketball championship of 2010 that Norcoms' football team became sufficiently inspired to defeat Lake Taylor and win the Eastern District Football Championship in 2011. Unfortunately, a loss at Booker T. Washington, Norfolk, VA. late in the season, allowed Churchland High to back into a tie with Norcom for the Eastern District title.

There were other factors involved in the revitalization of the Norcom athletic program. I proposed the following changes regarding athletics and received approval from Ms. Briley.

(1) A major problem at the time of our arrival at Norcom was the lack of eligibility for many good athletes. During an era of SOL testing accountability teachers' primary interest was appropriately focused on student performances in their classrooms, not on their performances on the courts and fields of play. Our response was to foster cooperation between teachers and coaches by teaming both in a collective effort to address relevant players' academic and/or behavioral issues. This process would be monitored by the Activities Director and Assistant Principal for Athletics.

(2) A second change involved Awards Day Recognition of Superlative Athletic Awards (Most Valuable by Sport). Prior to the change, all athletic awards were presented at the athletic banquet. In this way, only those athletes and their guests would experience the recognition of the yearly athletic awards. With the change, the faculty and full student body would acknowledge the award recognitions of Norcoms' Most Valuable Athletes recognized in each sport. This meant not only added support for the athlete, but it served as a recruitment tool for the various sports programs in the school. Some tried to make the argument that this strategy placed academics in competition with athletics. Nothing could be further from the truth. Curricular and Extracurricular are merely complementary aspects of the same mission—well-rounded students.

(3) We embraced the support and advocated the cooperation with alumni, parents of athletes, Aunt Sarah, Preston Harts, and The Norcom Hall of Fame Committee. These groups were among some of our most loyal fans and supporters. They also provided trophies and awards for our athletes.

(4) Lastly, we ventured to establish a meaningful nexus with our tributary middle schools (Waters Middle and Cradock Middle), with our presence and support at their sports

events and through our own successful sports performances and image. Our ultimate goal was to create a desire among the best athletes from our middle school feeders to aspire to attendance at Norcom above all others.

Orande Andrews became Activities Director following the departure of P. Moreno. Orande Andrews was employed as a history teacher and previously coached girl's track. Mr. Andrews was essentially the choice of Ms. Lynn Briley. He was selected from among about four individuals who interviewed for the position. Once assigned he mostly circumnavigated my supervision regarding financial oversight and deferred to Ms. Briley and Mrs. Buckley exclusively. As Administrator for Athletics, I brought this fact to Ms. Briley's attention, unfortunately to no avail. His breach of protocol never allowed my involvement accordingly. His behavior skirted my financial knowledge of and input involving the financial aspects of the school's athletic program, which was obviously warranted. On one occasion due to the discovery of unauthorized personnel disbursements, I drafted a letter to the central office for his dismissal. It was never forwarded as Ms. Briley (principal) rejected it.

The most outrageous of incidents occurred when a writer for The Virginian Pilot wrote this totally fabricated article telling how and why Mr. Andrews had hired the highly successful Coach Leon Goolsby. Any seventh grader knows that two of the most basic elements of journalism are obligation to facts and the discipline of verification. This article had neither. Andrews never could have hired Goolsby as he was a classroom teacher in 2006 when Goolsby was interviewed and offered the position by me. This can be easily substantiated by obtaining contracts from central office of Coach Goolsbys' date of contract then juxtaposed it to Andrews' (Activities Director) date of contract. When confronted about this fraudulent article he denied any input into the content of the article. I was completely befuddled by Ms. Brileys' response to the outrageous article. I personally heard her remark later "I'm tired of hearing about who hired Coach Goolsby". At the time, I could not understand how she could be so indifferent to this erroneous information and deceitful claim knowing full well what the facts were. How would the writer have received this false information and accepted it without second source verification? Maybe he (reporter) received it from another irrelevant source from within the building or elsewhere. However, no matter what the source, his information, and reporting was and remain totally bogus and probably false. Surely, a reputable newspaper such as The Virginian Pilot would not have tolerated such callus reporting. Besides on the day the article was released in The Pilot, Coach Goolsby must have seen it and sent me a text message saying "You gave me a chance when no one else would" indicating who actually interviewed, recommended, and placed the call to him informing him of his selection for the position.

The boy's varsity under Coach Goolsby's tutelage by 2010 had captured their first state championship to much appreciation and jubilation of the "Greyhound Nation". In 2011 with much of the core from 2010 returning, Coach Goolsby had the foresight to play a national schedule to which his team defeated every ranked opponent they encountered. These included the likes of Findley Preparatory, Las Vegas Nevada, legendary Damatha High School, of Hyattsville, MD., and were the champions at the Glaxo-Kline Christmas Tournament, Raleigh, NC. They were ranked the number one public high school in the USA in 2011 by MaxPreps.Com.

I was inspired and honored to write the article of 6/06/11 entitled "Norcoms' nod to community's role in its athletic excellence". The Virginian Pilot did a masterful coverage of the back-to-back championship runs of 2010 and 2011. The article tried to chronicle both the personal struggle and challenges of the athletes and the communities for their championships and their "Run to Glory".

Since my retirement in 2014, Norcom Boys Basketball under Coach Leon Goolsby and Assistant Coach Quinton Jones has captured three additional state championships.

I would be remiss if I didn't mention the contribution of my friend the late Henry "Barney" Stevenson Jr. and his vital role as an assistant basketball coach during the successful resurgence of the Norcom Basketball Program. As a Norcom alumnus, honored basketball player, and successful coach Barney should always be remembered for his: confidence in the players, dedication to the team and the monumental lifetime respect and love he perpetuated for the sport and the "Norcom High School Athletic Tradition."

Specialized Programs of Personal Design and Implementation

Behavior Review: *"An Interactive Discipline Strategy* at Norcom"

Safety, order, and good discipline are prerequisites to successful educational outcomes in the public school system of Portsmouth and elsewhere. For this reason, the school district produced the Portsmouth Schools Code of Conduct (2005-2006). This booklet served as a guideline for student behavioral expectations and the subsequent consequences if these were not adhered to.

Among code, guidelines were the directive for *"mandatory corrective action"* for those non-compliant students in every building of the district. By use of memo and by direction of Principal Briley I was tasked to develop a response to the School Board directive regarding (mandatory corrective action) found in the code of student conduct. Please find my response below.

The following is an abstract that relates a brief overview of the devised strategy and methodology appropriately named Behavior Review: *An Interactive Discipline Strategy.*

This brief describes the development and implementation of a behavior-contract-based strategy introduced at Norcom High School. Broad cores of school staff were used to positively direct and reinforce productive student conduct, attitudes, and behaviors. The Behavior Review Committee (BRC) served as a command center for review of discipline records, assessing behavior needs, development of interventions, and contract consummation. Behavior contracts between students and BRC become a springboard for constructive changes to undesirable behaviors. Review dates helped decide contract longevity and/or the need for revisions. Contract compliance and staff feedback were the most significant factors in the application of contractual incentives, modifications, and contract end date.

Some key artifacts used from program implementation were: (1) Behavior Review (Conduct Model) Flow Chart (2) Behavior Plan Contract (3) Behavior Plan Feedback Data Sheet (4) Behavior Intervention Worksheet (5) Behavior Review Counseling Component Process.

Student contracting with school entities was not a new concept. A contract method using a school-wide systematic approach resulting in sanctions may have been a new application for contract usage in this setting.

There were several positive results from the implementation of "*Behavior Review*". Some were purposefully sought and achieved while other results were unintended. Students who demonstrated the ability to meet the criteria of their contract for incremental periods between review dates often developed the skills to sustain that discipline. This precluded the need for further administrative disciplinary action. For those students who did not meet the required contract criteria and were thereby sent to "placement hearings" were less likely to receive leniency and more likely to be placed in the alternative school setting.

Unforeseen positive results were the expertise and proficiency developed by the Behavior Review Committee Coordinators. Most of whom were teachers aspiring to become administrators. Personally, for me, there was the opportunity along with the reigning (BRC) chairperson to present this developed program at the Virginia Association of Principals Conference in 2008 and to discuss its' merits at other venues across the state.

Because of the role of disciplinarian for many entry-level administrators, (BRC) committee coordinators were much better prepared at interviews for assistant principal positions. Their role as BRC coordinators provided them the experience to discuss authentic methods, applications, and results of a school based-discipline program. BRC Coordinators who advanced to administrative positions were Shantel Mayes, Damien Powell, Angela Bell, and Amy Strickland.

Mentoring BOYZIIMEN

Gang member affiliation and their subsequent behaviors have become an unfortunate reality throughout the urban United States. Usually, they are self-initiated groups of adolescent males with their own set of rules and norms not necessarily lawful. Portsmouth and Norcom High was no exception. Two such groups during my early arrival were The Goonies and (YNIC) Young N_ _ _ _ _s In Charge. I choose not to use the actual "N" word because I refuse to refer to myself as that which I so adamantly detest being referred to by others. Evidence of their presence was graffiti on bathroom walls and hallways, bullying and fights, and seizure of weapons (no firearms) through security checks and random searches. By the direction of the superintendent, we were informed to develop and prepare for a presentation of our school plan/program as a countermeasure for such problems.

My recommendation was to develop a mentorship program to advance and facilitate appropriate interventions. Our strategy was an effort to utilize a structured mentoring design in response to the educational and social demands for our difficult and most "at-risk students."

Mentoring is not an exact science. However, prevailing evidence and my previous experience suggested that a significant segment of youth at Norcom High could benefit positively from a well-structured and tailored mentorship program.

With the assistance of other staff members, I had previously developed a mentorship program in Portsmouth Schools during the '90s at Waters Middle. I recall while there Mrs. Rosa Wells Garris (principal) once asked me "Why did you start the Mentorship Program here? I replied quickly and succinctly "because I saw the need and wanted to do more". She simply responded "Good". However, this time around, I knew the need at Norcom would present much more of a challenge.

A TEAM effort usually produces the best results especially in the case of an extensive multilayered and complicated problems such as pseudo gangs and certainly bonafide ones. I was not yet 100% convinced that our schools were subject to true gangs. Later, I would become much less skeptical. I understood from my earlier experience with mentorship at Waters Middle that the support and involvement of the entire staff was warranted especially that of the male staff.

Establishing "The Men@Norcom" was an appeal to solidify the group under bannered recognition. Hopefully, we could "evoke greater mutual consciousness" within the group to blend the role of mentor beside that of *"teacher"* in an organized manner. This measure was needed for that elite group of students in desperate need found within our eyesight daily. We all then became the subject of a group photo in front of the school to consummate a commitment long overdue. Let me be clear, I would dare to say almost every man in the group was already mentoring on some level with students. We must remember the definition of TEAM "Together Everyone Achieves More". This was the proverbial "elephant in the room" and some answered the call.

BOYZIIMEN was the name selected for our newly organized mentorship program at Norcom. This was the namesake from the award-winning recording artists out of Philadelphia, PA. One of the first community resource persons that came to mind once again was Mr. Joe Wright. I felt extremely comfortable and confident soliciting the help of Mr. Joe "Righteous Wright" as I very respect-fully thought of him. He had previously assisted me with the mentorship program at Waters Middle. He did not disappoint. His wife received my call and explained she would relay my message. He immediately returned my call and expressed his desire to assist me in starting the BOYZIIMEN program at Norcom. He informed me that he would also bring another gentleman that might be even more helpful than he. Mr. Wright delivered with a presenter who had a past that offered authentic personal experience with gang affiliation, felony charges, and prison time. The presenter made it clear in his personal account that his undesirable lifestyle would not be his choice had he the opportunity to relive the experiences. He was emphatic that his was a lifestyle to avoid and not a badge of honor for anyone. His presentation was not a chapter out of "Scared Straight" but it could double as a significant effort in that direction.

After the guest speaker's presentation, I shared mentorship meeting procedures, topics of discussion, activities, and desired expectations. We likewise articulated roles for mentors and their interactive expectations with mentees. We further explained the role for parents, their valued continued participation, and their compulsory permission for student mentor participation. Our very first meeting was well attended by students, staff, and con-cerned parents.

Although there had been no indication of gang-related activity by girls there was often female conflict, fights, and too many incidents of unbecoming behaviors. I, therefore, felt that some constructive and impactful program should be available to our girls also. After consulting with several female staff members, Mrs. Michelle Blount committed to sponsoring a mentorship group for our female students. The group was given the name "Ladies of Distinction". The Ladies of Distinction quickly became positively recognized for emphasizing involvement in school activities, sponsoring events, field trips and projecting a very favorable image of their organization. This was carried out under the very capable leadership of Mrs. Michelle Blount, Mrs. Zelene Bell, Ms. Constance Christie, and other dedicated female staff members. BOYZIIMEN had become our newly organized mentoring program at Norcom for young men as Ladies of Distinction had become the same for young ladies. The two groups occasionally coordinated meetings and activities in a joint effort.

There were three high schools in Portsmouth, but we were the only school that had prepared a presentation as requested by the superintendent. I was the presenter of Norcoms' response to the threat of gang activity at the meeting in which school board members were presently hosted by Dr. Stuckwich (superintendent). One of the school board members had questions. His first question was for Ms. Briley. He stated, "We heard from Mr. Smith, how do you feel concerning the issue Ms. Briley"? She responded by acknowledging my experience with mentoring and she felt the plan outlined was a good start. His second question was directed towards the other two schools. He was interested to know their response to the issue. I recall Mr. Johnson (principal) from Wilson High School responded by posing the question "Couldn't good results with the Standards of Learning Testing (SOL Testing) serve as a deterrent to the problem? The superintendent didn't seem to answer yes or no but responded in an ambiguous manner. Churchland High School had no response during the open meeting. Maybe CHS had deter-mined they didn't have such problems and therefore had no reason to comply. If this were the case, I never understood the strange private response to me from a CHS assistant principal. He actually complained to me "why did you have to make the rest of us look so badly by presenting your entire BOYZIIMEN program you devel-oped at Norcom"? It was completely unbelievable that an admin-istrator from another high school in the city could suggest that I should not have complied with a central office directive because his school had not. His comment was highly inappropriate even as a joke because of the serious nature of the issue under discussion. Although, I never felt it was stated as a joke. Mentorship's group meetings, preparations, and activities initially fell to yours truly and the M@N participants, which quickly became difficult because of other required duties and responsibilities. Fortunately, as if by Divine intervention I was called by a former fellow employee whom I had informed previously that we needed an ISS coordinator. He informed me that there was a very gifted and dedicated young man with him by the name Quentin Jones. He was seeking employment and was wonderful as a coach, mentor, and role model for young men. Well, as he walked into my office that day and extended his hand I knew even before he spoke, he would be outstanding. As the conversation progressed, I discovered he had attended Norfolk State University. He later played pro baseball with the Atlanta Braves, coached baseball at NSU, and most importantly had a pas-sion for mentoring young men. After meeting Ms. Briley, Quentin (Mr. Versatility) Jones became our newly acquired ISS coordinator and our boy's mentorship advisor (extraordinaire).

BOYZIIMEN became the benefactors from the volunteerism of a group of very dedicated mentors from Groves Baptist Church in the Churchland community of Portsmouth. This group of men committed themselves to weekly meetings, each accepting mento-ring responsibility for one or more mentees after consent by their parents. They served as quasi big brothers/father figures/and advisors. I was invited to speak at their church and invited to do so from the pulpit of the church. The dedication of this group of men proved saintly.

The untimely deaths of several students occurred during my years at Norcom but none more tragic than that of Rashawn (Peanut) Finney. This heart-wrenching event happened during football season to a good student and our football captain. The entire Finney family had been outstanding athletes and good academic students both the boys and girls. They were well known throughout the region for their athletics.

Rashawn had become a "student of interest" for BoyzIIMen mentoring. Our interest was not based upon any misconduct in school but the potential benefits he may have gained for some reported behaviors away from school. I remember vividly the meeting we held with him and his very concerned mother. He was not boisterous or disrespectful in any way when he stated to us, he could not be in the mentorship program. He did however agree that he would help me in what he could do with the problems we were having in the building. It was that attitude that made many people respect him as I did. RaShawn lost his young life from gunshot wounds received at a party during the fall of 2008. My thought then and even sometimes now, why didn't I try with just a bit more determination, and couldn't I have done more?

The success of our program became increasingly reliant upon Mr. Jones with his very reliable volunteer, Coach Dale. Mr. Jones proved to be imaginative and tireless in his efforts as I receded to a more advisory role. Our BOYZIIMEN mentoring program continued forward movement receiving noteworthy media attention stories from both newspaper and magazine articles. One such lengthy article was printed in <u>The Tidewater Teacher</u> Magazine (November-December (2008)) exalting the programs' Christmas TOY project and other volunteer causes. A very well-done article on BOYZIIMEN was written by The Virginian Pilot author Cheryl Ross entitled "Mentorship Program Gives Teens a New Look at Character". The article covered objectives and methods of the program quotes from several of the mentees and pictures from a typical mentoring session.

Mr. Jones and I also participated and presented at a statewide school safety convention on behalf of Norcoms' BOYZIIMEN program. In 2008, the program was held at Booker T. Washington H.S. Norfolk, VA. Governor Tim Kaine congratulated us for our efforts with mentoring and we both were given opportunities for photographs with the governor.

In 2009, Mrs. Michelle Blount and I presented Authentic Methods and Strategies from Mentorship Programs at Norcom High at the Southern Association of Colleges & Schools-Council on Accreditation and School Improvement (SACS-CASI) conference in Williamsburg, Virginia.

We received an invitation to present at the national (SACS-CASI) Conference after Williamsburg but were consumed in hosting our own school accreditation review at the time of the nationals.

Establishing mentorship programs across the district as called for had become a conversation of interest among the dedicated mentors, appreciative parents, and forward-leaning participants. BOYZIIMEN had become a well-acknowledged initiative during a time of great need for such a program. We were encouraged especially by the community, and the overwhelming support we received from volunteers and especially from the men of Groves Baptist Church.

Many concurred that a significant segment of our youth could benefit from similar mentorship programs throughout the schools in the district. For these reasons, I informed Dr. Stuckwisch (superintendent) of the interest level held by stakeholders. He decided upon a convenient meeting date for him and me at Norcom one afternoon after school. During the meeting, I conveyed my mentoring background in the district, rationale, basic princi-ples, and strategies. This I explained and shared experiences from both the BOYZIIMEN program and likewise from the CAP (Cavaliers Achieving their Potential) Program initiated earlier in my career at Waters Middle. I presented a program brief over-view for the *"Divisional Proposal"*. The brief draft and reference included the Program Name (1) (Mentoring a Guided Process); (2) Training Targets for Mentors; (3) The Six Week (Bi-weekly Training Sessions at the EXCEL Campus) (4) and Listing of the six areas of Instructional Content). I did not feel it appropriate to present every comprehensive detail of program content, instructional practice, and method infringing even more on the superinten-dents' time. Besides, a part of that would become refining and revi-sionist aspects of the program with implementation as the program evolved. He listened, asked a few questions, and seemed to have been genuinely amenable to the complete proposal. That proved not to be the case. In a few days, I received a call from the office of Dr. Marie Sheppard (Assistant to the Superintendent). I was informed of a visit I would receive from her and Ms. Sara Sugars her assistant. Once in the meeting it was clear they were not there for clarification, but to totally upend the program. Assistant Sarah Sugars was like an attack dog. She began to say things like "this is not a program". She wanted all the details that day. She wanted to know how this would promote the schools' missions and how would you know when to end it. She finally said this is inadequate as a divisional proposal.

Dr. Sheppard didn't say very much but I knew they had been sent as a team. Maybe she was not speaking aggressively as was her cohort for good reason. She was keenly aware that the mentorship program (CAP) she inherited at Waters Middle as a neophyte prin-cipal was my and Mr. Collins's voluntary work. So, once I became clear on what this meeting was about, I relinquished any further desire to explain or defend. I just continued to listen quietly to the attempt at the "big tear down". When she finished, I calmly asked the question, since it's clear that I'm lacking the skills and knowledge to successfully implement this proposal let us (you and me) work together in bringing this much-needed program to our students of Portsmouth. I further stated I will gladly work under your very capable tutelage to make this happen as a well-devised team. For just a second there was silence because this response they had not anticipated. They couldn't say yes because our teaming on this matter was never a contingency. Their goal was to destroy this initiative clear and simple because this had been their directive. After the meeting, I never once received correspondence from neither the superintendent nor any related matter or likewise concern from Dr. Sheppard's' office including Ms. Sugars. However, BOYZIIMEN and Ladies of Distinction continued as relevant and viable mentoring programs at Norcom High School for the remainder of my tenure and beyond.

Local Media and Norcom H.S.

One of the ongoing dilemmas of Norcom's recent history has been the challenge of unfair negative media. It is true that Norcom has seemingly experienced more episodes of student conflicts and physical confrontations than any committed stakeholders would ever condone. It is also factual that sustaining full academic accreditation has been and still is an ongoing effort. Most, if not all, of the aforementioned are applicable for most inner-city schools across the nation for similar reasons. However, school administrators, teachers, and supporting staff have never wavered nor decelerated their efforts or energy for producing the desired instructional outcomes and required standards.

A fair assessment of any school must always consider the three C's. They are community, conditions, and clientele. I make no excuses, but Norcom and its' stakeholders deserve a more complete view and analysis of the issue. There are more factors to consider than a mere student entering a school building and SOL scores. How do the economic and geo-political factors on a student impact his/her readiness for learning? So, the obvious question becomes how do the immediate environment, circumstances of existence and resulting world view of the student prepare him or her to or not to comprehend the curriculum(s) offered and the instructional method(s) utilized?

Norcom as do many public schools across the nation receive Johnny and Susie Que's Publics' finest. My employment in both urban and rural school settings have revealed that some students arrive prepared for school and others not so much. This is usually no fault of their own. In fact, a significant percentage of those least prepared for academic prowess may have been better conditioned for the three F's (fear, fussing, and fighting). For this group, the academic setting would necessarily be a major departure when directed and re-oriented from the science and art of survival and towards those of academics (English, Math, Science, Social Studies, etc.).

In one instance a child is given the values of education to survive while another is inundated with the values of the streets to try the same. Whatever the learned values are upon enrollment they necessarily become a significant factor within our process to instruct, teach and redirect.

There were constant exaggerated media accounts of school disruptions and methods such as unauthorized fire alarms, fights described as brawls and melees, and "academic dumbing down". Seemingly, we were excessively targeted and highlighted in television reporting and print media especially during the time period for the release of test scores.

During the spring of 2010, following our first state championship, a grading system in which fifty became the base grade designed to decrease the senior dropout rate was implemented at

Norcom and other local school districts. This new policy inspired several egregious articles concerning Norcom when other districts were using similar methods.

Norcom somehow received most of the overly critical ink. Dr. David Stuckwich (superintendent) offered Norcom and Ms. Briley (principal) precious little public support against the barrage of criticism during these times of difficult reports from the media. Among the several articles written, a cartoonist attempted to use Norcom's recent state basketball championship to lampoon the aforementioned grading strategy. A much more callus and serious happening occurred for me on one occasion when the reports of unauthorized intruders were reported in the building. A full SWAT team dressed and armed accordingly was dispatched to the school. One such team member pointed a weapon with the red lazar directly at me as I descended the stairs. I yelled, "I'm an administrator here" before he finally lowered it. I didn't understand how he could have mistaken me as unauthorized in the building wearing a school badge, donned in a dress suit with a walkie-talkie in my hand but that's what happened. My conclusion was that these enforcers had been subject to tons of negative information concerning the school. This one seemed indifferent and insensitive to the fact that it was a school at all. It appeared that their work this day, which involved everyday people consisting of students, teachers, school staff, and administrators mattered not. How and where did this attitude come from? Was he responding to ideas conceptualized through the local media?

There were some excellent journalists and media types that I must mention. Among the most fair and objective were Cheryl Ross (a writer) and Jamesetta Walker (an editor), both of The Virginian Pilot Norfolk, Virginia.

Despite the sources of negative media we have incurred in the past, our resolve has thereby strengthened to receive our students with our mission foremost in mind without prejudice. Through

relentless pursuit for academic excellence, best instructional practices, development and application of curriculum to insure what is
learned is commensurate with what is warranted. Extra curricula
activities must be aligned with our renowned band, championship athletics, vibrant mentorship programs, stake holder pride,
and participation in Norcorm's continued progress and success in
public education of the highest magnitude.

Chapter 9

Growth in Consciousness

Conceptualization and Foundations of Consciousness Growth

I n 1967 I was sixteen years old, and slavery had been abol-
ished for slightly more than one hundred years. Yet, its residual
impact continued into my lifetime through segregation, discrimination, and overt acts of racism. Until this time, I had been aware
of the social divide, but it had little personal impact on me, at
least in my mind, which indicated my low state of consciousness.
Consciousness is the level of one's understanding and knowledge,
including expanded awareness of truth beyond the state of one's
physical/material existence.

Fundamental growth in consciousness is warranted in most
of us within the following categories: the physical (physiological)
mental (psychological) self, the historical-geo-political-commu-
nity of self, and lastly and most significantly the internalizations
of our cosmological and spiritual self (Wilson 1998; King 1995).
To be sure this level of consciousness is much more than a mere
departure from ignorance. Clearly, this level of awareness initi-
ates and enlightens one's understanding of he/she the being, of
their place and relationship to and within nature, the universe, and

195

divine order, especially as it relates to the earth her occupants and resources.

Spiritual consciousness exists beyond the material state of sensibility. We the "black humans" at our Classical best in Africa once possessed this level of consciousness. In ancient Kemet, a system of education known as the "Mysteries System" had as a foundation a nexus between the spiritual and material accountability for existence. As great as the material universe (Cosmos) is, the spiritual is far, far greater than that of any and all material existence. I believe spiritual states are necessarily the precursors to any and all material states of existence. Simply stated, before there was "something there had to be "nothing" that became something. Nothing was a "spiritual existence" before it became "something". Note my implication is that the spiritual existence both precedes and succeeds the material existence. Not difficult, all is Kemetic thought (philosophy).

I believe consciousness actualized at this level becomes the doorway to spirituality (spiritual consciousness) as discovered by our Kemetic ancestors. Please familiarize yourself with the work of Dr. Richard King including ***Black Dot***. We all have this struggle both individually and collectively. The sources are ancestry, nature, cosmos (universe), and "The Divine" (All/God). Hence "Man Know Thy Self" was inscribed on temples throughout ancient Kemet. It (consciousness/spirituality) was implicit in their belief system that in knowing oneself one knew the universe.

This level of spirituality is not to be confused with many contemporary religions although they have borrowed much from the Kemetic spiritual systems sources (ben-Jochannan 1991) and others. The evidence of Kemetic spirituality was interwoven into their routine and daily practices were not separated under a banner called religion. Kemetic Spirituality was not a set of "professed beliefs" for the purpose of (Sunday) identification, affiliation, association, and ceremonial or sanctimonious practice. It was an applied system acknowledging and accepting the divine and natural order upon which their scientific foundations, social institutions, and systems of people management were patterned, structured, administered, and **"lived"**. These were the basis of highly- advanced Kemetic classical cultures. The contributions in the many areas of arts, sciences, and philosophy not only contributed to world advancement but resulted in the unparalleled longevity of Kemetic civilizations juxtaposed all others. There is obvious evidence of confusion within the domain of contemporary western religion/theosophy in this regard.

Generally speaking, my parents did not and few Black parents to my awareness often discuss the devastating reality of the prevailing racial circumstances in a holistic or detailed manner with their children, no fault of their own. To be sure, this is no knock on our parents. My interpretation of their behavior of avoidance was linked directly to their feeling of inadequacy and helplessness regarding their set of racial conditions and circumstances. Other than their guidance with general caution and their persistence in acculturation with high morals, educational tenacity and good citizenship, there was little more control or impact they could have had in altering our experiences at the time.

Watching televised and other media reports of acts of racial hatred and injustice grew collective strength and materialized as the "Audacity of Hope" which sprang eternal as "pure" motivation from one generation to the next. The determined resistance of the sixties was no different. It implied change was nearing!

Instructions on African American history during my scholastic years (1957-1969) were excluded essentially from the formal curriculum. Any instruction in this area was basically limited to related displays, bulletin boards, and an occasional guest speaker for a one-week-a-year affair known as "Negro History Week". Dr. Carter G. Woodson, a Black historian, and humanist, was the impetus for establishing the second week in February beginning in 1926 for the annual recognition of Negro History Week (currently Black History Month initiated (1976). During that very limited desig-nated week, teachers would create bulletin boards with pictorial illustrations and related captions of African Americans. Famous performers such as Sammy Davis Jr. (dancer), Marian Anderson (singer), Joe Lewis (Boxer), Louis Armstrong (musician), Jessie Owens (Olympic athlete), and Jackie Robinson (barrier breaker in major leagues) were typical of those highlighted. All such Americans were undoubtedly talented and gifted but recognition during Negro History Week was slanted towards contributors in entertainment, show business, and sports. Some exceptions to this tendency were the aforementioned along with Carter G. Woodson, Harriet Tubman, Mary McCloud Bethune, Fredrick Douglas (abo-litionist), and scientist extraordinaire George Washington Carver who were recognized but did not fit the standard mold. Scientists, medical pioneers, political leaders, and international statesmen were generally underrepresented during this celebrated week.

Black leaders were mostly promoted and showcased according to the degree of willingness they accommodated the social order of the day or best fitted a stereotype of success for the Black human.

Unlike Booker T. Washington, Marcus Garvey and William Monroe Trotter were examples of Black political leaders who did not represent the standard stereotype, nor did they demonstrate such establishment behavior.

By the mid-1960s, Martin Luther King Jr. had become most prominent among civil rights activists in America. He borrowed much of his non-violent protest philosophy from Mahatma Gandhi who introduced this strategy earlier during British colonial con-trol of India.

Fortunately, African American newspapers such as the Norfolk Journal and Guide and the Baltimore Afro-American published arti-cles conveying a broader spectrum and perspectives of the move-ment. They included reports from Black Nationalist leader Malcolm

X and Elijah Muhammad's Black Muslim newspaper <u>Muhammad Speaks</u> which usually could not be found among local newspapers or mainstream media. These early indicators implied something was beginning to happen that would never allow the Jeannie to be placed conveniently back into the bottle.

During my undergraduate study at NCCU, I was introduced to several literary works such as <u>Jubilee</u> by Margaret Walker, <u>The Autobiography of Malcolm X</u> by Alex Haley, <u>The Rich and the Super Rich</u> by Ferdinand Lundberg, and <u>Before the Mayflower by Lerone Bennett Jr.</u> Heretofore, I had been primarily influenced and indoctrinated by Eurocentric literature, images, and lifestyles. These books were among the early sources, which helped broaden my perspectives and increased my thirst for "knowledge of self".

<u>Jubilee</u> was highly instructive for understanding the daily lives of the slave and the reality of the devastating impact of the institution. <u>Malcolm's Autobiography</u> demonstrated how acquired knowledge of self could inspire an individual to self educate, defeat his most learned adversaries in debate, express explanations of both national and international issues in such a manner that the masses could easily understand. While providing a fearless nationalistic leadership. Lundberg's book <u>The Rich and the Super Rich</u> made clear the role of the rich and super-rich as "the authentic power brokers and royalty" in the American economic and political system. <u>Before the Mayflower</u> became my first historical accounts of African American history from an Afrocentric perspective and source.

It was during my tenure at North Carolina Central University at Durham, N.C. (NCCU) that I learned the academic value of historiography. There is an understanding of history that involved more than mere dates and events void of meaningful explanation. Rather, historiography was demonstrated to be much more as an interpretation of history with validating reason and rationale.

I discovered that a major component of the historiography of Africa was the purpose and outcomes of its many ancient invasions and the subsequent more recent effects resulting from colonialism, imperialism, and racism directed toward the continent (Fanon, 1968; Rodney, 1982). Africa and its peoples in Diaspora continue to struggle with the aforementioned catastrophic and lingering effects of this history (see relevant illustrated chronological dates and events (p.240-241). Related and significant for these reasons, much of its past greatness has been skewed, erroneously defined, and excluded from the pages of western history. We must be reminded that "omitted African History is the missing pages of world history". Then and there it became clear for me that "world history cannot be factually and properly understood until African History and its peoples are properly included and validated accordingly".

My undergraduate studies thereby helped me connect the dots of my deprived state of self-awareness and served to increase my desire to awaken in the area of **"authentic knowledge of self"** and **"growth in consciousness"**.

What then is consciousness in this context? It is a concept as relevant today as ever, centered on the ancient African belief "Man Know Thy Self". Self-knowledge provides insight and confidence acquired from group collective historical memory, defense from others erroneously labeling and defining the group, and a keen awareness of group self-interest and self-preservation (Akbar, 1985; Wilson, 1998; 45). Specifically, this requires being centered and rooted in one's own historical reality by viewing, interpreting, and responding to the world according to their own authentic group values of self and not those projected upon them by others (Afrocentric).

My growth in consciousness continued during my first employment at Aurora High School as a public-school educator. However, my trajectory in consciousness continued as my energy was redirected in this regard from my own personal growth to that for my students and student athletes. There were two subjects taught by me that best loan themselves to this feasibility and served as the most fertile ground for sources of student growth. The two subject areas were African American Studies greatly and United States History to a slightly lesser extent.

One of my instructional goals for U.S. History, in addition to covering all curricular-related objectives; was to thoroughly compare the ideals of the nation with the reality of its practices and current outcomes. A critical introductory objective for African American History was the instructional presentation of the economic, political, and historical background of the inception of chattel slavery in America.

This is profoundly important in understanding key issues which continue to perplex many today. Their primary confusion is centered on the extremely insufficient understanding of "self". The self is much more than the "individual you". The self is the "ancestral and historical you" combined with the "current community of you". That is, that which produced you synthesized with that which sustains you.

It then becomes imperative here to understand that the "historical you" did not began in the Americas with chattel slavery. A critical learning objective for every student enrolled in African American history and otherwise is the knowledge of the African origin of the high cultures of classical African civilizations including Nubian (Ethiopian), Egyptian (Kemetic), the ancient Nok Culture later Ghana, Mali and Songhai kingdoms of West Africa rising after the beginning of the Christian era. There were many others to numerous to mention.

The Aurora High African American history student's annual Christmas Basket Elderly Appreciation and Delivery Project involved preparation and delivery of Christmas fruit baskets to elders in the community. This instructive activity became an act of self in support of "community of self". Implicit growth in consciousness occurred for students with the feedback received from their participatory service to the elderly with whom they shared a community. It likewise illuminated an awareness and reinforcement of the principle of "self". Their moment of epiphany (growth in consciousness) had arrived as they realized that their participatory service to the community elderly was simultaneously a service to themselves.

My eighth-year employment at Aurora High School ended with my enlistment in the U.S. Navy in 1981. This period of my life is more detailed in Chapter VII. Although I learned much during my Navy years it did not involve much regarding growth in consciousness. There were few opportunities during a tour of military duty to immerse myself into personal independent study. Later after my Navy separation in the mid-eighties, my opportunities rapidly expanded in this regard.

Brother George Welch

The greatest portion of such sources resulted from the opening of The Self Improvement Education Center (SIEC) of Norfolk, VA. It was owned and operated by George Welch pictured here with your author. Brother George as he was affectionately called had once been a keen student of the Honorable Elijah Muhammad. As founder of the SIEC of Norfolk, he was very passionately dedicated to the education of the African American community including its history, knowledge of self, and personal growth in consciousness. The SIEC provided a local source for Afrocentric books, literary materials as well as a place for meeting, studying, and collaborating on related topics.

Early friendships developed here were those with Edward Taylor and Charles Vincent (Monsungo) both of Norfolk, but Ed was by way of Los Angeles, CA. Ed and I became virtually brothers in our mutual study and research of what was typically referred to as "the knowledge". *"The knowledge"* was short terminology for "knowledge of self" extended into a social, natural, and divine (spiritual) order of comprehension and understanding. Authentic Knowledge of self (afrocentric) being "all subjects African" for continental Africans and those of African descent in the Diaspora.

Obstacles and Barriers

Since the loss of control of their homeland, many African's homes and elsewhere have been masterly misinformed concerning their ancestral home. This happening was not by chance. Even today we are still greatly unaware of its multitude of contributions and very significant role in the forward procession of history. More importantly is the nearly incomprehensive benefit we stand to realize by its recapture culturally, educationally, politically, economically, and spiritually.

Ironically, for thousands of years, before multiple waves of invasions and attempts at colonialism finally ended in successful European/Asian domination, Africa had become the light of the world. She dominated world agriculture, religion (spiritual systems), metallurgy, medicine, the physical and applied sciences, architecture, and the arts (Massey 1963; Walker 2006; Van Sertima 1976, 145-146). Through falsification of mainstream historical print media, contemporary misleading bombardment by negative televised images and through the persistent propagandistic rhetoric concerning Africa (the Mother Land) as a continent of savages, hopeless backwardness, in perpetual need of foreign aid and western assistance. This effort has shaped the perspective of the continent by others but more significantly, it has done precisely the same to many African Americans, as unfortunate as this reality has become. Consequently, many of her own have erroneously concluded much about Africa. The unwitting consumption of the very well-prepared "Kool-Aid" after having been separated from our "historical self" has been and continues mostly effective. This measure continues effective in deterring our interest and fidelity from the problem as it extends into the 21st century.

So, Africans, African Americans, and others in the Diaspora have continuously and gravely left unexamined and underestimated their own collective potential. This "must" change immediately. How? Only through a heightened growth in consciousness! As one wise man once correctly stated, "you can't love the tree and hate the roots". The correct corollary being you can't love yourself and hate the source from which you came. Accordingly, African humanity necessarily cannot hate Africa without ending hating themselves.

Roles of Study Groups and Cultural Performing Groups

As the study groups' quest for knowledge grew so did our active participation, relevant activities, and scope of involvement. There were weekly lectures at the center, a major increase in the availability of books, more Africentric items to purchase, and noted visitation from scholars and writers such as Yosef-ben Jochannan and Ishamusa Barashango.

Now, is an excellent time to show within my standard there is little to no difference in essence between the terms Afro-centric,

Afri-centric, or African-centered. All are interchangeable having essentially the same meaning. However, there is a very important caveat as it relates often to the terms Negro or even Black. Just because something is referenced with either of these descriptors, it could easily not meet the criteria of the previously mentioned three.

We soon grew to organize separate area study groups. Ed's group was based around Norfolk State University instructing and elevating the consciousness of NSU students. My group (The Kemet-Gnostics) was organized around a community-based membership and coordinated for a while with The African Cluster, a student-based study group at Hampton University. Our focus was centered mostly upon Egypt and pre-Egyptian Nile Valley civilizations. Monsungo with his wife and his performing Uruhu Dancers performed all over the Tidewater region and did much to elevate consciousness about African dance and culture. We selected the study group name (Kemet-Gnogstics) from the indigenous name of Egypt (Kemet) and the name of an early African Christian Sect Gnostics (Knower's of Truth). The study group proved to be a definitive consciousness builder and an outstanding group experience. Our meetings were held at various locations, including the local library, the Self Improvement Education Center, and occasionally at the homes of members. We would typically meet bimonthly to discuss the current reading/research topic(s) and sometimes analyze and exchange views hours beyond the scheduled meeting.

As our study and acquisition of self-knowledge grew so did our personal desire to inform and share with relatives, friends, and the general community of this new world of information that we had discovered.

During the first year of existence of the Kemet-Gnostics we responded to many requests. Most public interest in our study group included: the content of our focus of study; Kemetic (African) history, culture, and sciences also our methods of study and sources of information.

My mother had always impressed upon our family the quote "charity starts at home and spreads abroad". My corollary to her statement was that anything worth doing should begin at home and spread elsewhere as applicable. My immediate family therefore became the audience of my initial knowledge-sharing presentation. Later, that year I presented at the church of my life-long best friend (Minister Ken Hammond) in Williamston, North Carolina. The church event was followed by an event at Fairmont High School, Fairmont, N.C. at the request of my sister Jean. Lastly, that year I made an appearance on ABC television affiliate WCTI New Bern, N.C. with a short Kwanzaa presentation.

A strange incident worth mentioning occurred one Sunday evening at the home of a member hosting a study session. A young Brother appearing to be 25-30 years of age, entered our meeting with which none of us were familiar. He looked unassuming enough as not to generate suspicion. So, he sat attentively throughout the meeting without participation or engaging in any of our study topics. At the end of the meeting, as others were leaving, he addressed me as I was the presenter that evening. He explained that he just returned from the Middle East and had the personal mission of recruiting volunteers for combat in support of Muammar Qaddafi. I expressed with humility that our group was merely a study group of African history and culture. Further, I stated neither I nor any of our members to my knowledge would be interested in foreign combat or mercenary causes at this time. He didn't contest my response or even ask a follow-up question. He very quietly rose from his seat and left without a response. I have since wondered many times what that was about. Two scenarios came to mind: was he sincerely a recruiting agent on behalf of Qaddafi or was he a governmental agent trying to figure out if our study group might have a subversive tendency? I remain unsure until this day. I am however certain that the foci for our groups were the work of historians, scientists, and Afrocentric scholars from any and all academic disciplines.

The following group of historians, psychologists, psychiatrists, sociologists, and research scientists presented here are among the leading thinkers and Afrocentrics of world scholarship. I like to think of them as "high priest/priestess" or "tutors in consciousness supreme". Their "Afrocentric contributions" in the fields of world history, psychology, ethics, religion, social theory, and unified scientific theorem have been immeasurable in the revival of the once disregarded African role in these areas of human existence. Their scholarly research, findings, and struggle against significant odds, have resulted in the "growth in consciousness" for those of us continental and Diasporas Africans in search of our world identity and authentic selves.

Master Contributors to Consciousness Growth:
George G. M. James
(1893-1956)

Professor George G. M. James was born in Georgetown, British Guiana, South America. He studied at Durham University in England and did postgraduate work at Columbia University. He taught at Livingston College in Salisbury, N.C. and Johnson C. Smith College, Charlotte, N.C., Georgia State College, Alabama A&M, and the University of Arkansas, Pine Bluff.

Professor James is best known for his contentions set forth in his monumental and earth-shaking book concerning the genesis of Western civilization entitled Stolen Legacy. Here he asserts in (James 1988, 1) "the term Greek philosophy, to begin with, is a misnomer, for there is no such philosophy in existence". What have become known as Greek Philosophy created by such men as Socrates, Plato, Aristotle, Pythagoras, and others were not the founders of the philosophical, theosophical, or scientific discoveries known as such? He further states in (1988, 7) ..., the book Stolen Legacy "is an attempt to show that the true authors of "Greek

Philosophy" were not the Greeks; but the people of North Africa, commonly called Egyptians; and the praise and honor falsely given to the Greeks for centuries belong to the people of North Africa and therefore to the African Continent". Likewise (ben-Jochannan 1988, 375-376) cites "the Egyptian Mysteries System" (education system) and its three-step philosophy to a salvation process (1st) Mortals-initiates not yet having achieved inner vision, (2nd) The Intelligences-initiates having attained inner vision and received "mind" or "nous and (3rd) Sons of Light-those who had assailed to "spiritual consciousness" were the true source of Greek Philosophy.

Cheikh Anta Diop
(1923-1986)

Diop later greatly amplified Dr. James' assessment as a "Stolen Legacy" by the Greeks. He exponentially verified his conclusions by using a multi-faced academic approach, culturally based, historically-sound with a scientifically supported methodology for its substantiation. His brilliant use of science in his roles as, linguistic, archeologist, anthropologist, chemist, and historian extraordinaire has contributed greatly to the rescue and restoration of the (African-centered) perspective of authentic Egyptian (Kemetian) history and the role of ancient Egypt (Kemet) in world history (Diop 1974, 1989).

Many nineteenth and twentieth-century western Egyptologist propagated ancient Egypt (Kemet) as a product of European or Semitic culture. Would the prevailing racist views of Hegel and like-minded Western Egyptologist continue to carry the day? Furthermore, it was usually described geographically as a Middle Eastern nation as opposed to an African nation in order to avoid the association.

However, Diop took issue with this view and set out to scientifically disprove what he called "the falsification of African history". It was his contention that the Nile Valley civilization of Egypt (Kemet) was founded and administered by its indigenous Africans (Blacks) of antiquity. Further, Hyksos and those of other races who came later as conquerors had virtually no impact on the development or establishment of Egypt's (Kemet's) "classical high culture". The pyramids of Giza, sphinx, and other magnificent Egyptian structures of architecture and the required science, mathematics, and engineering fundamental to their development, had long been in place by the time of arrival of the first wave of invaders (Walker 2006, 80), (Williams 1987, 39). In fact, their intrusion significantly resulted in a dark age decline as described by Leo Africanus "...invaders of an obscure race marched with vengeance on our land (Kemet). By sheer manpower, they quickly seized our land. They hurriedly set fire to our cities...and abused our people with cruel brutality (ben-Jochannan 1988, 272).

Diops' conclusions were based upon a multi-faceted methodology to prove his historical positions. He utilized the most recent method for archeological artifact dating by use of radio-carbon results at his lab (LC14). He surveyed applicable ancient art images and examined physical anthropological artifacts; mummy melanin content test, osteological bone measurements and blood type identification (Diop 1989, 9). He asserted that Egyptians by self-definition called themselves "Kmtyw or Kemetiu (Black People) stemming from km the ancient Egyptian word for Black as indicated by their temple scripts and hieroglyphs (Mdw Ntr) in tombs (Diop 1989, 20).

Thirdly, he offered documented eyewitness reports by Greek and Latin writers such as Aristotle, Didorus, Herodotus, and Lucian describing Egyptians with African characteristics such as thick lips, broad nose, woolly hair, burnt skin, and thin legs (ben-Jochannan 1988, 156; Diop 1989). Continuing, he points out the linguistic relationships among other African cultures with Egypt. Wolof, a Senegalese language, located in extreme West Africa far from

Egypt (Kemet) was but one of several examples (Diop 1989, 22). Additionally, he demonstrated similarities among ancient Kemet and other ancient African Cultures, such as matrilineal focus, cosmology, architecture, divine kingship, music, instruments, dance, circumcision, and religious practices (Diop; 1989, 23).

Finally, Diop very appropriately stressed the most obvious fact. Egypt is geographically located in Africa but has been placed within the Middle East construct for contemporary revisionist reasons.

The United Nations Educational Scientific and Cultural Organization (UNESCO) convened a weeklong conference in1974 to study "the Peopling of Egypt and the Decipherment of the Meroitic Script. Among the participants were the most renowned and accomplished names in European scholarship on Ancient African history. They included: W. Kaiser, Germany; J. Lechlant, France; R. El Nadoury, Egypt; S, Sauneron, France; T. Save Soderbergh, Sweden; P.L. Shinnie, Canda and last but not least Cheikh Anta Diop and his protégé Theophile Obenga of Senegal. All had reputations in their respective countries for their work and all had international recognition with the exception of Diop and Obenga (Asante 2007, 31-32).

Suffice to say after a multifaceted catalogue of data illustrated by supporting slide visuals and the tons of evidence from the many academic disciplines: of documented history, anthropology; especially melanin content testing of mummies, archeology, linguistics and radiocarbon dating of artifacts by Diop and Obenga were overwhelming even for the international scholars.

By the end of the conference and with the evidence that had been consumed by the international media, it was clear that no longer could the interconnections between ancient Egypt and the rest of Africa scientifically be disregarded. But most importantly, the ancient civilization of Kemet could only be recognized as an Indigenous Black culture in accordance with the massive relative evidence presented by African scholars Diop and Obenga.

Yosef ben-Jochannan
(1918-2015)

Dr. Ben was not a traditionalist as a historian, historiographer, or thinker. Africa and the glory of ancient Egypt had been mostly written and interpreted by European scholars prior to Dr. Ben, Dr. Diop, and several of their contemporaries. His controversial but exceedingly thorough body of work has done much to challenge and confront the very foundations and genesis of Western Civilization. He insisted on a method of lecture and rendering of instructions with emotions and often humor, as he captivated his audiences with encyclopedic volumes of knowledge of ancient Kemetic and African culture. It was during the summer of 1988 that I received the most humbling request of my lifetime to date. I was informed by my cohort Edward Taylor that I had been invited to provide remarks at the retirement ceremony of Dr. Yosef ben- Jochannan at City College of New York, (C.C.N.Y.). My presentation was a brief one but the honor for me was absolutely surreal. In addition to Dr. Ben, I had the distinct privilege that evening to meet many other scholars and dignitaries of familiarity but had no idea I would ever personally meet: Dr. John Henrik Clark, Dr. Leonard Jeffries, Ashra Kwesi, Professor James Smalls, Dr. Asa Hillard, Dr. Richard King, Dr. James Turner, Dr. Adelaid Sanford, and Dr. Amos Wilson.

He has written and published many books and articles to this end. Some of the most significant are: The <u>Black Man of the Nile and his Family</u>, <u>We the Black Jews</u>, <u>African Origin of the Major Western Religions</u>, <u>Africa (Mother of Western Civilization)</u>, and <u>A Chronology of the Bible</u>.

My first awareness of Dr. Ben as he was affectionately known, came by way of videotape lecture while on an educational tour. He was instructing a group of African American tourists on the history and significance of ancient Nile Valley civilization(s). The tape consisted of an evening lecture following a day tour of ancient temples, monuments, obelisks, statues, etc., at their many ancient places along the Nile River.

Dr. Yosef ben Jochannan

In his aforementioned major works, he challenged the old Eurocentric Historian guard by refuting assertions of Egypt as an Indigenous European or Asian culture. Dr. Ben and others have disproved this belief to no creditable contention (Ben-Jochannan 1973; Diop1974; Walker 2006). He similarly states African systems of spirituality as the forebears of Judaism, Christianity, and Islam. All three religions had their foundations heavily borrowed from the Pyramid Texts, writings from Egyptian Temples, and The Egyptian Book of the Dead (Ben-Jochannan 1970; Jackson 1985; Karenga 1993).

Needless to say, Dr. Ben's academic and professional life was not made easy by the educational establishment. Related to his bold, contentious, and Afrocentric research, scholarship, and lectures he was reported to have once been **"fired in writing on toilet paper".**

John Henrik Clark
(1915-1998)

Dr. John Henrik Clark committed his scholarship, professional and personal life as an Africanist in dedication to teaching, directing, and preparing young scholars and laypersons in the areas of our greatest deficits, "knowledge of self, self-reliance, and nation-building".

He has written, edited, or co-written more than 30 books, pamphlets, and articles in the area of African history, culture, and challenges of the Diaspora. Some of his most noted works include: My Life in Search of Africa, Christopher Columbus, and The African Holocaust—Slavery and the Rise of European Capitalism, African World Revolution—Africans at the Crossroads, African

People in World History: Lecture, and Who Betrayed the African World Revolution? And other Speeches.

Dr. Clark has become an institution and beloved by his students and audiences for his humble demeanor and personality; as proved when he allowed this photo with yours truly at a retirement ceremony at City College, N.Y. in 1988. Even more so, he is known for his powerful storehouse of knowledge emanating from the depth of his insatiable reading, research, and recall of historical data. A unique example was demonstrated in the now famous debate of (March 29, 1996) with Mary Lefkowitz of Wesley College. In her 1996 book Not Out of Africa—How Afrocentrism Became an Excuse to Teach Myth as History, Lefkowitz referred to African Origins of

Civilization, the Egyptian Mysteries System, and the book Stolen Legacy by James as myths. This as you can surmise did not sit well with Dr. Clark. During the debate, it was revealed that Dr. Lefkowitz had never been to Africa. She appeared completely overwhelmed to the point of embarrassment on the subject for debate by Dr. Clarks' massive scholarship and background in this area. Dr. Clark made it clear in the opening of the debate "I'm not here to debate with anyone; I debate with my equals all others I teach".

Dr. Clark also provided Malcolm X (Malik El Hajj Shabbaz) with consultation and perspectives in the area of African and African American history during the lifetime of Malcolm's activism and leadership. In the related picture here (1988), I had the overwhelming pleasure of meeting and engagement in conversation with Dr. Clark at Dr. Ben Jochannan's retirement ceremony at City College.

Ivan Van Sertima
(1938-2009)

My introduction to the work of Dr. Van Sertima came by way of a videotape presentation (1987) by Aishwa Kwesi. Later in 1990, I was privileged to attend a lecture by him at William and Mary College in Williamsburg, Virginia. Van Sertima was a native of Guyana, South America, and employed at Rutgers University. His pioneering study in anthropology and linguistics of ancient America, Europe, and Asia are chronicled as his major works. The cover of the book, The African presence in Ancient America: They Came Before Columbus, displays the large Africoid heads found in modern day Mexico.

Dr. Van Sertima's extensive research has become quite significant in the mounting archeological evidence showing African presence in America predating the European African slave trade and Columbus's discovery by centuries.

Dr. Van Sertima asserts the pyramids of La Venta in (Olmec Mexico) along with mummies, hieroglyphic writing and many

---

---

other African-related artifacts cannot be coincidental (Van Sertima 1976, 32-33). Their presence in ancient Mexico shows shared pyramid construction knowledge and the homage paid to them by the Olmec people through the construction of the giant Africoid heads in their appreciation and honor.

His major works includes: The African presence in Ancient America—They Came Before Columbus, The African Presence in Early Europe, Golden Age of the Moors, Early America Revisited, Great Black Leaders, Egypt Revisited, Black Women in Antiquity, African Presence in Early Asia, and Blacks in Science.

Maulana Karenga
(1941- Present)
(Founder of Kwanzaa)

During the late eighties (1988), I had the great privilege and honor to meet Dr. Karenga, the founder of Kwanzaa. Master historian, scholar, writer, Advanced Study of Classical African Civilization (ASCAC) charter member, cultural warrior, Afrocentric thinker, and all-around visionary at a lecture and book signing at Williamsburg, Virginia.

Between his two scheduled lectures, he autographed books for lecture attendees. During the autographing session, he spoke freely even indulging in conversation, and allowed pictures to be taken with him. During my time with him, while talking and sharing a photo, I noticed a suited European man wearing an identification badge labeled CIA (Central Intelligence Agency). Immediately I asked Dr. Karenga was he aware. "Yes," he responded. "They are always around". Strange I thought, seemingly they would have had activities of more governmental importance than tracing around behind Dr. Karenga.

His founding of KWANZAA a cultural holiday for Africans and Africans in the Diaspora has become a celebrated focal point in many places across the globe. "First fruits of harvest celebration" are foundational to the holiday. The core aspects are gathering for reverence, commemoration, recommitment, and celebration in building family, community, and viable culture for the Black community. Dr. Karenga selected values for Kwanzaa are commensurate with the desires and aspirations of many continental Africans and African Americans including the guiding principles of MAAT. These were the struggle for freedom and justice, rebuilding community, and contributing to a new historical trajectory for mankind (Karenga 1989, 31-45).

The Seven Principals (NGUZO SABA) which are the values of emphasis for Kwanzaa celebrated one each day during the period December 26th through January 1st are:

1. Umoja (Unity)
2. Kujichagulia (self-determination)
3. Ujma (Work and Responsibility)
4. Ujamma (Cooperative Economics),
5. Nia (Purpose),
6. Kuumba (creativity)
7. Imani (faith) (Karenga 1989, 45-73).

Since the start of the Kwanzaa Holiday and in support of its purpose and tradition, I have been honored to meet Dr. Karenga; a brilliant, scholarly, and humble man. Since our acquaintance and having become motivated by his scholarship and dedication I better understand the value of the Kwanzaa celebration as a cultural holiday. These are some of the outlet merchants with whom I dealt in the promotion and distribution of Kwanzaa related articles and artifacts: The Self Improvement Education Center, Norfolk, VA., Liberation Book Store, Harlem, N.Y., The Know Book Store, Durham, N.C., Blacknificent Book Store, Raleigh, N.C., Pyramid Books, Boynton Beach, FL. and Washington, D.C., Baltimore, M.D.

Some of his major books include Introduction to Black Studies, Selections from the Husia: Sacred Wisdom from Ancient Egypt, The African American Holiday of Kwanzaa, A Celebration of Family, Community & Culture, MAAT: The Moral Ideal in Ancient Egypt, Essays on Struggle and Position and Analysis, The Foundations of Kawaida Theory.

Finally, it is important to remember Kwanzaa is an African/African American cultural holiday. It **is not a religious holiday** in competition or contradiction with the celebration of Christmas or Hanukkah. It is my steadfast belief that Kwanzaa will inevitably experience exponential growth in the U.S. and elsewhere. As the African human become more conscious of his/her "authentic self" he/she will appreciatively gravitate towards the celebration of Kwanzaa; commensurate with their growth in consciousness, more decisively adhere to the principals of Kwanzaa, and cohere almost intuitively with their authentic reality.

Molefi Asanti
(1942- Present)

Dr. Molefi Asanti is a professor and leading voice of African and African American Studies in the nation. In 1988 Dr. Asante founded the nations' first doctoral program in African American Studies at Temple University.

Dr. Asante presenting at Juneteenth 2019 –Richmond, VA

He has become very influential in the field of intercultural communications, and many consider him the father of Afrocentricity. The term dates back to the '70s with Dr. Asante's first major work introducing the concept in Afrocentricity: The Theory of Social Change. Since its introduction, Dr. Asante has authored several other books on the subject. (Karenga 1993, 34) notes clearly that the Afrocentricity construct has become one of the most conceptually important frameworks to emerge in Black Studies in recent development. (Asante 1990, 8) states the Afrocentric method pursues a world voice distinctly African centered in relation to external phenomena. During a lecture, at which this author was present, at Norfolk State University in 1987, Dr. Asante explained thoroughly that Afrocentricity was both a methodology and a desired outcome of its application. Dr. Karenga indicates Afrocentricity should not however be thought of as a counter measure for Eurocentrism and misnomered "Afrocentricism" (Karenga 1993).

Some of his more than fifty published books include The Afrocentric Idea. Malcolm X as Cultural Hero and Other Afrocentric Essays. Historical and Cultural Atlas of African Americans. The Egyptian Philosophers. The Book of African Names. As I Run Toward Africa. African Pyramids Knowledge. Handbook of Black Studies. Revolutionary Pedagogy, The American Demagogue. Kemet Afrocentricity and Knowledge. Classical Africa. The Afrocentric Manifesto. Afrocentricity. African Intellectual Heritage. Cheikh Anta Diop: An Intellectual Portrait and Painful Demise of Eurocentricism. Please include me among the multitude from the African world thankful for the work and scholarship of Dr. Molefi Asante.

Dr. Asante has become an authoritative scholar in his field of study. During the eighties, he appropriately and convincingly testified as an expert witness in defense of Dr. Leonard Jeffries. Dr. Jeffries had come under attack unjustly as Black Studies Department Chairperson at City College, New York.

Dr. Asante had recently returned from Africa and presented in Richmond, VA. during the Juneteeth Celebration of 2019. Here he was kind in entertaining one of my many questions.

Chancellor Williams
(1893-1992)

Dr. Williams was a historian, sociologist, writer and Africanist of high order and discipline. He attended Howard University and American University where he acquired a Ph.D. in sociology. He also did research in African history at Ghana University before writing his major work <u>The Destruction of Black Civilization—Great Issues of a Race From 4500 B.C. to 2000 A.D.</u> This work detailed much of the history of the Asian and European wave after wave of invasions into North Africa from periods B.C.E. (Before the Christian Era) into modern times. The many invaders include Hyksos, Assyrians, Persians, Greeks, Romans, and Arabs (Williams 1987, 40). In accordance with the racial differences with each invasion so was a change in the racial make-up of the Egyptian population from the original indigenous one (Black Africans). The pyramids of Giza, the Sphinx (Harmacus), the Ramses Colossus were all in place before the first invasion by the Hyksos 1675 BCE (ben-Jochannan; 1971: 275). It is for these invasions that many have erroneously claimed Egypt in all its wondrous glory a European or Semitic civilization. This claim has been disproven and debunked several times over through melanin content testing of some of the oldest occupants remains, linguistics, radiocarbon dating, etc. (Diop1974; 1991); and more traditional archeological, anthropological and primary source documentation (ben-Jochannan;1971), (Walker; 2006) and many others. Dr. Williams made this assessment of available documents, records, and artifacts in support of this issue. Accordingly ... "Apart from the remarkable contributions of archeology in the 19th and 20th centuries, there has always been more than sufficient written records to reconstruct the history of the Blacks from the earliest times" (Williams 1987, 361). The inconsistency would seem to indicate the will of the writer and a desire for revisionist interpretations.

The multitude of invaders over the millennium's behavior ranged from savage and inhumane to less so and even conciliatory. However, as noted historian John Henrik Clark often stated in his lectures, "Africa always had something that others wanted and sometimes needed but didn't want to pay for." This included the theft of the big four trending from antiquity to currently: 1) mind/ mentality (science, math, and high culture) 2) materials (rubber, cocoa, timber, etc.) 3) minerals (gold, diamonds, titanium, etc.), 4) even African man and African woman human prowess and power (slaves).

It is worth noting biographically, that Dr. Williams had the legendary Africanist Leo Hansberry as a contemporary, teacher and consultant who was much more than a capable resource. He says, "Standing alone and isolated in the field for over thirty-five years, William Leo Hansberry was the teacher who introduced me to the systematic study of African history and, of equal importance, to the ancient documentary sources" (Williams 1987, 361). Dr. Chancellor Williams, through his three editions of The Destruction of Black Civilization, reveals history of invasions and destruction of libraries, temples, and many artifacts from African antiquity. Although the results were catastrophic; the Indigenous people of Africa created high civilization and culture in such abundance and grandeur, but all was never destroyed; despite the effort to seemingly do so.

Robin Walker
(1967- Present)

London born, Dr. Robin Walker historian, educator and lecturer has become England's most outstanding scholar in the fields of African History and Egyptology.

Dr. Walker increased his notoriety exponentially with his publishing of the book "When We Ruled" 2006. As one of the most comprehensive accounts of Ancient Africa of the 20th century, this work is rapidly becoming an international classic. He covers topics over vast areas of the mother continent presenting thousands of years of important and relevant world history. Among his many topics and foci are Origin of the human race, Ancient Ethiopia and Southern Africa, Pre-dynastic Kemet, Ancient Kemet and Ancient West Africa.

He has researched and developed a chronology of African history dating from 88,000 B.C.E. (Before Christian Era) to 1994 C.E. (of the Christian Era).

Dr. Walker's historical knowledge and detail, coupled with sprinklings of emotion and humor are very reminiscent of the qualities and mannerisms of noted historians Dr. Yosef ben-Jochannan, and Dr. John Henrik Clark. These are proven methods by the masters to educate and motivate Black audiences.

Major books by Dr. Robyn Walker include: If You Want to Learn Early African History Start Here Blacks and Science, African American Contributions to Science and Technology, The Rise and Fall of Black Wall Street and The Seven Key Empowerment Principles, African Mathematics: History Textbook and Classroom Lessons, When We Ruled.

Professor James Smalls
(1945-Present)

Professor James Smalls is an Afrocentric historian, scholar, lecturer, writer, and Pan African activist of high regard. He is well known as an *"activist intellectual"* for his lifelong involvement and dedication to differing aspects and components of the liberation movement.

Professor Smalls's legacy is bolstered by his affiliation with Malcolm X, the Muslim Mosque Incorporated, and the Organization of African American Unity (OAAU). He is currently an active member and a former regional president of the Advanced Study of Classical African Civilization (ASCAC). Other related memberships and arenas of service were the Student Non-Violent Coordinating Committee (SNCC) and National Association for the Advancement of Colored People (NAACP).

As a member of the City College faculty of N.Y., he was a valued instructor as a member of the Black Studies Department. Here he taught such subjects as Malcolm X, the Urban Community, and Traditional African Religion. Professor Smalls is also a priest of the Yoruba, Oyo, and Ife traditions. Over the course of my study and research, I have had the honor to attend several lectures and presentations by Dr. Smalls.

He has produced the booklet Know Your History Booklist and is currently developing work related to Lectures on Malcolm X and Post Slavery Trauma Syndrome.

Professor Smalls currently conducts educational and cultural tours to Africa and stays on the battlefield for the liberation of African peoples around the world.

Frances Cress Welsing
(1935-2016)

Dr. Welsing, a third-generation medical doctor (psychiatrist) in her family developed the Cress Theory of Color-Confrontation and Racism (White Supremacy). The purpose of her theory was to psychologically, functionally, and descriptively give Afrocentric meaning, and understanding to white (European) racism and white supremacy practices.

(Welsing 1991, ii) states her definition of racism (white supremacy) as follows: The local and global power system structured and maintained by persons who classify themselves as white, whether consciously or subconsciously determined; this system consists of patterns of perception, logic, symbol formation, thought, speech, action, and emotional response, as conducted simultaneously in all areas of people activity (economics, education, entertainment, labor, law, politics, religion, sex and war). The ultimate purpose of the system is to prevent white genetic annihilation on Earth-a planet in which the overwhelming majority of people are classified as non-white (black, brown, red and yellow) by white-skinned people. All of the non-white people are genetically dominant (in terms of skin coloration) compared to the genetically recessive, white-skinned people. Global power formations and realignments will emerge such as European economic and military unification and USA and Russian linkage.

She spoke and lectured all over the country and abroad with numerous radio and television appearances on such shows as Phil Donohue and others. She seemed always relaxed and under control with her message and responses no matter how hostile the audience.

The Cress Theory of Color-Confrontation and Racism (White Supremacy) is delineated in her book, The Isis Papers: The Keys to the Colors.

Dr. Welsing would famously say she had just one speech but all who ever heard it would attest it was emphatically on point! In addition to the methodical step by step explication of her definition of terms and people activity impacted by "white supremacy", there were coded symbols deciphered from within the global system of "white supremacy" explained as well.

This author had the distinct honor to assist her once to the place she was designated to deliver the keynote speech of the evening on the campus of Howard University. Strangely, about ten minutes into her speech I became drastically ill and was forced by it all to leave her lecture. I recall she looked over in some bewilderment as if, why are you leaving? I felt terrible and thought, only if I could explain, I meant no disrespect!

Amos Wilson
(1941-1998)

Dr. Amos Wilson was an afrocentric thinker, psychologist, social worker, prolific writer, and professor of Psychology at the City University of New York. He was immensely analytical from a psychological perspective regarding children's mental health and development, black-on-black violence, race, and class, economics in contemporary Africa, race, and economics in America, and the crisis of Black leadership. He emphasized that the side of the brain an individual uses most is determined by which side an individual or group is rewarded by society for its usage. His contention was that Blacks have been rewarded more for right-side activity i.e., singing, dancing, music, and sports (Wilson 1981, 12). Another major area of his research was Black-on-Black crime as elucidated in his major work, Black-on-Black Violence: The Psychodynamics of Black Self-Annihilation in Service of White Domination.

Some of his major books included: Falsification of African Consciousness, Black on Black Violence, Awakening the Natural

Genius of Black Children, Blueprint for Black Power: A moral Political and Economic Imperative for the Twentieth Century and Issues for Manhood in Black and White.

Dr. Wilson often did public lectures and was known as a forceful and dynamic speaker and as an Afrocentric advocate of causes for sound mental health, liberation, and "authentic Black power".

Wade Nobles
(Present)

Dr. Nobles is Professor Emeritus of Africana Studies and Black Psychology of San Francisco State University, San Francisco, CA.

He is a founding member of the Association of Black Psychologist, founder and executive director of the Institute for Advanced Study of Black Family Life and Culture, a charter member of Advanced Study of Classical African Civilization (ASCAC), writer, lecturer, and a leading voice in African-Centered Scholarship.

Dr. Nobles has been out-front in establishing the foundation for the Black Psychology Movement. Among his academic efforts have been to show the underlying culture and belief system of African Americans is rooted in African philosophy and African ethos. As Nobles says (Nobles 1985, 54) "it is our contention that Black culture in the United States is the result of a special mixture of our *continued African orientation operating* within another cultural milieu which is primarily defined by the philosophical assumptions and underpinnings of the Anglo-American community". Major aspects of this continuum include the belief in the oneness with God and the entire universe; the cultural belief that there should be no distinction between the religious belief and daily routine (stated differently not merely ideals professed as religion but behaviors commensurate with one's daily actions), and kinship or collective unity which creates togetherness and *conceptual idea of the Extended Self.*

Dr. Nobles and associates have become the warriors against *transubstantive errors* (cultural misinterpretations) and *conceptual incarceration* (lack of ability to expand cognitively, intellectually, and spiritually due to limitation by incarcerated thought (the encasement) limitation of understanding by virtue of the terms, concepts, and paradigms utilized in explanation of cultural, material, and spiritual phenomenon) (Nobles 1985, 101-108). The devastating consequences of both are formidable challenges to our potential expressed by Dr. Nobles and his colleagues on behalf of African people.

A list of major books by Wade Nobles are: African Psychology: Towards it Reclamation, Reascension? and Revitalization, Seeking the Sakhu: Foundational Writings for an African Psychology, African Psychology in Historical Perspective and Related Commentary, Africanity and the Black Family: The Development of a Theoretical Model and The Island of Mimes: Haiti's Unfinished Revolution.

Na'im Akbar
(1944- Present)

Dr. Akbar is an afrocentric thinker, professor, psychologist, writer, lecturer, a member of the Association of Black Psychologist, member of the Advanced Study of Classical African Civilization (ASCAC) and founder of his own Mind Productions Publishing Company. While collaborating closely with peers he has become a pioneer and forward thinker in the field of Black Psychology and knowledge of self.

Dr. Akbar did much to enhance and broaden perspectives of self within an Afrocentric concept. Accordingly, (Akbar 1985, iv-v) states "The Community of Self talks about self, me, and ourselves. The context is the African-American experience...stands as one of the strongest examples of high human principles being able to endure despite environments of extreme opposition." He brings clarity for the need and benefits of extension of self from the individual to the group and community.

Dr. Akbar presents in Raleigh, NC --1987

Many within the academic community as well as casual thinkers believe that slavery is totally passé. However, Dr. Akbar points out "slavery was "legally" ended in excess of 100 years ago, but over the 300 years experienced in its brutality and unnaturalness constituted a severe psychological and social shock to the minds of African Americans" (Akbar 1984, 7). His work also suggests the use of certain psychological religious images depicting the Christian god deity as Caucasian to Africans incarcerated many African slaves' minds. African slave image presentation and manipulation once established in the Western hemisphere became a viable tool in supplanting a geo-political socio-economic (slave) status for a fictitious "divine" one. Stated in other words Christian theology was used to reinforce the social and economic status of slavery as defined intent and purpose. Inference here stated differently, even

God wanted Africans to be slaves in America. This became and remains a devastating reality for many African Americans.

Some of Dr. Akbar's body of written work includes <u>Chains and Images of Psychological Slavery</u>, <u>The Community of Self</u>, <u>Breaking The Chains Of Psychological Slavery</u>, <u>Know Thy Self</u>, <u>Visions for Black Men</u> and <u>Light from Ancient Africa</u>.

Psychological warfare for the mind of man has been and still is a potent tool for those wanting to subjugate, dominate and render others to a perpetual state of confusion and subordination. This author had the enlightening experience of meeting.

Professor Carol Barnes
(Present)

Professor Barnes is a polymer chemist; researcher, lecturer and writer concerning the chemical properties of melanin. Professor Barnes is a pioneer in the field of melanin research who has determined from his research and analysis that this extraordinarily complex biopolymer (melanin) is responsible for much more than pigmentation and color among the races of mankind. Professor (Barnes 1988, 36-38), (Edelstein 1971, 311-312) lists the following ten important properties of this primal organic compound:

1) Melanin is an incredibly old chemical and has been involved in life processes for eons
2) Melanin is composed of varying amounts of different smaller chemicals (precursors) such as tyrosine, tryptophan, melatonin, and serotonin
3) Melanin can produce electrical charges and various bonding properties such as ionic, metallic, and covalent
4) Melanin responds to and absorbs light, sound (music), and electrical energy
5) Melanin is an extremely stable chemical

6) Melanin is centrally involved in controlling ***physical and mental body*** activities
7) Melanin is present at the site of tissue repair, regeneration (cuts/wounds), and infectious diseases
8) Melanin in the brain ***increases from the lower primates up through man and peaks in the Black Human***
9) Melanin is capable of undergoing many chemical reactions at once through what scientists call oxidation-reduction reactions. These reactions may give the Black Human their smooth movement and rhythm
10) Melanin can produce or neutralize radiation or free radicals (reduce the incidence of skin cancer).

Professor Barnes asserts many biological and environmental advantages in the chemical compound melanin. The Black Human produces by far the greatest quantity of melanin among all groups (Barnes 1988, 22-23).

His major work: MELANIN: The Chemical Key to Black Greatness.

Richard King
(1946-2013)

Dr. Richard King M.D. was a psychiatrist, historian, writer, lecturer, Egyptologist, and Afrocentric researcher and scholar.

He studied with Alfred and Bernice Ligon at the Aquarian Spiritual Center in Los Angeles where he acquired an additional interest in Egyptian spirituality. Later Dr. King became known for his study and research in the vast field of melanin also referred to as Black Dot (Archetype of humanity). He especially researched the area of the ancient Kemites knowledge and consciousness as it relates to melanin. Dr. King as a psychiatrist studied the African origin of biological psychiatry.

According to (King 1994, 9) Black Dot is an ancient symbol for blackness. His research and scholarship revealed the ancient Kemites determined Blackness to be the universal solvent of all and was seen as the one reality from which lives loom spun. All colors, all vibratory energies were but a shade of black. Black was the color of outer space; birthplace and womb of the planets, stars and countless galaxies, black holes; color of carbon (the key element, carbon atoms link together to form black melanin found in all living matter. Melanin is the black seed of all humanity, the archetype of humanity, the hidden doorway to the collective unconsciousness. An extensive line of profound ancient Kemetic scientists studied for thousands of years until they discovered the hidden doorway to advanced laws and rhythms that span the universe. These profound African priest-scientists were able to visualize knowledge from their intuitive mind's timeless collective unconscious and memory banks. (King 2001, 10-11) asserts black people are awakening from the spell of mental slavery, ignorance of self, and an inability to focus the mind spiritually.

Black Dot in the form of melanin, is the hidden doorway through which a reborn people must pass to restore their historical greatness. I had the distinct honor to have met Dr. King at Dr. ben Jochannan's retirement ceremony in 1988.

Major books by Dr. Richard D. King MD are: African Origin of Biological Psychiatry, Melanin: A key to Freedom and Why Darkness Matters.

R. A. Schwaller De Lubicz
(1887-1961)

Schwaller de Lubicz was a French-born philosopher and Egyptologist whose work is highly regarded by many Afrocentric historians. De Lubicz contributed significantly to the symbolic and esoteric orientation believed to be much of the Pharaonic Precepts of ancient Kemet. He was not the traditional Egyptologist of his day. He examined and intently studied the art and architecture of the Temple of Luxor (Thebes) for more than fifteen years and came to very different conclusions than did his contemporaries. De Lubicz discovered a much more systematic and sophisticated method of awakening latent knowledge (esoteric) and evocation by the use of structural design and artistic Measures in Ancient Egyptian.

Egyptian (Kemetic) temples (De Lubicz, 1977). His writings from his work at the Temple of Luxor were translated into English in his book <u>The Temple in Man</u>. Important differing views held by de Lubicz included: (1) Symbolism is the method of transcription (conveying) of the thought of the Ancient Egyptians, in writing and in figuration as well as in the architecture; (2) that the temple is constructed (contrarily to our current principals of architecture) on several axes; that each axis has a meaning, and that this meaning dictates the meaning of the parts subordinate to it and; (3) there is, in pharaonic Egypt, geodetic, astronomical, and physiological knowledge surpassing that which Egyptology had heretofore not been able to concede (de Lubicz 1977, 132).

He further advanced his views of ancient Egyptian (Kemetic) philosophy, science, and theosophy in other related works including <u>Symbol and the Symbolic Ancient Egypt, Science, and the Evolution of Consciousness</u>, <u>Sacred Science</u> and <u>Nature Word</u>.

Schwaller de Lubicz contributed immensely to the understanding of the richness, sophistication, higher level of consciousness, and spirituality of ancient Egypt (Kemet) as a non-traditionalist in the field of Egyptology.

<u>Asa Hillard III</u>
(1933-2007)

Dr. Asa Hillard III was an African American-education-specialist, an Afrocentric scholar, master teacher, professor,

231

writer, lecturer and a founding member of the Advanced Study of Classical African Civilization (ASCAC). In addition to his in-depth knowledge of ancient Kemetic history and culture, he was a tireless warrior to bring this academic content to the curriculums of the public schools of America. Among other reasons, Dr. Hillard felt that Ancient Kemet in all its glory and accomplishments should be acknowledged and reclaimed by its historical authentic owners. He believed that infusion of African Classical Culture would become a source of African identity and a much-warranted catalyst for group unity. Group cohesion is a prerequisite to effective action and group action is certainly rooted in a shared culture. He collaborated tirelessly with several school districts across the nation with this methodological intent as an objective.

In 1990, he was instrumental in leading the sponsorship of the first Annual Conference for the purpose of infusing African and African American content in the school curriculum within the state of Georgia (Hilliard 1995, 219). During the same time period, the old guard attempting to protect the exclusive curriculums created a backlash by critiquing and attacking this effort as irrelevant pluralism. He continued his advocacy for a more Afrocentric curriculum for African American students absent standardized testing and until such time they abandoned their biased tendencies.

Major works by Dr. Asa Hilliard include The Teachings of Ptahhotep; The Oldest Book in the World, The Maroon Within Us: Selected Essays on African American Community Socialization and The Re-Awakening of the African Mind.

Marimba Ani
(Present)

Professor Ani with her anthropological African-centered scholarly background successfully accomplished what many felt was inevitable if the African World is ever to recover from her past consisting of waves of invasions and destruction of the Black classical culture of ancient Egypt (Kemet), chattel slavery, and colonialism. This also includes the worldwide legacy of European domination by racism and oppression of recent times. In review of the evolving process of "oppression eradication", the oppressed must complete an accurate and objective analysis (critique) of the culture which have marginalized, enslaved, and oppressed them. Dr. John Henrik Clark points out in the book's introduction that most books about Europeans deal mainly with what Europeans think of other people, "In this book, Professor Richards (Ani) has analyzed the European and their influence on the world". According to Professor Marimba Ani this cannot and should not be attempted by the use of the very Eurocentric terms, concepts, belief systems, and paradigms that hamper and entrap (conceptually incarcerate) the very message in which she is attempting to redefine and construct. She has thereby selected key terms from the most widely used African language (Swahili) as appropriate revolutionary response and framework of verbal expression to better convey meaning from a more African-centered reference.

In her book, Yurugu: An African Centered Critique of European Cultural Thought and Behavior, she details, dissects, and analyzes European Cultural Thought from an African-Centered perspective. "African people must come to know the nature of European thought and behavior in order to understand the effect that Europe has had on our ability to think victoriously" (Ani 1994, 2). Professor Ani makes analytical usage of several Swahili terms to discern; communicate, impart meaning and bring clarity to her audience. I will attempt here to relate a much-abbreviated definition of the key Swahili terms utilized.

1) Asili – the developmental germ or seed of culture (that from which all other components derive)

2) Utamawzo – culturally structured thought (component of the asili)
3) Utamaroho – the energy source of a culture that motivates the collective behavior of its members
4) Yurugu – a being in the mythology of Dogon/African origin which is responsible for the disorder in the universe (a being conceived in denial of the natural order).

Professor Ani masterfully illustrates the process and germination of the Asili, and its mandates upon the Utamawzo fueled by the Utamaroho using several analogous flow charts in her African-centered analysis of (Yurugu).

Major works by Marimba Ani include: Let the circle be unbroken: The Implications of African Spirituality in the Diaspora, Yurugu An African - Centered Critique of European Thought And Behavior.

Jacob Carruthers
(1930-2004)

Dr. Carruthers was a pioneer in the Afrocentric movement as a challenge to the standard Eurocentric interpretation of Ancient Egypt. One major area of focus in this regard was an emphasis on language and writing. The written Mdw-Ntr (hieroglyphics) was an area he felt was critical for study and analysis for the purpose of rescue and restoration of Black classical culture. With others, he founded the Kemetic Institute in Chicago to serve as a major resource for African-centered study and research. Later he along with John Henrik Clark, Asa Hillard, Leonard Jeffries, Yosef ben-Jochannan and Maulana Karenga founded The Advanced Study of Classical Civilization (ASCAC) research organization for the reclamation of our classical African culture.

Major works by Dr. Carruthers include Intellectual Warfare, Essays In Ancient Egyptian Studies, MDW NTR: Divine Speech,

Science and Oppression, Kemet African Worldview: Jacob Carruthers with Maulana Karenga.

Gabriel A. Oyibo
(1952-Present)
God Almighty Grand Unified Theorem (GAGUT)

Dr. Oyibo is a Nigerian-born mathematician and scientist of the highest order. He received his Ph.D. in Aeronautics and Mathematics from the Renhsselaur Polytechnic Institute and founded GAGUT (God Almighty's Grand Unified Theorem Gij,j=0) also called (The Holy Grail of Mathematics and Physics).

Renowned scientists such as Isaac Newton, James Clerk Maxwell, and Albert Einstein tried unsuccessfully to resolve the issue of the Grand Unification Theory (Gij,j=0). This theory is also known as "the theory of everything" which *combined the four known forces* in the universe, which are: gravity, electromagnetic, strong, and weak forces, and also accounts for any forces yet to be discovered.

Professor Oyibo has also showed the unification of all 118 elements in the Periodic Table; by illustrating that the 117 elements following hydrogen in the Periodic Table of Elements are merely nuclear compounds of hydrogen.

For clarification, Hydrogen has the atomic number 1, Helium 2, Lithium 3, Beryllium 4, Boron 5, Carbon 6... and so on in the Periodic Table reflecting the number of positively charged protons in the nucleus of the atom balanced by the same number of negatively charged electrons circling the nucleus. Hydrogen (Africum) thusly is identified by GAGUT as the *unifying building block* of the remaining 117 elements and their atomic numbers 2-118 (actually compounds) as indicated by their respective atomic numbers in the Periodic Table of Elements. Be reminded that the 118 elements are the elemental building blocks of all known matter in the universe. He also advances the genesis of Chemistry

(Khemistry), thusly, the Mystery of the Kemites (Khemistry) dating back to Pharaoh Shabaka and his re-discovery of Memphite Theology from what became known as the "Shabaka Stone". Kemites is the Indigenous name of the ancient Africans. Dr. Oyibo likewise unified the mathematical, biological, and social sciences linking them back to Khemistry.

He references *biology* as a study of cells (chemical compounds) which are the building blocks of life. *Psychology* is the study of the behavior of cellular constructed life. *Sociology* is the study of cellular constructive group actions and interactions. *History* then becomes the study of cellular-constructed humans (bio-systems) recorded events over time. All are unambiguously related to subsets of chemistry (Khemistry).

In the process of developing a science of how to construct forms geometry evolved as a building block in mathematics by application of its fundamental components: points, lines, and planes. Curves, squares, pyramids, obelisks, and structured matter are perceived through geometrical design. Dr. Oyibo states constantly that Geometry equals mathematics and becomes much of the language of GAUGAT along with the other mathematics, which Dr. Oyibo asserts as subsets of geometry. Trigonometry is the mathematical study of lines (sides) that create angles and their relative functions. Arithmetic displays positive and negative integers on a geometric *number line,* which can be added, subtracted, multiplied, or divided. Algebra is an advanced form of arithmetic using some of the same operations often solving for an unknown but can be solved from the *geometric number line* as well. Calculus is an advanced form of mathematics similar to Algebra but more complex because of its ability to decipher problems involving, changing rates of speed by use of derivatives and unusual measurements; often using *x and y axes* (geometric lines) represented by positive and negative integers.

Dr. Oyibo's earth-shaking GAGUT (theory of everything) clearly demonstrates the unification of the following: all known energy in the universe (the four known universal energy sources); all matter (hydrogen, as the building block and other elements as nuclear compounds of hydrogen), and the definitional relationship of all the sciences (mathematical, natural and social) which provides the language and conduit to convey and express the principles of Gods' Almighty's Grand Universe.

Conclusions

In my estimation, there is a fundamental similarity and nexus between Dr. "Oyibo's (Physical and Mathematical Sciences) GAGUAT" with Dr. Wade "Nobles (social scientist) Principle of Ontological Consubstantiation". "That is" all that which is part of the universe on some level is of the "same stuff" there is no such thing as "other" accordingly. One of the greatest marvels of the universe is of its oneness: energy, matter, and science. The Human species will either learn this cosmic lesson or perish because of an ignorant indifference to it. African-centered scholarship must continue diligence to ensure the continuance of African self-knowledge (nous/clear understanding), of whom he/she is in the world, (consciousness), and authentic interpretations of world events, and their historical roles therein (worldview). The social institutions upon which civilization is constructed thereby lie in the balance.

I believe consciousness and its varying levels are realized by seeking and allowing the acceptance and ascension of truth to prevail as the guiding force for individual behavior and that of affiliated group members' collective behavior. Truth is thereby the sustenance and essence of a consciousness, which leads to an "enlightened -evolved-understanding (realization of divine universal principles); the application of enlightenment within this truth (social application of divine principles) becomes a source and method worthy of "true religion". Simply stated, there is no daylight or schism between science and true spirituality. Truth deniers accordingly become their own worst enemies and those of the people. Attempting to understand and explicate the interconnection between cosmological content and man's respective place therein has been an ongoing challenge since the dawn of recorded history for the African mind and mentality.

A new and exciting way of scientifically viewing the cosmos or universe more uniformly and succinctly has appeared with the "theorem of all" discovered by Nigerian native Dr. Gabriel Oyibo. All known matter, energy sources and related sciences have been unified under a single theorem (GAGUT). His discovery had been unsuccessfully sought by such renowned western scientists as Sir Isaac Newton, James Clerk Maxwell, and Albert Einstein. Each managed to identify a piece of the elusive scientific puzzle; but Dr. Oyibo has successfully demonstrated the collective unity of gravity, electromagnetic force, and the strong and weak forces related to quantum theory (subatomic particles).

The work of the forward-thinking scholars presented in this chapter represents the most productive effort attempting to rediscover and reconnect to the many millenniums of African knowledge and discovery once lost, destroyed, or otherwise ignored. This group best represents African-centered perspectives and discovery paving the path for a return to African-centered consciousness in their variant fields of the twenty-first century.

Dr. Oyibo and the other aforementioned African-Centered Scholars have shown a masterful return to the world stage of research, scholarship, and ideas. People of African descent are rediscovering from their own classical-cultural platforms. The Afro-centric processes and methods presented have successfully provided the "jackal principal process" for discernment of contemporary sources, information, and conclusions. This new and exciting construct smashes "conceptual incarceration" and avails rising young scholars with the tools to amazingly navigate transformational boundaries. The spiritual infusion of possibilities within the academic domain of the 21st century and beyond" is thereby boundless for generations to come given the "consciousness to meet the challenge".

Rationale of Chronology

Critical chronological events of African history illustrates the underlying relevance and need to confront and challenge the "old guards" historical revisionism with the discipline of objectivity from antiquity (ancient) to present (contemporary) time.

CRITICAL CHRONOLOGICAL EVENTS OF AFRICAN HISTORY FROM ANCIENT TO MODERN TIMES

Unification of Upper And Lower Egypt (Kemet)	Menes or Narmer Founds 1ˢᵗ Dynasty c.5660-4188 BCE. Creation Old Kingdom
Great Pyramids of Gira Constructed	Fourth Dynasty c.4824-4678 BCE
First Immediate Period	c. 4188-3448 BCE. Political/ Social Upheaval
Mentuhotep II Restores Political Order and Governance	c. 3448BCE. Eleventh Dynasty and Middle Kingdom Begins
Second Intermediate Period	c.3182-1709 BCE .Fall of the 13ᵗʰ Dynasty and Middle Kingdom
Hyksos first foreign Invaders to rule in Kemet	c.2545 BCE.
Ahmose I Defeat Hyksos Pharaoh Ahmose and Queen Nefertari Reunify Kemet	c.1709 BCE. Establish the Glorious 18ᵗʰ Dynasty and the New Kingdom Begins
Assyrian Invasion	c.663 BCE.
Shabaka Establish 25ᵗʰ Dynasty and Battle Assyrians	c.730-656 BCE. Last Unification of Kemet under Home Rule (African) before losing her through current time

Other Invaders Persian Invasion Greek Invasion Roman Invasion Arab Invasion	c.525 BCE. c.32 BCE. c.30 BCE. c.639 CE. Current
European Slave Trade of Africans begins	1441 Twelve Africans Kidnapped and given as a present to Prince Henry of Portugal Scores of millions to the Americas between the 16th-19th centuries
First African Slaves to American Colonies	1619 Jamestown, VA.
Three Fifths Compromise	1787 U.S. Constitutional Covention
Black Humans counted as 3/5 of a man regarding	Congressional Representation for slaveholding States
Berlin Conference Colonization of Africa Planned By Europe and U.S.	1884-1885. Africa divided between European Nations. No African Nation By Europe and U.S. Present
U.S. Supreme Court Invaldates Key Component of Voting Rights Act of 1965	2013. States with records of previous Violations of voting rights of African Americans no longer had to receive Preclearance from the Fed to make changes to voting process or practices.
Presidential Election of 2016	Donald Trump elected 45th president of United States

*Bibliographical References
(Karenga 1993)
(Walker 2006)
(Williams 1987)

Chapter 10

Reflections and Perspectives

Summary

My initial perspectives on the significance of learning and education began in the remote surroundings of (Eastern North Carolina) embedded by my parents, church family, and the North Winterville, N.C. Community. Whether listening to the family as readers and/or storytellers, participating in Sunday school, or just the constant encouragement from community elders, the importance of education was consistently emphasized as the key to self-improvement and "upward mobility".

By the time my formal education had begun in the elementary grades (1957) the Brown Decision had been the "law of the land" for public education several years, although not yet de facto implemented. Understandably, I was not cognizant nor focused on this reality at the time. What I do recall is a special ambiance at school during those years. The prevailing "educational atmosphere" within our segregated status involved keen concentration on preparation, performance, qualifications, and achievement. We were persistently coached by our teachers and administrators to this end. The usage of such "terms of success" were essential in a new world Black educators believed to be on the horizon. Throughout both the elementary and high school experiences, discipline, and academic diligence focused us on the challenge of an emerging integrated society where if success was to be actualized, "we could not merely be good; but were required to be better" than our across-town Caucasian counterparts. Robinson and Historically Black High School Teachers elsewhere, perceived these as prerequisites in order to persist and take full advantage of the opportunities they assumed soon to be within our grasp.

My early home, community, and grade school experiences brought three important attributes to mind suggested as needed by psychologist, Dr. Wade Nobles. They afforded me *character.* I gleaned from family, the Black church, and the segregated but proud Black community *competence.* I learned from the excellence demanded by segregated grade school at (RHS) and the *confidence* I constructed from 360 degrees of my total youthful Black experience. All served as necessary layers for an emerging desire for mental growth and awareness as I completed grade school in 1969 America.

N.C. Central (1969-1973) became the venue seemingly for significant growth in consciousness. As a history major at an HBCU (Historically Black College/University) one would assume to become the recipient of a much greater volume and detail in the area of a useful "initiation into self-knowledge for the "Black Human". My conversance with such knowledge could then begin the enhancement of an appropriate worldview and a much better understanding of "my place therein". This thereby became the beginning of my quest for "self-knowledge and consciousness" until now stifled and engulfed by Eurocentrism.

During summer recess from undergraduate studies, a neutral educational experience through summer employment under the auspices of PACE (federally funded program) provided me as a college student with a "transformative learning experience" in the basics of work ethic and consideration for co-workers. It was from the group of "blue-collar" workers employed at the Pitt County Schools Maintenance Department who conveyed many highly principled skills and values I would cherish for a career and lifetime. It was through their modeled behavior, the value and pride placed on manual skilled labor, outstanding work ethic and their genuine concern for the safety and wellbeing of fellow co-workers that so impressed and imprinted upon me.

Unfortunately, and significantly much of my formal education and acculturation had in fact been *"miseducation"* by virtue of unwitting acceptance of false academic content, possessing major deficits in "knowledge of self", and by default internalizing cultural definitions of others as my own with devastating effects ("conceptual incarceration"). Much to our detriment these cognitive influences have been and remain the successful enemies of growth in consciousness for the African American and others similarly conditioned. A "mental slavery" of sorts invariably then becomes the perpetual outcome positioned in the place of "consciousness growth". The rewards and material benefits within such a system can never become favorable for the victims of miseducation. Those who are so acculturated are doomed to forever remain ignorant of themselves. Dr. Carter G. Woodson indicated the many adverse effects of such a cultural predicament in his 1933 classic "The Miseducation of the Negro". This makes clear why there can never be a reasonable expectation that those responsible for the miseducation of a people will ever correct the glaring misdeed that has so successfully served its purpose.

For this very reason, I was immediately attracted to The Self Improvement Education Center of Norfolk, Virginia owned and operated by Brother George Welch. Many sources of books and study materials were accessible as we organized and prepared Afrocentric-oriented study groups. My study and collaboration here with similarly like-minded thinkers followed a direct path into the wonderful studies of ancient Nile Valley Cultures with a primary focus on Kemet (Egypt). Our research and study came from many sources especially the relevant work of scholars and academics presented previously in chapter nine.

The '80s was a period of heightened interest national in scope on the study of Classical Kemetic (Egyptian) culture from a new and much needed perspective. The surge in this area and method of research was generated by divergent and exciting scholars and writers. Also, their writings were supported and reinforced by; orienting related publications, organizations, and conferences such as The Journal of African Civilization, Advanced Study of Classical African Civilization (ASCAC), Melanin Conferences, and local study groups founded across the nation.

An individual may ask sincerely from a point of reference why as a Black Human would you be so interested in the study of Black Classical Civilization? I would give the following basic reasons:

1) To rediscover the specifications and historical cultural foundations from the African ancient past (to know what people of African descent were able to know and accomplish during the time of their best collective mind cooperation)

2) To develop an awareness and greater consciousness from the body of work made available from, contemporary Afrocentric Scholarship (e.g. chapter nine) of world events, chronology, historiography and scientific; reason, rationale, and discovery mostly exclusive of foreign and derogatory input)

3) In order to reclaim vital awareness of the value for the moral standards established under the highest authentic spiritual system practiced by man under the African Spirituality (MAAT).

The ancient Kushites foundational contributions around the globe cannot be ignored forever and the magnificence of Ancient

Egypt (her daughter) with her high sciences and spiritual systems became "the light of the world". This was before her destruction by the multitude of invasions she incurred over the millenniums.

Africa and African people have not always existed in their current predicament of exploitation and deprivation, nor were they once portrayed and perceived as lackeys and cultural misfits. Since African people initially laid the foundations of sedentary civilization in which others followed, there was no rationale for racism against the Africans in the ancient world. Instead, there was much cause and justification for cultural borrowing from their emulation of them and identification with them. There is a long-standing adage in Western Civilization "The Romans conquered Greece, but the Greeks conquered the Roman mind". Meaning although the Greeks were eventually conquered by their more northern European family members (Romans), much of what the Greeks had mastered culturally (arts, sciences, architecture, mathematics, etc.) was acculturated by the Romans. There is still one very significant aspect to this generally accepted truth. Does the remarkable question become from whom in the ancient world did the Greeks acquire much of what was passed to the Romans and subsequently to Western Europe? Stolen Legacy offers intriguing evidence on this historical foundational question.

Only since the advent of the European Atlantic Slave Trade and the colonization of Africa have these racist ideas and theories evolved within the context of revisionist history. Despite the racism against the African human concocted during slavery and colonialism, it was never based upon anything more than economic rewards and the need to justify western attitudes and behavior. The clarity of African contributions to world culture and humanism despite the savage, brutal and despicable acts normalized against them thoroughly contradicts the revisionism and purposeful misinformation until today see (Welsing 1991, Chapter 9). I would have suggested the following discovery for the perpetrators and their enablers from <u>The Book of Amenomope</u> (Sacred Wisdom of Ancient Egypt) "Beware of robbing the poor and of oppressing the weak and helpless. Raise not your hand against the aged nor address an elder with improper speech. Let not yourself be sent on an evil mission nor stand in the company of those who have performed them" (Karenga; 1989:58).

Much from the early cultures of the Nile Valley was borrowed extensively by western civilization (see James chapter 9). Our studies did much in the way of clarifying many of the false narratives, misunderstandings, and viewpoints regarding the history of the African people. The work of Diop, Ben Jochannan, Chancellor Williams, Van Sertima, Robin Walker, and others established the African Origin of Civilization (see chapter 9). We now acknowledge the Ancient African culture of the Upper Nile (Kush) as an ancient African culture even predating Kemet (Egypt) and historically determined to have been her source. The high Nile Valley Cultures which once thrived in this region were remarkable in their cultural accomplishments. Their agriculture, astronomy, philosophy, mathematics, science, engineering, and architectural accomplishments resulted from their acquired, compiled, and applied knowledge over millenniums of unbroken progression. Such advancements made the region a wonder during its existence and evoked desire, invasion, pillage, and destruction by others. The High Cultures of the Nile Valley existed for thousands of years peacefully before an incursion by foreign invaders. Their continuous invasions began with the mostly nomadic Hyksos followed by other warlike invaders such as the Assyrians and Persians: later by Greeks, Romans and finally the Arabs who remain presently. None of which were Indigenous nor responsible for developing the high science or skills nor played any role in constructing the many magnificent structures such as the Pyramids, Sphinx of Giza nor the Colossus of Ramses II at Abu Simbel despite their erroneous revisionist historical claims (Ben-Jochannan 1988; 273).

Chancellor (Williams, 1987; 117-118) cites the end of the Twenty-fifth Dynasty 656 B.C.E. as the time ending Blacks dominance in world history. (Diop, 1974; 221) states the Assyrian destruction of Thebes "marked the end of the Nubian Sudanese Twenty-fifth Ethiopian Dynasty...also the decline of Black political supremacy in Antiquity and in history".

The aforementioned dates of descent by Blacks from world power and influence were further exacerbated by two subsequent major catastrophic historical periods albeit by more than two millenniums later.

The two other events were the African Slave Trade, which for more than 400 years uprooted and victimized more than 12 million Africans (Davidson 1961). The second was the colonization of most of Africa or the forceful settling on their land while forcing the Indigenous people into subservient and slave-like roles while likewise raping their land of its valuable minerals and resources. Africa is seldom identified as such but is unquestionably known to be the most abundantly endowed continent with natural resources. That does not exclude its people. This is why Dr. John Henrik Clark often said in his lectures that "Africa from antiquity until the present has always had something of value others wanted but did not want to pay for" accurate then and even more so currently.

The destruction and loss of control of Mother Africa coupled with the loss of possession of their many compiled library volumes of classical African knowledge and Culture (from ancient times through colonial occupation) has been categorically and emphatically much worse than catastrophic. This is a monumental understatement.

Never erroneously think that the African human never successfully defended his land and culture. The wave upon wave of ignorant and merciless invaders during ancient time were mostly successfully challenged, dismissed, and expunged by the Indigenous Africans for a long period of time. This repulsion continued through the end of the twenty-fifth dynastic period (Diop 1974, 221; Ben-Jochannan 1988, 273-275; Williams 1987, 41-42; Walker 2006, 208-210).

Over millenniums of time the results of the invaders and their amalgamation with the indigenous stock was significant. Finally, the current occupants resulting from their status as the last invaders (Arabs) remain to the present. It is therefore not historically accurate to state or imply that other races never ruled or occupied Egypt. However, it is extremely inaccurate to suggest the invaders contributed positive impact on Egypt's underlying science, mathematics, or philosophy quite the contrary. The long-standing existence and application of an African source and knowledge base had culminated into the high culture that existed long before the foreigners' destructive arrival.

It is clear that much of the Indigenous African high culture was mutilated, vandalized, destroyed, and/or claimed by others which can be found in museums across the globe. In many instances, the nose was knocked off or otherwise removed from many ancient African statues in an attempt to disassociate the likeness of the statues with their true African origin. One of the most egregious examples was the case of the Sphinx (among the oldest of Egyptian monuments). Many scholars believe that a cannonball was used to shoot off its' nose by Napoleonic soldiers in1798 during French imperialism into Kemet.

It should be underscored that many formidable cultures have existed in other geographical regions of the "Mother Continent" since the demise of the Nile Valley high cultures. Archeological evidence and artifacts abound throughout Africa showing the previous existence of many great civilizations throughout the "birthplace of mankind" in West, South, and Central Africa. Included are those of ancient Nigeria, (Nok Culture); Ghana, (Benin); Zimbabwe and Tanzania (Great Zimbabwe), and many others.

Ancient African civilizations of the Nile valley produced high cultures employing architecture, science, mathematics, and complex spiritual systems in ancient times. Most foreign invaders wanted the African cultural greatness but had not the scientific or spiritual basis to comprehend or sustain it.

The multitude of attacks on African high culture from Asian and European invaders during ancient times was followed by a second phase; European Atlantic African Slave Trade, European colonialism and the third phase and current phase, is institutionalized and global racism for the purpose of justification and reinforcement of the initial two. The second and third phases have currently existed for more than five centuries (15th-20th) C.E. The results were death and destruction in the form of chattel slavery in the Americas and European colonization of Africa during (19th-20th C.E.). These have become the historical evidence of the African and all-African Peoples holocaust.

In recent times the West has only begrudgingly begun to acknowledge the foundational and successful academic challenge set forth. Western Civilization must give significant recognition to the role of Africa and its people for their many and foundational contributions and involuntary sacrifices to the West (Primarily European Civilization) including learning from Classical African Cultures, economic enrichment from 400 years of slave labor and many trillions from African natural resources exploitation. What would the sum be if all of this could be calculated into today's dollars? The results would be beyond astronomical to state the minimum!

By way of Afrocentric scholarship, the false and revisionist sources of structured misinformation regarding Classical African Civilization has only recently been effectively challenged and debunked both scientifically and historically. The loss and separation from African classical culture through invasion, slavery, colonialism, and revisionist history has made for a long journey back to the world stage. Such scholars are highlighted in Chapter Nine. These are mostly contemporary scholars, who have assembled on the battlefield for historical truth and accuracy despite perpetual Eurocentric academic indifference, and often outright hostility.

Monuments, temples, obelisks, colossal structures, and writings in stone all sources for growth in consciousness by the Black Human were greatly depreciated through purposeful misinterpretation, destruction, and theft of most things African. Many such artifacts have gone from scarce to outright non-existent following the destruction and fall of classical African culture. Books, manuscripts, art, and valuable cultural items, were burned, seized as contraband, and carted off to museums and capitals of conquering nations across the globe.

In review of ancient and contemporary history, the record reveals conclusively that the African Human has done nearly all that has been asked of him and her and even demanded of them for the benefit of others most often to their own detriment and well-being.

The proper growth and proliferation of Black research have endured a difficult and arduous evolvement back to the world stage. The reclamation of relevant artifacts, ancient writings, Kemetic philosophical interpretations, and new archeological finds will speed the retrieval of knowledge and consciousness lost and/or stolen through the annals of time. The Black human will emerge into higher consciousness through internalization of the following three growth processes.

Consciousness Growth Essentials for the Black Human

1) By grasping the classical African meaning and usage of will, intent, character, politics, economics, and spirituality for moral guidance and perspective

2) By cultivating a value system for purpose, sensitivity, and desire to utilize Afrocentric Scholarship and historiography as sources and methods of researching, analyzing, and developing knowledge of self on multiple levels and

3) By Learning to use the Afrocentric, rationale, process, and authenticity in development of a world view, spirituality, and connectedness to the cosmic order once again.

Remember, knowledge is power, but "consciousness" is much more. It synthesizes and elevates knowledge, power, and wisdom into something far greater. In the distant past it was called "initiation and enlightenment" today we call it the "exclusive road map" back to world leadership. HOTEP!

BIBLIOGRAPHY

Akbar, Ni'am (1985) The Community of Self, Jersey City, NJ: New Mind Productions.

Akbar, Na'im (1984) Chains and Images of Psychological Slavery, Jersey City, NJ: New Mind Productions.

Akbar, Na'im (1996) Breaking the Chains of Psychological Slavery, Tallahassee, FL: Mind Productions & Associates, Inc.

Akbar, Na'im (1999) Know Thy Self, Tallahassee, FL: Mind Productions & Associations.

Allen, T. Harrell (1999) Lee's Last Major General: Bryan Grimes of North Carolina, Mason City, IA: Savos Publishing Company.

Ani, Marimba (1994) YURUGU: An African-Centered Critique of European Cultural Thought and Behavior.

Asante, Molefi (2007) Cheikh Anta Diop (An Intellectual Portrait), Los Angeles: University of Sankore Press.

Asante, Molefi (1990) Kemet, Afrocentricity and Knowledge, Trenton, NJ: Africa World Press Inc.

Barnes, Carol (1988) MELANIN: THE CHEMICAL KEY TO BLACK GREATNESS: The Harmful Effect of Toxic Drugs on Melanin Centers Within the Black Human, Houston: C. B. Publishers.

ben-Jochannan, Yosef (1988) Africa (Mother of Western Civilization), Baltimore: Black Classic Press.

ben-Jochannan, Yosef (1973) A Chronology of the Bible, Baltimore: Black Classic Press.

ben-Jochannan, Yosef (1991) African Origins of the Major Western Religions, Baltimore: Black Classic Press.

Bennett, Lerone Jr. (1966) Before the Mayflower (A History of the Negro in America 1619-1964), Chicago: Johnson Publishing Company, Penguin Edition.

Bradley, Michael (1981) The Iceman Inheritance (Prehistoric Sources of Western Man's Racism, Sexism and Aggression), Toronto, Ontario: Dorset Publishing Inc.

Breitman, George (1965) Malcolm X Speaks, Selected Speeches and Statements edited with Prefatory Notes by G.B. New York: Grove Press, Inc.

Budge, Wallis E. A. (1895, 1967) The Egyptian Book of the Dead, New York: Dover Publications 1967.

Carruthers, Jacob (1984) Essays in Ancient Egyptian Studies. Los Angeles: University of Sankore Press.

Carruthers and Karenga (1986) Kemet and the African Worldview (Research, Rescue and Restoration, Los Angeles: University of Sankore Press.

Chandler, Wayne (1999) Ancient Future (The Teachings and Prophetic Wisdom of the Seven Hermetic Law of Ancient Egypt), Baltimore: Black Classic Press.

Cheatham, James T. (1897) A History of The Grimes Plantation Grimesland, Pitt County North Carolina, Baltimore: The Lord Baltimore Press.

Churchward, Albert (1990) The Origin And Evolution of Religion VOL. 1-A, New York – Chesapeake: ECA Associates Publications.

Churchward, Albert (1990) The Origin And Evolution of Religion VOL. 1-B, New York - Chesapeake: ECA Associates Publications.

Clark, John Henrik (1994) Who Betrayed (The African World Revolution? and other speeches), Chicago: Third World Press.

Davidson, Basil (1961) The African Slave Trade (Pre Colonial History 1450-1850), Boston/Toronto: Atlantic, Little, Brown and Company.

De Lubicz, Swaller, R. A. (1977) The Temple in Man (Sacred Architecture and the Perfect Mann), Rochester, Vermont: Automn Press.

De Lubicz, Swaller R. A. (1978) Symbol and the Symbolic (Ancient Egypt, Science and the Evolution of Consciousness), Rochester, VT: Inner Traditions International.

De Lubicz, Swaller R. A. (1982) Sacred Science (The King of Pharonic Theocracy), Rochester, VT, VI: Inner Traditions International.

Diop, Cheikh Anta (1974) The African Origin of Civilization (Myth or Reality), United States of America: Lawrence Hill & Company, Publishers Inc.

Diop, Cheikh Anta (1989) "Origin of the Ancient Egyptians" Journal of African Civilizations 10:Summer 9-37.

Diop, Cheikh Anta (1987) Black Africa, The Economic and Cultural Basis for a Federated State, Westport, CT: Lawrence Hill & Co. and Trenton, N.J. Africa World Press.

Dubois, W.E.B. (1970) The Selected Writings of W.E.B. Dubois, New York and Toronto: The New American Library Inc.

Edelstein, L. M. (1971) , Melanin " - A Unique Biopolymer", Pathobiology Annual. Vol. 1.

Fanon, Frantz (1968) The Wretched of the Earth, New York: Random House.

Fanon, Frantz (1967) Black Skin, White Masks, New York: Grove Press.

Finch, Charles (1998) The Star of Deep Beginnings (The Genesis of African Science and Technology), Decatur, GA: Knenti, Inc.

Franklin, John Hope (1947) From Slavery to Freedom (A History of African Americans), New York: Alfred A. Knopf Publishing. House.

Garvey-Jacques Amy (1968) Philosophy and Opinions of Marcus Garvey, Vol. I & II, New York, Macmillian Publishing Company.

Hardee, Wilbur (2000) The Life and Times of Wilbur Hardee, San Jose, NY: Writers Club Press.

Hillard, Asa (1995) The Maroon Within US (Selected Essays on African American Community Socialization), Baltimore: Black Classic Press.

Houston, Drusilla (1926, 1985) Wonderful Ethiopians of the Ancient Cushite Empire, Baltimore: Black Classic Press 1985.

Jackson, John G. (1972) Man, God and Civilization, Secaucus, NJ: Citadel Press.

James, George G. M. (1988) Stolen Legacy, San Francisco: Julian Richardson Associates.

Jr. Hill, Paul (1992) Coming of Age African American Rites of Passage, Chicago: African American Image.

Josephus, Flavius (1900) The Complete Works of Flavius-Josephus, Chicago: Thompson and Thomas.

Karenga, Maulana (1989) Selections from The Husia (Sacred Wisdom of Ancient Egypt), Los Angeles: University of Sankore Press.

Karenga, Malana (1993) Introduction To Black Studies, Los Angeles: University of Sankore Press.

Karenga, Maulana (2006) MAAT: THE MORAL IDEAL IN ANCIENT EGYPT, A STUDY IN CLASICAL AFRICAN ETHICS: Los Angeles, University of Sankore Press.

Karenga, Maulana (1989) The African American Holiday of KWANZAA (A Celebration of Family, Community & Culture), Los Angeles: University of Sankore Press.

King, Richard (2001) African Origin of Biological Psychiatry, Chicago: Lushena Books, Inc.

King, Richard (1994) Melanin: A Key to Freedom, Hampton, VA: U.B. & U.W. Communications Systems, Inc.

Kunjufu, Jawanza (1985) Countering the Conspiracy to Destroy Black Boys, Chicago: African American Images.

Madhubuti, Haki R. (1991) Black Men Obselete, Single, Dangerous: The African American Family in Transition, Chicago: Third World Press.

Massey, Gerald R. (1963) Ancient Egypt (The Light of the World), London: The African Publication Society).

Nobles, Wade (1985) Africanity and the Black Family (The Development of a Theoretical Model) Oakland, CA: The Institute for Advanced Study of Black Family Life and Culture, Inc.

Poole-Lane, Stanley (1990) The Story of the Moors in Spain, Baltimore: Black Classic Press.

Rashida, Runoko and Sertima Ivan V. (1988) African Presence in Early Asia, New Brunswick (USA), NJ: Transition Books, Rutgers.

Rodney, Walter (1982) How Europe Under-Developed Africa, Washington, D.C.: Howard University Press.

Suggs, Henry Lewis (1988) P. B. YOUNG Newspaperman; Race, Politics, and Journalism in the New South 1910-1962, Charlottesville: University Press of Virginia

Van Sertima, Ivan (1976) (The African Presence in Ancient America) They Came Before Columbus, New York: Random House.

Van Sertima, Ivan (1988a) African Presence in Early Europe, New Brunswick (USA) and Oxford (UK): Transition Publishers 1988.

Van Sertima, Ivan (1988b) Blacks in Science: Ancient and Modern, New Brunswick (USA) and London (UK): Transition Books.

Walker, Robin (2006) When We Ruled, Baltimore: Black Classics Press.

Welsing, Frances Cress (1991) The Isis Papers (The Keys to the Colors), Chicago: Third World Press.

Weston, Rubin Frances (1972) Racism in U.S. Imperialism; The Influence of Racial Assumptions on American Foreign Policy, 1893-1946, Columbia: University of S.C. Press

Williams, Chancellor (1987) The Destruction of Black Civilization (Great Issues of a Race From 4500 B.C. To 2000 A.D.), Chicago: Third World Press.

Wilson, Amos (1998) Blueprint for Black Power (A Moral, Political and Economic Imperative for the Twenty-First Century New York: African World Infosystems.

Wilson, Amos N. (1981)"The Psychological Development of the Black Child," Black Books Bulletin, 7, 2: 10-12.

Wilson, Amos (1993) The Falsification of African Consciousness: Eurocentric History, Psychiatry and the Politics of White Supremacy, New York: African World Infosystems.

Wright, Bruce (1993) Black Robes White Justice, New York: Carol Publishing Group.

Yette, Samuel (1975) The Choice, New York: Berkley Publishing Corporation.

CAPTIONS

The captions here represent and capsulize key themes, modalities and the essence of African-Centered-Thought (Afrocentricity). This includes the increasing avail of its supporting research and scholarship as well.

"Consciousness growth is much more than a mere departure from ignorance" but, must include "expanded awareness in truth"

Spirituality exists beyond the material state of sensibility... In ancient Kemet, a system of education known as the "Mysteries System" had as its foundation a nexus between the spiritual and material accountability for existence.

...As impactful as formal education is on the individual, general culture may have a much greater impact than all the grade schools, colleges, universities and "formal bastions of organized education" combined.

We must be reminded that the omitted and misunderstood pages of African History are the missing and confusing pages of World History